FREE PRESS
PAPERBACKS

UP FROM
CONSERVATISM

*Why the Right
is Wrong for America*

MICHAEL LIND

FREE PRESS PAPERBACKS
Published by Simon & Schuster

New York   London   Toronto   Sydney   Singapore

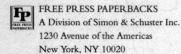 FREE PRESS PAPERBACKS
A Division of Simon & Schuster Inc.
1230 Avenue of the Americas
New York, NY 10020

First Free Press Paperbacks Edition 1997

FREE PRESS PAPERBACKS and colophon are trademarks
of Simon & Schuster Inc.

Designed by Carla Bolte

Manufactured in the United States of America

10   9   8   7   6   5   4   3   2   1

Library of Congress Cataloging-in-Publication Data

Lind, Michael, 1962–
    Up from conservatism : why the right is wrong for America /
Michael Lind.
        p.   cm.
    Includes bibliographical references and index.
    ISBN 0–684–82761–1   ISBN 0–684–83186–4 (Pbk)
    1. Conservatism—United States.   I. Title.
JC573.2.U5L58   1996
320.5'2—dc20   96-8097
                                                       CIP

ISBN 0-684-82761-1
    0-684-83186-4 (Pbk)

FOR PETER VIERECK

O tu ch'onore scienza e arte

Contents

Introduction

The Triumph and
Collapse of Conservatism

merican conservatism is dead. This is not to say that the conservative moment in American political history is over. Just as left-
liberal Democrats continued to advance their agenda in the 1970s and
1980s—years after their ideology degenerated into an empty creed—so
the right wing of the Republican party may continue to expand its influence for some time to come. But those victories will be a result of
external factors—the collapse of the left, the disorientation of the political center, the long-term conversion of the white South to the GOP,
inertia—not of vigor or dynamism on the part of conservatives. Even as
the Republicans came to power in Congress for the first time in nearly
half a century, the mainstream conservative movement in the United
States was cracking up. The project of sustaining a mainstream, centrist
conservatism distinct from the far right in its positions, and not merely
in its style, has failed. Its remnants are like fragments of a comet that
continue in their destructive course even after the comet has disintegrated.

The conservative intellectual movement was the first element of
mainstream conservatism to fail. Intellectual conservatism fell apart beginning in 1992, as a result of the rise of the far right of Pat Robertson,
Patrick Buchanan, and antigovernment militias. For more than a quarter of a century, beginning with the efforts of William F. Buckley, Jr.
and Barry Goldwater in the 1960s to distance themselves from the John
Birch Society, the mainstream conservative movement had been careful

to separate itself from the radical right. In the 1990s, televangelist Pat Robertson, in the manner of the demagogic radio priest Father Coughlin in the 1930s, put together a powerful grass-roots political movement, the Christian Coalition, while disseminating the familiar ideology of the far right: a conspiracy theory blaming wars and revolutions on a secret cabal of Jewish bankers, Freemasons, Illuminati, atheists, and internationalists. Faced with a challenge to the integrity of the conservative movement far greater than that posed by the John Birch Society, the leaders of intellectual conservatism—William F. Buckley, Jr., Irving Kristol, and Norman Podhoretz—chose unilateral surrender. They devised tortured exonerations of the anti-Semitic theories purveyed by Pat Robertson and denounced former conservative critics of the TV preacher like me as "liberals" and even "Marxists." The result was an exodus of the major young intellectuals formerly associated with the right and the revelation that the conservative intelligentsia had become little more than public relations specialists for the GOP.

The crack-up of the Republican electoral coalition followed the decline of the conservative intelligentsia by a few years. Again the cause was the rise of the far right. For decades, the Republican right had been trying to define national politics as a contest between conservative populism and liberal elitism. This strategy had its roots, like so much of modern American conservatism, in McCarthyism (which was as much a populist revolt as an anticommunist crusade). It had become central to Republican politics as a whole in the 1970s and 1980s, when Richard Nixon and his successors learned from George Wallace how to pose as defenders of the "silent majority." Conservative populism, of course, was an oxymoron; from Burke onward, conservatives have been defenders of elites and establishments, and American conservatives, in particular, have been defenders of the prerogatives of the rich and the business class. Nevertheless the snobbery and preference for government by judicial decree of the left-liberals who dominated the Democratic party from the 1970s to the 1990s made the conservative strategy of diverting populist anger from Wall Street and the rich, its traditional targets, to government, feminists, blacks, gays, and intellectuals seem almost plausible.

All this came to an end in the early months of 1996. During his race against Bob Dole for the Republican nomination, Patrick Buchanan exposed conservative populism as the fraud it is by becoming a consistent populist: denouncing affirmative action *and* Wall Street, homosexuals *and* corporations "downsizing" their work forces, feminists *and* rich country-club Republicans. He denounced Bob Dole as "the bellhop of the Business Roundtable." The Republican establishment was horrified. Buchanan, after all, ever since his days as a Nixon speechwriter, had been one of the architects of Republican "culture war" populism. He, more than anyone else, should have understood that conservative populism was not to be taken seriously, that it was merely a method of persuading white working-class voters to vote their prejudices rather than their economic interests. Suddenly, though, he had become a consistent cultural and economic populist, in the tradition of George Wallace, Charles Coughlin, Huey Long, Tom Watson, and William Jennings Bryan.

With a few exceptions (chiefly Jewish neoconservatives offended by his constant stream of anti-Semitic innuendo) the leaders of the conservative movement had tolerated or actively supported Buchanan over the years. *National Review* even endorsed him in the race against Bush for the Republican presidential nomination in 1992. As long as Buchanan directed abuse at racial minorities, homosexuals, immigrants, the United Nations, feminists, and avant-garde artists, the conservative movement had a place for him. When he began criticizing millionaires and corporate executives, though, the conservative elite was shocked, *shocked,* to discover that Buchanan is a rabble-rousing demagogue. Panicked by Buchanan, the Republican establishment belatedly discovered that conservatism had nothing to do with populism. Many of the very conservative politicians and intellectuals who a year or two before had been deriding liberals as the party of "the elites" suddenly rediscovered the importance of elitism, hierarchy, tradition, institutions. "Someone needs to stand up and defend the Establishment," declared the crown prince of the Republican intelligentsia in Washington, William Kristol, former chief of staff of Vice President Dan Quayle and now editor of Australian media mogul Rupert Murdoch's American conservative journal the *Weekly Standard.* "In the last couple of weeks, there's been too much pseudo-populism, almost too much concern and attention for, quote, the people. . . . After all, we conservatives are on the side of the lords and barons. . . . We at the *Weekly Standard* are pulling up the drawbridge against the peasants."[1]

Who on earth had confused conservatism and populism anyway? Well, among others, William Kristol's own father, Irving Kristol, the leading figure of the foundation-subsidized Washington conservative intelligentsia. In the *Wall Street Journal* in the spring of 1995, Irving Kristol called for a populist conservatism: "But the most important phenomenon of the postwar years, certainly so far as conservatism is concerned, was the rise of the so-called 'religious right.' This, above all, has re-created American conservatism into a populist movement. . . . [A] democratic populism can be a corrective to those defects of democratic politics arising from our secular democratic elites."[2, 3]

Even before Washington conservatives like William Kristol repudiated the conservative populist strategy that the Republican right had pursued since the days of Nixon, conservative populism was revealed as a fraud by the deeds of Newt Gingrich and his allies in the Republican Congress elected in 1994. When they came to power, the Republican congressional leaders claimed they were leading a "revolution" against the rule of special interests on Capitol Hill. Within weeks, it was clear that nothing had changed apart from the substitution of Republican special interests for Democratic ones. Gingrich and other Republican leaders began a massive shakedown of Washington lobbyists, warning that if they did not fund the Republican party they would lose access to Congress. When a bipartisan coalition of Republicans and Democrats tried to introduce campaign-finance-reform legislation, Gingrich sought to prevent the subject from coming quickly to a vote by turning the matter over to a commission.

The First Hundred Days of the Republican Congress turned into the greatest romp for business interests since the Gilded Age. A few conservative reformers, like House Budget Commission Chairman John Kasich, had promised to go after corporate welfare. Then corporate PAC money began pouring into Republican coffers, and the crusade against corporate welfare was put off indefinitely by the same method employed to thwart campaign-finance reform—a proposed independent commission. Instead of balancing the budget by getting rid of subsidies and tax breaks for corporations and the rich, the House Republicans concentrated on eliminating programs for the powerless poor. While leaving untouched $50 billion in tax breaks for big business, and subsidies like the $2.6 million the federal government pays to promote the products of the E & J Gallo Winery, the Republican "revolutionaries" saw to it that more than half of the $9.4 billion in cuts in the House budget proposal came from low-income housing programs.[4] While proposing to increase the federal deficit by several hundred billion dollars through new tax cuts that would have chiefly benefited the rich,

Gingrich's Republicans posed as friends of wage-earning Americans by pointing to a "profamily tax cut" that would have given each American the handsome sum of an additional $9.60 a week. Even though full-time minimum-wage workers do not earn enough to reach the poverty line, Gingrich and Dole—each with an enormous salary compared with those of most Americans, and a generous government health care plan—argued that the economy could not afford an increase in wages for the poorest workers.

With "conservative populism" like this, it was only a matter of time before working-class and middle-class conservatives rebelled under the leadership of someone like Patrick Buchanan. For a few weeks during the Republican primary campaign, the two wings of mainstream conservatism—the social and economic conservatives—were embodied respectively by Patrick Buchanan and Steve Forbes, the angry lower-middle-class populist and the billionaire's son. Even if the Republicans manage to cobble together the populist-libertarian alliance in the fall of 1996 and after, the damage has been done. By April 1996, public approval of the Republican party had fallen to the lowest point recorded by CBS/New York Times pollsters in twelve years of polling.[5]

The crack-up of the Republican coalition along class lines has revealed that there is no conservative majority in the United States. For that matter, there is not much of a conservative minority either. The conservatives in the Republican party are divided rather sharply into a culturally and economically populist far right and a more or less consistently libertarian right. Since the 1960s, the conservative movement has tried to unite these two factions by means of a conservative ideology that unites cultural populism with economic libertarianism. As a formula this has been useful (and may be useful again). The problem is that hardly anyone on the right really takes it seriously. Religious fundamentalists tend to be suspicious of big business and international finance, as well as of big government; economic conservatives tend to be liberal on social issues, even if they suppress their views on matters like abortion and gay rights in the interests of Republican unity. Whatever Republican politicians and intellectuals may claim, the number of Americans who are consistent believers in conservative ideology—who sincerely believe both that abortion should be outlawed and that there should be further massive tax cuts for the rich—is quite small. Such consistent ideological conservatives are not only a minority of the American people and a minority of the Republican party; they are a minority on the right itself, squeezed as they are between the two big blocs of far-right populists and libertarians.

If you think about it, the status of consistent "movement" conservatives as not merely a minority but a tiny sect on the right shows the failure of the American conservative movement. Modern American conservatism is usually dated from 1955, when William F. Buckley, Jr. founded *National Review* (in reality, it originated with the red-baiting of Joe McCarthy, of whom the young Buckley was an associate and defender). The conservatives have had almost half a century to win a majority of Americans over to their views, and they have failed miserably. The success of the Republican party in reaching parity with the Democrats does not represent a victory for conservatism, since most Republicans oppose the anti-abortion stand of their own party leadership.

In the mid-1990s as in the mid-1950s, the views of mainstream conservatism seem weird and repugnant to most Americans. The average American, it is safe to say, considers Franklin Delano Roosevelt one of the greatest presidents of all time. For conservatives, however, FDR was an evil figure who ruined American society. In his 1995 address to the American Enterprise Institute, conservative columnist George Will mocked FDR's January 1944 State of the Union message, in which FDR said: "We cannot be content, no matter how high that general [American] standard of living may be, if some fraction of our people— whether it be one-third or one-fifth or one-tenth—is ill-fed, ill-clothed, ill-housed or insecure." Will sneered, "This was a summons to permanent discontent on the part of citizens and government." Unlike FDR, it appears, conservatives can be perfectly content if one-third of the American people are "ill-fed, ill-clothed, ill-housed or insecure." According to Will, "Conservatism depends on eliciting from citizens a public-spirited self-denial." If they had been virtuous, if they had shared "a thoughtful reverence for the nation's founding," destitute Americans in the 1930s would have rejected New Deal reforms like Social Security while quoting *The Federalist Papers.*

Hardly anyone in this country, apart from George Will and other members of the tiny conservative intelligentsia, thinks this way. Hardly anyone believes that old people who cash Social Security checks and college students who apply for student loans are morally corrupt parasites who have abandoned republican virtue and the ideals of the Founding Fathers. The very idea is bizarre. But conservative ideology is made up of ideas that are equally strange. It seems strange to most

Americans to argue that doctors who perform abortions should go to prison for murder, while restraints on the sale of "cop-killing bullets" represent a tyrannical law that should be repealed. Yet if you are a "movement conservative" this is what you are supposed to believe.

In almost half a century, then, the conservative movement has failed to create a conservative majority in the United States. But its effect has been profound and destructive nonetheless. Historians of the twenty-first and twenty-second centuries are likely to record that the only lasting effect of the conservative movement of William F. Buckley, Jr., Irving Kristol, and George Will was to legitimize the powerful far right that awakened at the end of the twentieth century in the United States. By choosing to appease the far right of Pat Robertson, Patrick Buchanan, and the militias, the conservative leadership has unwittingly helped an incompatible rival movement to replace it.

Today the right is defined by Robertson, Buchanan, and the militia movement. The "right" now means the overlapping movements of the "far right:" the religious right, the populist right, the paramilitary right. The remnants of the Washington–New York conservative movement, the Buckley-Goldwater-Reagan right, simply do not matter. Washington-based conservative operatives like William Kristol and William Bennett can provide quotes to reporters and write op-eds, but they do not speak for any constituency. In the 1960s, *National Review* intellectuals formed the vanguard of a grass-roots movement based on organizations like Young Americans for Freedom (YAF). In the 1990s, the conservative intellectuals, bereft of a social base, continue to exist as a group only because of subsidies from foundations and corporations for their little magazines and think-tank careers. They are generals without an army.

The only movement on the right in the United States today that has any significant political influence is the far right. In the manner of the southern right from the Civil War until the civil rights revolution, which operated both through the Democratic party and the Ku Klux Klan, or the modern Irish Republican movement, with its party (Sinn Fein) and its terrorist branch (the IRA), the contemporary American far right has both public, political wings (the Christian Coalition, the National Rifle Association, Project Rescue) and its covert, paramilitary, terrorist factions. Although the Christian Coalition and Operation Rescue officially denounce violence, the fact remains that a common worldview animates both the followers of Pat Robertson and Pat Buchanan and the far-right extremists who bomb abortion clinics, murder federal marshals and county sheriffs, and blow up buildings and trains.

That worldview is summed up by three letters: ZOG. ZOG stands for "Zionist-occupied government," the phrase used by far-right white-supremacists, anti-Semites, and militia members for the federal government. When Pat Robertson warns about "the new world order" and describes conspiracies of famous Jewish bankers like the Rothschilds and Freemasons to destroy the United States and Christianity; when Patrick Buchanan talks about "Israel's amen corner" in Washington and rails against the surrender of American "sovereignty" to NAFTA, the World Trade Organization, and the UN, they are legitimizing the paranoid worldview of the opponents of ZOG. And when mainstream conservatives, in turn, make excuses for the conspiracy theories of Robertson and Buchanan, they lend further legitimacy to the worldview of the far-right lunatic fringe.

It is easy to sound hysterical, by exaggerating the power of the far right. Consider the following facts, though. The United States, for more than a decade, has been suffering from wave after wave of right-wing terrorism: the bombing of abortion clinics; the murder of doctors who perform abortions; the murder of federal, state, and county law enforcement officers by right-wing extremists like Gordon Kahl, David Koresh, and his followers; the bombing of the federal building in Oklahoma City; the derailing of an Amtrak train by "sons of the Gestapo"; racist murders committed by neo-Nazis in the U.S. Army stationed at Fort Bragg, North Carolina. The ideology of the new terrorists of the right, down to the details of the supposed conspiracy to impose a "new world order," is almost indistinguishable from that of the "legitimate" or political far right that formally disavows their deeds. As of this writing, the FBI is besieging the "Freemen," a group of far-right extremists in Montana who stockpiled ammunition allegedly to commit acts of terrorism against the federal government. In light of this epidemic of right-wing terror, talk about a threat from the left seems like a sick joke.

Nothing like today's convergence of overt far-right politics and underground far-right terrorism in the campaign against the federal government and "the new world order" has been seen in the United States since the late 1930s, when Father Charles Coughlin, Gerald L. K. Smith, and others led a powerful far-right populist movement united by hatred of the new "Jew Deal" of "Franklin Delano Rosenfelt" and admiration for Hitler and Mussolini. Pat Robertson's maunderings about

Kuhn and Loeb and other New York Jewish bankers financing the Russian Revolution, and Patrick Buchanan's sneering references to "Israel's amen corner" and the "Brandeis football team," could almost be lifted from the texts of Father Coughlin's speeches of the 1930s. And the modern militia movement itself has a predecessor in Coughlin's paramilitary "Christian Front," described by one authority as a "national militia-style organization." In 1940 the FBI raided one Brooklyn Christian Front unit and discovered bombs, rifles, thousands of rounds of ammunition. Charged with a plot to destroy Jewish newspapers, blow up bridges and railroads, and assassinate members of the federal government, the "Brooklyn Boys" were acquitted by a sympathetic jury, though not before one member committed suicide out of despondency at being kept from traveling to Europe to fight for Hitler.[6]

The main forces on the right in the 1990s, then, have more in common with the far right of the 1930s than with the mainstream right of the 1980s. A decade ago, when I joined the conservative movement as a protege of William F. Buckley, Jr., I could not have imagined that by the mid-nineties Republican presidential candidates would feel compelled to seek the blessing of Pat Robertson; that Patrick Buchanan would be the spokesman for the grass-roots right in the Republican party; and that conservatives in Congress, pressured by the National Rifle Association and the paramilitary militia movement, would ignore the pleas of police officers across the country and attempt to repeal the ban on assault weapons, which are used not to hunt animals but to slaughter people.

How did this disaster happen? How did the conservative movement—which briefly, in the 1980s, seemed on the verge of becoming the vehicle of mainstream Americans—become identified with, indeed overshadowed by, the radical right? The purpose of this book is to explain the shipwreck of American conservatism.

In the first half of this book, I describe the conservative movement and its place in contemporary American politics. Since the 1960s, I argue, the United States has undergone both a political realignment and a social revolution. The realignment has not been a Republican partisan realignment, but a bipartisan conservative political realignment that has benefited Jimmy Carter and Bill Clinton, the most conservative Democrats since the 1890s, as well as moderate and conservative Republicans. This realignment, I argue, is not the inevitable result of great historic forces, but rather the contingent (and avoidable) result of the defeat of the New Deal liberals and the victory of the New Politics/New Left faction within the Democratic party between 1968 and 1972. Since then there has been a gaping hole in the center left of the U.S. political spectrum where New Deal liberalism was once located; the only options for Americans have been, and still are, left liberalism and, on the other side of the missing center left, neoliberalism (moderate conservatism) and radical conservatism. For two decades, conservative Republicans have run from, and neoliberal Democrats have run against, left-liberal Democrats. A comparison of today's political spectrum with that of the 1948 election is instructive: today there are political heirs of presidential candidates Henry Wallace (left liberals), Thomas Dewey (neoliberals and moderate Republicans), and Strom Thurmond (radical conservatives); but today there is no faction in the American political class consisting of the political heirs of Harry S Truman.

This conservative political realignment has been accompanied by a social revolution: the rise of the American overclass. The "overclass" is a new national elite, based in the university-credentialed professions, that has arisen from the merger of the old northeastern Protestant establishment and upwardly mobile Americans from other regional and ethnic backgrounds. The decreasing dependence of politicians on political machines and unions, and their increasing reliance on large individual and corporate donors and ideological and professional groups, has meant that the political influence of the numerically small overclass has grown at the expense of the middle class. Rising overclass influence has effects all across the political spectrum; it results in the empowerment of overclass leftists and overclass centrists as well as overclass conservatives, at the expense of left-wing, centrist, and right-wing wage-earning Americans alike. The predominance of the overclass in American politics explains the near-unanimity on economic policies that benefit the affluent and the gentleman's agreement within the political-journalistic elite that the differences between "left," "liberal," and "conservative" will chiefly turn on matters of social and cultural policy, like abortion and arts funding, rather than bread-and-butter issues.

The bipartisan conservative realignment and the overclass revolution have alienated a substantial group of former New Deal Democrats, the so-called radical center. Members of the radical center, who combine moderate conservative social views with support for social democratic policies that benefit working people, have not been represented by any political faction since the demise of the FDR-Truman-Johnson liberals at the hands of left-liberal McGovernites. The left-liberals offend the radical center with their cultured radicalism; the neoliberals and radical conservatives, though differing on social issues, agree on a laissez-faire economic agenda that sacrifices the interests of wage-earning radical centrists. In Chapter Two, I argue that there were two opportunities for the formation of a mature, centrist American conservatism that would have answered the needs of the radical center and prevented its members from destabilizing the political order with their alienation and anger. The first chance for a unifying "one-nation conservatism" came in the late 1940s and early 1950s with the "new conservatives" or vital center liberals like Reinhold Niebuhr, Arthur Schlesinger, Jr., and, most important, Peter Viereck. The second chance for one-nation conservatism came in the late 1970s and early 1980s with the influx into the Republican party of the neoconservatives (many of them former vital center liberals). In each case potential one-nation conservatism was defeated by a radical conservatism on which the two greatest influences were Jacksonian populism (midwestern in the 1950s, southern and southwestern in the 1980s) and the inverted Marxist ideology of ex-leftist radicals (like Willmoore Kendall and James Burnham in the 1950s and Irving Kristol, Norman Podhoretz, and Michael Novak in the 1980s). For almost half a century, the American right has not been "conservative" in the sense in which Edmund Burke and Daniel Webster used the term, but rather a bizarre synthesis of the traditions of William Jennings Bryan and Karl Marx (perfectly symbolized today by the alliance between Pat Robertson and ex-leftist Jewish neoconservatives).

In Chapter Three, I describe how the present-day conservative movement is organized in three divisions: the grass-roots right, the brain-trust right, and the big-money right. The high degree of coordination of the right-wing political-media machine can be seen from the unanimity with which every major conservative publication and leader sprang to the defense of Pat Robertson after I drew attention to the Christian Coalition leader's anti-Semitic conspiracy theories in the spring of 1995—a story I tell in Chapter Four. Pandering to the Protestant fundamentalist right, I argue in Chapter Five, is an essential part of the conservative elite's strategy—inspired by that of southern Bourbon Democrats—of using the so-called culture war to divert the attention of voters from the ongoing class war of the overclass against wage-earning Americans. From the segregationist Dixiecrats of the early twentieth century, the southern politicians who dominate the Republican party of the 1990s inherited the combination of radically plutocratic economic policies with a demogogic culture-war politics based on manipulating public anxieties about race, "family values," and imaginary threats of federal tyranny.

In the second half of the book, I examine the major themes of the conservative culture war and show how conservative economic policies promote the right's class war. In Chapter Six, I subject the right-wing myth of the "new class," which owes its inspiration equally to Jacksonian populism and inverted Marxism, to critical scrutiny. Three other conservative myths, about taxes, education, and illegitimacy, are dissected in Chapter Seven. The revival of social Darwinism and racism on the mainstream right in the 1990s is the subject of Chapter Eight. In Chapter Nine I trace the roots, in the tradition of southern Jacksonian Democrats, of the antigovernment radicalism that has replaced the tradition of Hamilton, Webster, Lincoln, and Theodore Roosevelt in providing the constitutional theory of the Republican party. All of these culture-war themes, I argue, distract attention from the damage being done to the middle class by conservative economic policies—a subject I discuss in Chapter Ten.

In the epilogue, "Up From Conservatism," I speculate on the alternatives to the radical right. In the long run, a sweeping middle-class revolution checking the exorbitant privileges of the newly ascendant overclass will be necessary if the United States is not to permanently become a more stratified, divided, and poorer country. In the medium-term future, the priority must be to reconstruct a centrist "national liberalism," inspired more by the Progressives than by the vital center liberals or the New Deal liberals. Until a new national liberalism becomes a force in politics, though, the best course is to support the center right (the neoliberals) against the radical right (on economic policy) and the left-liberals (on civil rights and social issues). Until a version of the Progressive–New Deal–vital center tradition can be restored, neoliberalism will be the least of three evils.

There are two issues I do not address in this book. The first is foreign policy (a category in which I would include immigration and trade policy). Since the cold war ended, there has been no single conservative foreign policy line—nor, for that matter, has a new liberal grand strategy emerged. From the late 1940s through the mid-1960s there was a bipartisan foreign policy consensus; since 1989 there has been a bipartisan foreign policy dissensus. The three-way argument in foreign policy among globalists, realists, and isolationists is one that cuts across the liberal-conservative divide—not along it. At some point a new conservative foreign policy consensus may crystallize; until then, foreign policy will continue to be peripheral both to the leaders of the radical right and to their adversaries.

The other issue that I do not address in this book is the private lives of public figures. In recent years, all too many conservatives have disgraced themselves in their effort to impute sexual and financial wrongdoing to liberals like Anita Hill and the Clintons. For opponents of conservatism to make an issue of the private lives and financial histories of conservative leaders like Newt Gingrich and Bob Dole is an understandable, but mistaken, reaction. To establish that a politician is a hypocrite is not to establish that he is wrong. A politician who divorces his wife and abandons his children may nevertheless be right to praise intact families. A conservative politician who dodged the draft may nevertheless be correct in arguing that the Vietnam war was justified. If conservative policies are good for the country, then they should be adopted, even if individual conservatives exhibit human failings. Conversely, the sterling character of conservative leaders would not be sufficient to recommend a program that harms the American republic. It is better to be governed well by sinners than to be misgoverned by saints. FDR's adultery and Lyndon Johnson's shady business dealings did not prevent FDR and Johnson from being greater leaders and doing far more for ordinary Americans than Calvin Coolidge or Ronald Reagan, who may well have been better practitioners of the private virtues. In this book I hold conservative leaders accountable for their ideas and their public deeds, not for their private lives or private dealings. Conservatives can have the gutter if they want it.

In the first issue of *National Review,* in 1955, the young William F. Buckley, Jr., called on conservatives to "stand athwart History and shout, Stop!" It is time now for intelligent and patriotic Americans of all persuasions to stand athwart History and shout Stop! to the out-of-control train of conservatism as it drags the nation toward disaster.

The danger is not that conservative policies will succeed, if success is defined as improving the wages of average Americans and the quality of

American public life and discourse. There is not the slightest chance of conservative success, thus defined. The danger, rather, is that when the inevitable failure of conservative governance occurs, an angry populace will conclude that mainstream conservatism as well as liberalism has been discredited—and that the extremists of the populist and fundamentalist right will be well placed to take advantage of popular alienation and wrath, having gained an unprecedented degree of legitimacy as a result of the "no enemies to the right" policy adopted after 1992 by the mainstream conservatives. Make no mistake, the present Republican spree on behalf of the corporate elite and the richest families in America will sooner or later provoke a backlash—if not from a renewed liberalism, then from the sinister sort of far-right populism symbolized by Patrick Buchanan.

Indeed, it seems increasingly likely that the now moribund mainstream conservative movement of 1955–1992 will be viewed by historians as nothing more than the icebreaker for a resurgent radical right. Historians of the next century may well record that the conservatism of Buckley, Kristol, and Podhoretz was an ephemeral offshoot from the main line of descent on the American right, a line that leads from Father Coughlin through Joe McCarthy and George Wallace to Pat Robertson and Patrick Buchanan. Though they claim to be students of the French and Russian revolutions, all too many of the thinkers and strategists of the conservative movement appear to have forgotten that those who begin revolutions are seldom the ones who finish them. Indeed, they are often among the first victims of the brutal forces they unleash upon the world.

Chapter 1

Realignment and Revolution

The New Map of American Politics

The election of the first Republican Congress in forty years in 1994, following a quarter-century of Republican domination of the presidency, inspired many of the leaders of American conservatism to proclaim that the future belongs to the right. It remains to be seen, of course, whether the Republican party can recapture the White House in 1996, or even hold onto its majority status in both houses of Congress. This uncertainty has not prevented jubilant conservatives from claiming that the United States is in the midst of both a realignment and a revolution. The realignment, optimistic right-wingers claim, is a "partisan" one, which will install the Republican party as the majority party for a generation or more. This partisan realignment, according to House Speaker Newt Gingrich and others, is itself a reflection of a revolution that transcends mere electoral politics—a social and economic revolution being driven by emerging technologies. Liberalism, the worldview of the "second wave" of smokestack industry, must give way to conservatism, the ideology appropriate for the age of the "third wave" information revolution.

The conservatives who claim that the United States is undergoing both a realignment and a revolution are correct. However, they have misidentified both of these phenomena. The realignment is a bipartisan conservative political realignment, which may or may not take the form of a lasting Republican partisan realignment. The revolution is not so much a technological revolution as a social revolution—the rise of the overclass, a new American oligarchy.

15

What is more, neither the bipartisan conservative political realignment nor the overclass revolution is a new phenomenon. The conservative realignment began in the mid-1970s; it has given us not only Republicans to the right of Eisenhower and Nixon but the most conservative Democratic presidents since Grover Cleveland: Jimmy Carter and Bill Clinton. Nor did the rise of the overclass begin in the 1990s; its origins lie in the expansion of the university-credentialed elites in the years after World War II, and its effects have been increasingly apparent since the 1960s.

The interaction of the conservative political realignment and the overclass revolution are responsible for the emerging pattern of the American political scene—a pattern in which the center of gravity of American politics is at once to the right of center (the political realignment) and very high in the socioeconomic scale (the overclass revolution). To put it another way, the winners in contemporary American politics are right-wingers and the well-to-do; the losers are Americans of middling views and of the middle class. Most Americans sense that Washington responds neither to their views nor to their economic interests. Their anger, though tapped by Republicans in 1994, is really anger against the entire political class, Republican and Democrat alike.

In this chapter, I will describe both the realignment and the revolution that are reshaping the American polity. The bipartisan conservative realignment is the result of a civil war within the Democratic party. The destruction of mainstream New Deal liberalism by left liberalism in the 1960s and 1970s backfired, hurting the left and benefiting both moderate and extreme conservatives. The post-1960s conservative realignment reflects the collapse of the mainstream liberal center, rather than the persuasiveness or popularity of conservative ideas. The rightward shift of the political spectrum has taken place at the same time that the importance of parties and political machines has declined and the importance of money to pay for campaign advertising has grown—both trends that have benefited the minority of Americans who belong to the affluent and well-organized overclass. The chapter concludes with a discussion of the peculiar pattern of political groupings that has emerged in the last decade of the twentieth century, a pattern in which there are not two major political positions, but five—left-liberals, libertarian conservatives, the far right, the moderate middle, and the radical center.

Whatever else it may have been, the 1994 congressional election was a repudiation of the Democratic party. Not a single Republican incumbent, in Congress or a governor's mansion, was defeated. For the first time since the election of the Eighty-third Congress in 1952, the Republican party gained control of both houses of Congress, with a greater majority than they won in any election since 1946. Their Senate majority was soon increased when two Democratic senators, Richard Shelby of Alabama and Ben Nighthorse Campbell of Colorado, changed parties. The GOP sweep was not limited to Congress. The Republicans won twenty-four of thirty-six governor's races. As a result, for the first time since 1970, the Republicans won a majority of governorships, as their share rose from nineteen to thirty. As a result of the election, the percentage of Americans in states with Republican governors went from 38.4 percent to 71.8 percent—the highest percentage since the early years of Reconstruction, before most of the Confederate states were readmitted to the Union.[1] Indeed, for the first time since President Rutherford B. Hayes pulled federal troops out of the former Confederacy and Republican puppet regimes in the southern states collapsed, the Republicans gained a majority of southern seats in the House (sixty-four to sixty-one) and the Senate (twelve to ten).

Few experts expected the Republican upset. In hindsight, however, the warning signs were visible in 1992. In an unusual three-way race, a Democrat won the White House—but with the smallest percentage of the vote (43.0) since Woodrow Wilson in the three-way race of 1912 (41.8), when Theodore Roosevelt, like Ross Perot, split the Republican presidential majority. Clinton's *winning* vote matched the average percentage of *losing* Democratic presidential candidates from 1968 to 1992. Even worse, Clinton had no coattails; the Republicans picked up ten seats in the House. Clinton began his term with only fifty-eight Democrats in the Senate, a margin so slight that he was unable to prevent Senate Majority Leader Robert Dole from filibustering most of the administration's proposals to death. Democratic victories in the 1992 congressional elections, moreover, shifted the party toward demographic groups associated with the party's left wing. In 1992 the number of black representatives grew from twenty-five to thirty-eight, and the group of Hispanic members of the House rose from eleven to seventeen; at the same time, the number of women in the Democratic House contingent rose from twenty-eight to forty-seven. The president who had run as "a different kind of Democrat" had to govern with a Democratic majority in Congress that was not only smaller but more liberal than before.

Elections in the aftermath of November 1992 brought additional bad news for the Democrats. Senator Wyche Fowler of Georgia lost a runoff election against Republican Paul Coverdell. In a special spring 1993 election for the Texas Senate seat vacated by Lloyd Bentsen when he became treasury secretary, Democrat Bob Krueger, who had been appointed by Texas Governor Ann Richards, was defeated by Republican Kay Bailey Hutchison. In fall 1993, Democratic governors in Virginia and New Jersey lost to Republican challengers, and the two largest cities of the United States, New York and Los Angeles, dominated for generations by the Democrats, elected Republican mayors. Then in 1994 conservative Republicans won special races for Congress in Kentucky and Oklahoma. Like pebbles clattering down a mountain slope, these events warned of the landslide to come.

In light of the magnitude of their victory in 1994, many Republican leaders and some political scientists have interpreted the midterm election as a "critical" or "realigning" election inaugurating a new era of Republican hegemony in American politics. For most of its history the United States has been dominated by a single party. The Republicans (or National Republicans) controlled Congress and the presidency for twenty-six of the twenty-eight years from 1801 to 1829. Between 1829 and 1861, the Democrats controlled both political branches for eighteen of thirty-two years; the opposition simultaneously controlled the presidency, House, and Senate for only two. From 1860 to 1932, the Republicans controlled White House, House and Senate for forty-two of seventy-two years, while the Democrats had unified control for only ten years. From 1933 to 1968, the Democrats controlled all three political bodies for twenty-one of thirty-five years; the Republicans held both branches for only two (1953-55).[2]

Instead of a two-party system, then, the United States has had five or six one-and-a-half-party systems. The political scientist Samuel Lubell, in 1951, described the succession of American party systems with a metaphor from astronomy: "Our political solar system . . . has been characterized not by two equally competing suns, but by a sun and a moon. It is within the majority party that the issues of any particular period are fought out; while the minority party shines in reflected radiance of the heat thus generated." During periods of one-party dominance, the minor or "moon" party tends to succeed in presidential elections only when it nominates bland, nonpartisan figures, like military heroes, as the Whigs nominated William Henry Harrison in 1840 and as the Republicans nominated Eisenhower in 1952.[3]

The eras of one-party dominance have been divided by what American political scientists, following V. O. Key in 1955, call "critical" elections. The contemporary American political scientist Walter Dean Burnham has called critical elections America's "substitute for revolution." According to most scholars, the critical elections have been those of 1800 (Jeffersonian Republicans), 1828 (Jacksonian Democrats), 1860 (Lincoln's Republicans), 1896 (McKinley's Republicans), and 1932 (FDR's Democrats). Was the 1994 election such a critical election? Some observers argue that the Republicans are on the verge of consolidating a new majority, united by racial, cultural, and religious rather than economic issues.

This interpretation seems doubtful. The rising unpopularity of Newt Gingrich and the Republican Congress in the first year of their rule is evidence for the existence of a fickle and dissatisfied majority, not a nation of eager converts to right-wing Republican ideology. If a partisan realignment has not taken place, then what explains the magnitude of the change wrought by the 1994 midterm election? The answer becomes obvious once we step back from a narrow concentration on American politics and take in the rest of the world. In 1992-94, a "vote-quake" of electoral rebellion that has been shattering parties and political orders throughout the industrialized world finally transformed the landscape of American politics.

Since the end of the cold war, the political systems of the industrial democracies, one by one, like houses in the path of a wildfire, have flared and collapsed into smoldering rubble. In country after country, long-dominant parties have been overthrown in voter rebellions and, in some cases, completely dissolved. The Social Democrats in Sweden, the Christian Democrats in Italy, the Socialists in France, the Liberal Democrats in Japan, the Progressive Conservatives in Canada—all have been shattered or liquidated. The discrediting of socialism, even democratic socialism, by the collapse of the Soviet Union might explain the demise of the Swedish Social Democrats and the French Socialists—but it cannot explain the simultaneous implosion of pro-business, center-right parties, like the Japanese Liberal Democrats or the Canadian Progressive Conservatives.

What seems to be occurring, more or less at the same time, in countries with quite different political and cultural traditions, is a rebellion of the electorate against the local political class as such—left, right, and center. The chief beneficiaries of these anti-system revolts in Europe and Japan have been mavericks like Italy's prime minister Sylvio Berlusconi, and national-populist movements, mostly on the right, ranging from Jorg Haider's party to far-right nationalist parties in France and Preston Manning's Perot-like Reform party based in western Canada. The only dominant parties in the West that are still standing are Helmut Kohl's Christian Democrats in Germany and the Conservatives in Britain. Kohl's coalition partners, the Free Democrats, are endangered, and the Conservatives may fall in the next British election.

In 1992 and 1994, the anti-system revolt came to America. If the United States had a unified government with a parliamentary system, the dominant party probably would have been decimated as completely as its equivalents in Europe and Asia. Because of the separation of powers and the division of government between the two parties, however, the angry electorate—to be precise, the angry independents—could not obliterate the entire political class with one shot. The rebels did the next best thing, mobilizing behind Perot to throw out the incumbent president in 1992, and turning to throw out the dominant party in Congress two years later. Among its other merits, this theory explains the peculiar fact that in 1992 the Republicans *gained* in Congress even as a Democrat was elected to the White House; voters were attacking the party identified with each branch for a quarter of a century. (If I may, I would like to claim some credit as a minor prophet: in 1993 I wrote an op-ed for the *Washington Post,* in which I argued that anti-system politics of the European and Japanese variety was emerging in the United States and that the Democrats, as the dominant party, were likely to be devastated. The editors thought my prediction was unconvincing, and the essay, although set in galleys, was rejected at the last moment.)

What is behind this extraordinary series of more or less concurrent political rebellions in the First World? The culprit, it seems, is the world economy. The post–World War II era of high productivity growth ended in 1973. For a generation slow growth has resulted in declining real wages in the United States and in high unemployment in Western Europe (the same phenomenon may now be occurring in Japan, whose protected domestic economy until recently was following a unique trajectory). The free-market reforms of politicians like Reagan, Thatcher, and neoliberals of various stripes in Europe have failed to jump-start the engine of western prosperity. What is more, the liberalization of the former Soviet bloc and Third World economies since 1989 has created an ever-growing pool of cheap but often skilled labor. Squeezed by low productivity growth, western workers increasingly find themselves forced to compete directly with low-wage workers in poor countries. Small wonder that the fastest-growing political movements in the industrial democracies are those of radical populists like Ross Perot and Patrick Buchanan appealing to public disenchantment with political and economic elites.

The good news for the New Politics/New Left Democrats, then, is that they were not finished off by a Republican realignment; they were killed by a worldwide political earthquake being driven by global economic upheaval. The bad news for them (though not necessarily for the country) is that the post-1968 left-liberal Democratic party is still dead.

In 1994, New Politics/New Left liberalism was dealt a deathblow. Some conservatives make the further claim that the 1994 election marked a repudiation, not only of post-1960s left liberalism, but of the New Deal liberalism in the tradition of FDR, Truman, Johnson, and Humphrey. In this view, 1994 marked the end, not only of the era that began in 1968, but of the era that began in 1932.

In old Perry Mason episodes, one plot is used again and again. The defendant sincerely believes he murdered someone sleeping in the dark; his lawyer Perry Mason, however, proves that the victim was already dead when stabbed or clubbed by his client. Perry Mason's client goes free, because it is not against the law to murder someone who is already dead. Today's conservatives are like Perry Mason's client. As much as they might like to claim credit for killing the New Deal coalition of Franklin Delano Roosevelt in 1994, the fact is that the New Deal Democratic party was killed between 1968 and 1972. The killers were George McGovern and his allies and supporters in the New Politics movement. By turning the Democratic party into an alliance of affluent whites and minorities based on identity politics rather than bread-and-butter issues, the left-liberals, without intending to, turned the country over to the center right and the far right.

This is a disaster of the first order. The New Deal liberals, between FDR and Johnson, were responsible for most of what is worthwhile about contemporary America. The contemporary Republican right frequently claims that its goal is to restore the Golden Age of mid-twentieth-century America. Conservatives seem not to notice that this era, from 1945 to 1973, happened to be the Golden Age of New Deal liberalism—and the Dark Ages for a marginalized American conservatism that had little influence (except for its contribution to anti-communist witch-hunts). The prosperity of the American middle class, endangered by the free-market dynamic that produced the Great Depression, was restored and increased by the federal government during the three waves of the New Deal liberal reform: Franklin Roosevelt's original New Deal (Social Security, welfare for widows with children, and workfare programs like the Civilian Conservation Corps for the able-bodied poor), Harry Truman's Fair Deal (the G.I. Bill and the federal home-mortgage interest deduction intended to allow middle- and low-income families to buy homes), and Lyndon Johnson's Great Society (Medicare, Medicaid, and student loans). Most of the New Deal liberal entitlements benefited middle-class and working-class Americans. Far from encouraging welfare dependency among the black poor, the early New Deal programs—at the insistence of southern Democrats in Congress—were designed to exclude black Americans (for example, by means of exemptions for the agricultural and menial-service jobs in which most blacks then worked). Had black Americans benefited as much as white Americans from New Deal liberal policies encouraging high wages, home ownership, and wealth formation, the black community would undoubtedly be better off today.

The third and last of the great New Deal presidents, Lyndon Johnson, undertook a task more difficult than his predecessors Truman and FDR had faced—a task, indeed, more difficult than that faced by any president since Lincoln. Johnson tried to complete the New Deal by giving all Americans access to guaranteed health care and higher education, while at the same time completing the unfinished business of the Civil War and Reconstruction: civil and political rights for all Americans, regardless of their race. The deeply rooted racism of many working-class and middle-class white Democrats, and of the Democratic political class in the segregated South, had deterred previous New Deal Democratic presidents; FDR had never dared take on segregation, and Truman's reluctant and moderate civil-rights reforms led Strom Thurmond and other southern Democrats to defect in the presidential election of 1948. To make matters worse, Johnson had to promote the completion of the New Deal and the Second Reconstruction while fighting an unpopular and disastrous war in Vietnam.

Johnson failed, of course. Though Johnson was one of the greatest presidents in American history, even his mastery of the political process was insufficient to avert a debacle. But then, no president could have succeeded—not FDR, not Lincoln, not even Washington—in the circumstances in which Johnson found himself. Still the shipwreck of the

Johnson presidency need not have meant the shipwreck of New Deal liberalism. Had history turned out differently, had the FDR-Truman-Johnson-Humphrey wing survived as the dominant force in the Democratic party into the 1970s and 1980s, the continuing vitality of New Deal liberalism might have given credibility to the moderate Eisenhower-Rockefeller wing of the GOP. In such an America, it seems doubtful that Ronald Reagan would have been elected in 1980 or that a Republican Congress would have come to power in 1994. If the Democrats during the past generation had been identified, like Lyndon Johnson and Hubert Humphrey, with race-neutral civil rights reform, generous entitlements for wage-earning Americans, and a foreign policy that avoided the extremes of pacifism and paranoia, then a second, integrationist phase of the New Deal might have succeeded the segregated first phase. Racial quotas and supply-side economics alike might have been equally unknown. Had color-blind New Deal liberalism survived, it is unlikely that the United States, on the verge of the twenty-first century, would be in the control of a Washington cabal of reactionary white politicians from the South and West and their corporate sponsors.

History, of course, has turned out differently—thanks as much to the New Left of the 1960s and 1970s as to the New Right of the 1970s and 1980s. The radicals of the 1960s, who became the mainstream "liberals" of the 1970s and 1980s, thought that nothing could be worse than "cold war liberals" like Lyndon Johnson, Hubert Humphrey, and Daniel Patrick Moynihan. They soon found out otherwise. The New Politics/New Left Democrats destroyed New Deal liberalism in the name of "the revolution" and "the movement," and discovered, too late, that the beneficiaries of their insurgency would be a revolution and a movement quite different from their own.

To understand the rise of the New Left within the Democratic party, we must go back to the 1948 presidential election. The election became a four-way race when the Democratic party disintegrated into three groups. The core group of New Deal liberals supported President Harry Truman. They were in favor of a continuation of New Deal reforms to benefit middle-class and working Americans; a vigorous but selective policy of "containment" of the Soviet Union in Europe and around the world; and civil rights for black and other nonwhite Americans.

The Truman Democrats had enemies on both the left and the right. The "progressives" (not to be confused with turn-of-the-century Progressives like Theodore Roosevelt and Herbert Croly) rallied behind their own presidential candidate, Henry Wallace. For years Wallace had been at odds with the Democratic party leadership, because of his pro-Soviet stance and his belief that American liberals should ally themselves with socialists and communists in domestic politics. Wallace had served as FDR's vice president, but FDR had dropped him from the ticket in 1944 and replaced him with Harry Truman. Under Truman, Wallace had served as agriculture secretary, until Wallace's reflexive pro-Soviet statements led Truman to fire him. Wallace became editor of the *New Republic* (which despite its Progressive origins had become a magazine of the pro-communist left) and ran for the presidency against his former rival and boss Truman, at the head of a coalition of radical liberals, socialists, and communists.

Wallace's Progressives broke with Truman's centrist liberals chiefly over foreign policy—the Progressives wanted to appease Stalin's Soviet Union, not contain it. Conservative Democrats rebelled against Truman and his allies on the basis of a domestic issue, civil rights. Angry at the success of liberals like Hubert Humphrey in including a civil rights plank in the 1948 Democratic platform, a group of southern segregationist Democrats stormed out of the Democratic convention and formed their own states' rights or Dixiecrat party, whose nominee was then-South Carolina governor J. Strom Thurmond. In the four-way election of 1948, the Dixiecrats carried only four states in the Deep South (these overlapped with the states carried by Barry Goldwater in 1964 and George Wallace in 1968; they have become the core of the moderate Republican presidential majority).

The 1948 election, then, presented American voters with a clear choice of four distinct, and incompatible, political ideologies—three of them in the Democratic party. On the extreme left were the Wallace Progressives, and on the extreme right the Thurmond Dixiecrats. Competing for the center were Harry Truman's center-left Democrats and Thomas Dewey's center-right eastern establishment Republicans (who had defeated the conservative midwestern Republicans led by Senator Robert Taft).

Thanks to Truman's narrow victory, the dominant faction in the Democratic party from 1948 until 1968 consisted of what Arthur Schlesinger, Jr. called "vital center" liberals and what their enemies called "cold war liberals." In foreign policy, the vital center liberals rejected the Left's policy of appeasing the Soviet Union and the Right's crackpot policy of "rolling back" Soviet gains in Europe by force, in favor of a patient policy of containment, which took the form of the commitment of U.S. forces to Europe as part of NATO and of U.S. defense of South Korea and South Vietnam against communist takeovers. In domestic policy, the vital center liberals rejected the extremes of socialism and laissez-faire in favor of "the mixed economy" or what in Europe is known as "the social market," a system combining private property and free enterprise with necessary government regulation and government provision of economic security (Social Security) and economic opportunity (the G.I. Bill, student loans, small business and home ownership subsidies). The distance between Democratic vital center liberalism and Dwight Eisenhower's moderate "modern Republicanism" was so small that the 1950s came to be known as the era of "the end of ideology" and the age of "consensus."

The greatest threat to the vital center liberals came not from the right but from the left, from two sources: the New Politics Democrats and the New Left Democrats.

As early as the 1950s, what the political scientist James Q. Wilson has called educated, affluent, and ideologically driven "amateur Democrats" were waging war on the urban and small-town political machines that were the backbone of the Roosevelt-Truman Democratic party. (Harry Truman himself was a product of the notorious Pendergast machine of Kansas City, named after "Boss" Tom Pendergast.) The nomination of Adlai Stevenson in 1956 was the first victory of what came to be known as the New Politics movement. In 1960, John F. Kennedy managed to appeal to both the upper-middle-class reformers (he was a Harvard man) and the ethnic voters (he was Boston Irish). The New Politics liberals, however, loathed Lyndon Johnson; genteel northeastern liberals were repelled as much by Johnson's southwestern populist persona as by his escalation of the war in Vietnam and his old-fashioned New Deal liberalism.

The influence of the New Politics reformers can be seen in the form taken by the War on Poverty during the Kennedy and Johnson years. The War on Poverty differed from the Great Society programs, which were universal entitlements whose chief beneficiaries were the middle and working classes—Medicare and student loans. The War on Poverty united highly educated white liberal reformers with black and Hispanic activists in alliances against the urban political machines representing working-class whites. The provision of the Economic Opportunity Act of 1964 that mandated "maximum feasible participation of the residents of the areas and the members of groups served" meant that War on Poverty programs, instead of being carried out by City Hall, were contracted out to nongovernmental community groups in largely black and Hispanic neighborhoods in cities like New York and Chicago. The technocratic rhetoric of "maximum feasible participation" masked what was, in effect, at once a class war and an ethnic war within the Democratic party. By means of federal community action, upper-income reformers, disproportionately Protestant and Jewish, subsidized the creation of black and Hispanic counter-machines to undermine the Democratic urban machines controlled by mostly Catholic ethnics (who had tended to freeze blacks out of both political and economic opportunities).

To the left of the New Politics reformers were the New Left radicals. It is no exaggeration to say that the New Left was disproportionately, though not exclusively, a Jewish phenomenon, with its origins in the radicalism that Eastern European Jews brought with them when they immigrated to the big cities of the Northeast in the late nineteenth and early twentieth centuries. Although Jews account for less than 3 percent of the U.S. population, a majority not only of the leaders but of the members of the New Left were Jewish, according to the most thorough study.[4] Jews, along with Scandinavians and Germans, had long contributed to the ranks of American socialism and radicalism far out of proportion to their numbers (this is reflected to this day in the progressive politics not only of American Jews but of the plains states settled by Nordics, like Minnesota). The New Left radicals of the sixties claimed to be spokesmen for their age group and rebels against authority. In fact, they were highly unrepresentative of young people of their generation—most working-class Americans in the sixties were not radicalized. At the same time, they were in a way utterly faithful to authority—not government authority, but family authority. Many of the New Left radicals were "red diaper babies," children of left-wing Wallace Democrats, Trotskyists, or Stalinists, and grandchildren of socialists and communists. In opposing the Vietnam war, they were merely reenacting the opposition of their left-wing parents to the Korean War and (during the Popular Front period) to World War II, and the opposition of their radical grandparents to Woodrow Wilson and U.S. entry into World War I. The "rebellion" of the sixties radicals, in short, resulted from conformity to the tradition of the tiny subculture from which the New Left emerged.

The struggle between the left and the center within the Democratic party, then, was simultaneously a class struggle and an ethnic struggle, between college-educated Jewish and mainline Protestant radicals and progressives on the left and the representatives of working-class, Catholic, and southern evangelical Protestant Democrats in the center. During the 1968 Democratic convention, the ethnocultural and class war within the Democratic party broke into open violence in the streets of Chicago, as affluent white student radicals fought battles with Mayor Richard J. Daley's working-class white police. Although the crumbling Democratic machines retained enough power to nominate Hubert H. Humphrey for president, the New Deal Democratic party was in its death throes. Complaints that the nomination process was undemocratic led the Democratic National Committee in 1971 to approve the new rules for delegate selection proposed by a commission chaired in succession by South Dakota senator George McGovern and Minnesota representative Donald Fraser. The new rules mandated affirmative action in state delegations to party conventions for blacks, women, and young people in "reasonable relationship to the group's presence in the population of the state." The power of the old machines was shattered, and the power of the "groups" or "caucuses"—feminists, antiwar activists, blacks, Hispanics, homosexuals—was institutionalized.

The defeat of the Wallace left by the Truman center in 1948, it turned out, had given New Deal liberalism only a twenty-year renewal. The final defeat of New Deal liberalism by New Politics left-liberalism was symbolized by one incident at the 1972 Democratic national convention. Throughout the New Deal/vital center era the Chicago Democratic machine had been one of the great power centers in the national Democratic party. In 1972, however, Major Richard J. Daley and his delegation of Chicago Democrats were found guilty of violating new Democratic party rules by not having enough blacks and women in their ranks, and were unceremoniously tossed out of the convention by left-liberal supporters of George McGovern. The Daley delegation was replaced by a new delegation from Chicago that included a young black activist named Jesse Jackson. The new slate of fifty-nine Democratic delegates from Chicago had only three Polish-Americans and one Italian-American.[5]

From Andrew Jackson to Lyndon Johnson, the Democratic party had been an alliance of southern white Protestants and largely Catholic immigrants from Europe and their descendants in the northern cities. In only a few years, the southerners and ethnics were displaced by a new coalition of affluent northern whites, disproportionately Jewish, secular, and mainline Protestant, and blacks and Hispanics. Such a coalition in the New York mayoral race of 1969 permitted John V. Lindsay to defeat the champion of the white ethnic Democrats, Mario Proccacino (who popularized the term "limousine liberals" for the affluent white reformers who were remaking the Democratic party). In Los Angeles a few years later, a similar coalition dependent on black votes and the donations of liberal Jews provided the critical support for Mayor Tom Bradley.

Here, in order of degree of partisanship, are the groups that voted Democratic in 1994: blacks (92 percent), Jews (78 percent), the poor, making less than $15,000 (63 percent), Americans with no religious affiliations (63 percent), members of union households (61 percent), Hispanics (60 percent), high school dropouts (60 percent), unmarried women (56 percent), and Asian-Americans (55 percent). Here, conversely, are the most partisan Republican voters, as revealed by the midterm election: Protestants (60 percent), whites (58 percent), Americans with some college (58 percent), high-school educated Americans aged thirty to forty-four (58 percent), married people (57 percent), Americans earning more than $50,000 (57 percent) and more than $39,000 (54 percent). As these figures indicate, the class-based "have/have-not" dichotomy of the New Deal era has been replaced, in the age of identity politics, by an "are/are-not" dichotomy. The "ares" are white, heterosexual, married, Christian, middle-class; the "are-nots" are not-white, not-heterosexual, not-married, not-Christian, not-middle-class. The data from the 1994 election indicating the most loyal Democratic groups are blacks and Jews merely confirm a pattern that emerged in the late 1960s and early 1970s, as a result of the triumph of the New Politics/New Left liberals over the New Deal/vital center liberals. As early as 1980, following the election of Ronald Reagan, Wilson Carey McWilliams observed, "The periphery of the New Deal coalition [progressives, blacks, and Jews] has become the heart of the Democratic party, and the historic Democratic party—Northern Catholics and Southern whites—has been moved to the periphery."[6]

The McGovern campaign, and the associated reforms of the nominating process, turned the Democratic party among whites into an hourglass alliance of the top and the bottom of the socioeconomic scale. One ranking of white voters in the 1972 election in terms of high, middle, and low socioeconomic status (SES) revealed that McGovern's highest percentages of the white vote were in the high SES (32 percent) and low SES (32 percent) categories and lowest in the middle SES group (26 percent). Between the Democratic landslide in Congress in 1964 and the post-Watergate Democratic landslide of 1974, the Democrats lost lower-status white voters and became increasingly a party of upper-income whites allied with nonwhite Americans.

The affluent white left-liberals who, with their black allies, were taking over the Democratic party viewed working-class whites and the political bosses who represented them with contempt. Writing in the *New York Review of Books,* Elizabeth Hardwick sneered at the typical lower-middle-class white American man, who "comes home to his payments on the car, the mortgage on his house in the bland development, to his pizzas and cottony bread and hard-cover pork chops, to his stupefying television, his over-heated teenage daughter, his D-in-English, car-wrecking son: all this after working himself to exhaustion." Idealizing the urban poor, Hardwick explained that the black woman on welfare "hopes for something more alive, original and creative" as a result of education for her children, in contrast to the moronic working-class white, who wants only to " 'stomp on'—the kind of term they like—the free and inspired teacher, bottle up the flow of ideas, further degrade the already bad textbooks."[7] Garry Wills could think of no better way to damn George Wallace than to associate him with the white lower middle class and working class. Wallace, according to Wills, looked like "a handsome garage attendant. . . . He comes out rubbing his hands on an invisible garage rag (most of the pit grease out of his nails), smiling and winking, Anything-I-can-do-for-you-pretty-girl? His hair is still wet from careful work with comb and water in the gas station's cracked mirror (main panel in the men's room triptych, rubber machine on one side, comb-and-Kleenex dispenser on the other)."[8] Liberals like Hardwick and Wills felt no inhibitions about describing white working people in terms that they would have denounced as racist had they been applied to working-class blacks or Hispanics. For a quarter of a century, the identification of left-liberalism with the snobbery of the white overclass has given credibility to the claims of conservative politicians from Nixon to Quayle to represent "the forgotten majority" against a supercilious "cultural elite."

In 1982, the Democratic National Committee gave its sanction to seven groups by naming them as "official caucuses": women, blacks, Hispanics, Asians, gays, liberals, and business/professionals. White working-class men—the most important constituents of the New Deal Democratic party of Roosevelt, Truman, and Johnson—were not given a caucus. To former student radicals and feminists, blue-collar whites were militaristic and misogynistic "hardhats"; to black civil rights leaders, they were racist "Bubbas." Scorned by the new leaders of the Democratic party, working-class whites would seek champions in independents like George Wallace and Ross Perot and in Republicans like Richard Nixon and Ronald Reagan.

In 1994, the ex-Democratic white working class exacted its greatest revenge on the post-McGovern Democratic party to date by throwing it out of Congress. In an election in which liberals and conservatives were unusually polarized, the Republican victory resulted from the votes of independents. Independents voted for the Democrats in the elections of 1988, 1990, and 1992, by 54–46; they voted 56-44 for the Republicans in 1994. Who are these independents? In the Midwest, the independents who turned against the Democrats in 1994 are described by Harold W. Stanley as "younger, white, working-class men motivated by economic issues." For independents in 1994, it seems, the issue was still "the economy, stupid." The "jobless recovery" of 1994 had not been translated into rising living standards; 75 percent of the voters in 1994 said they were worse off economically than they had been in 1992.

Analyzing the election of 1994, Ruy Texeira and Joel Rogers have documented a remarkable shift by non-college-educated whites away from the Democrats. "Between 1992 and 1994," they write in the *American Prospect,* "Democratic support declined 20 points (to 37 percent) among white men with a high school education and 15 points (to 31 percent) among white men with some college." At the same time, non-college-educated white women deserted the Democrats. The problem is not "angry white men," but an angry white working class, whose members, male and female alike, correctly believe that they are still suffering a decline in real income and living standards—and, justly or not, blame the Democratic party.

From 1968 onward, working-class white ex-Democrats have been the key to Republican presidential hegemony. In 1994, the same alienated voters cast the deciding votes in the election that delivered Congress to the Republican party. Call it Mayor Daley's revenge.

A case can be made, then, that we are still in the political era that began in 1968. The election of Bill Clinton was a fluke, caused by the entry into the 1992 presidential race of Ross Perot (the expression of post-cold war anti-system radicalism). The Democratic party is still the top-and-bottom party it has been since McGovern, disproportionately black, Jewish, and northeastern, a coalition of the affluent and the poor; the Republican party is still the predominantly southern and western white Protestant party bequeathed by Nixon, an alliance of the white top and the white middle against the nonwhite base. The ex-Democratic white working class, particularly in the economically depressed industrial regions of the country, is still up for grabs and drawn to candidates like Brown, Buchanan, and Perot who espouse a combination of radical political reform and economic nationalism. The very language of our politics—for example, Newt Gingrich denouncing "countercultural McGoverniks"—has scarcely changed since the 1972 election. The Republicans are still running against George McGovern, and they are still trying to convert permanently the fickle followers of George Wallace.

As this suggests, the divisions within American politics are not a simple matter of liberalism versus conservatism, or left versus right. One useful, though inadequate, approximation of the complex pattern of today's politics is provided by Figure 1.

Mapping economic views and social views on different axes produces four different political philosophies: left liberalism, conservatism, neoliberalism, and what might be described as national liberalism.

| | | Economics | |
		Liberal	Conservative
Social Issues	Liberal	Left Liberalism	Neoliberalism
	Conservative	National Liberalism	Conservatism

FIGURE 1

The term "liberal" today usually refers to left-liberals. If you are liberal both on economic issues (you favor higher taxes on the rich and more government services) and on social issues (you want to decriminalize marijuana and favor gay marriage), then you are a left-liberal.

As left liberalism is consistently liberal, so conservatism is consistently conservative. If you are an economic conservative (you favor low taxes on the rich and cutbacks on entitlements for the middle class) and a social conservative (you think that abortion should be outlawed and the media should be censored), then you are a mainstream conservative.

Neoliberalism might also be called moderate libertarianism (radical libertarianism is something different). If you agree with the conservative economic agenda of slashing taxes, rolling back entitlements, and furthering free trade and high levels of immigration, and at the same time agree with the left-liberal social agenda of preserving legalized abortion, decriminalizing drugs, and legalizing gay marriage, then you are a neoliberal.

The last of the four positions is national liberalism, which might also be described as a populism of the center rather than of the far right. National liberalism unites moderate social conservatism with moderate economic liberalism. If you agree with left-liberals that all working people should have guaranteed health care and paid maternity leave, and you also agree with conservatives that racial quotas should be abolished and that the police need to have greater powers to crack down on criminals and panhandlers, then you are a national liberal.[9]

These four viewpoints are highly idealized, of course. The political views of most Americans tend to be less consistent. Still, the fourfold division of American political philosophies into left-liberal, conservative, neoliberal, and national liberal is a great improvement over the liberal–conservative dichotomy.

The important thing to note about the fourfold division is this: of the four distinct positions, only three—left-liberalism, neoliberalism, and conservatism—are represented today in the two major parties and the media. The Democratic party includes both left-liberals like Massachusetts Senator Edward Kennedy and neoliberals like Bill Clinton. The Republican party, though predominantly conservative, has a few neoliberals of its own, such as New Jersey Governor Christine Todd Whitman and Massachusetts Governor Bill Weld, both of whom combine economic conservatism with liberal views on matters like abortion and gay rights. Outside of the political arena, left-liberal, neoliberal, and conservative perspectives are well represented in political journalism. The *Nation* is a left-liberal magazine; the *New Republic* is best identified as a neoliberal magazine; and *National Review,* the *American Spectator, Commentary, Policy Review,* and the *Standard* are conservative magazines. Left-liberals, neoliberals, and conservatives, then, all have elected politicians to carry their banner, and magazines in which the strategy of their cause can be debated.

National liberalism has neither politicians nor journals of opinion. There are no politicians, of either party, who at the same time favor universal health care and oppose racial quotas. There is no national liberal version of the *Nation,* or the *New Republic,* or *National Review,* in whose pages national liberals can hammer out a strategy for promoting a synthesis of economic liberalism and social conservatism. The closest thing to an organized national liberal movement that American politics has seen in recent years was the 1992 candidacy of Ross Perot, who was naturally attacked by left-liberals as a rightist and by neoliberals and conservatives as a leftist (and by all three factions, both inaccurately and unjustly, as a "fascist"). Perot's mixture of liberalism and conservatism was highly idiosyncratic, however, and as of this writing, despite his efforts to found a new party, the Independence party, the Perot movement remains a one-man show.

From 1932 to 1968, New Deal/vital center liberals like FDR, Truman, Kennedy, Johnson, and Humphrey spoke for the national liberal constituency in American politics. Since the downfall of the New Dealers, however, there has been no elite group that identifies with the millions of wage-earning Americans whose views clearly make them national liberals. The reason is that American politics is increasingly becoming a monopoly of a social elite—the American overclass. Left-liberalism, neoliberalism, and conservatism are all compatible, in one way or another, with either the social views or the economic interests of the overclass. But national liberalism, with its mixture of social conservatism and economic liberalism, represents a direct threat to overclass social views (which tend to be liberal) and overclass economic interests (which are promoted by neoliberal and conservative policies). Indeed, the one thing that left-liberals, neoliberals, and conservatives all fear more than each other is the reemergence of national liberalism as a political force, as in the era of FDR, Truman, and Johnson.

What is the overclass? The term was first used in English in the middle of the twentieth century by Gunnar Myrdal, who translated both "overclass" and "underclass" from his native Swedish. Though "underclass" has been widely employed to describe the hereditary inner-city poor, Myrdal's coinage of "overclass" fell on stony ground. Now and then, between the fifties and the nineties, the term popped up in the left- and right-wing press, independently invented by analogy with "underclass" by people who did not know that Myrdal had already introduced the term. I helped to launch the term into public discussion in 1995 with the publication of my book *The Next American Nation,* in which I discuss the subject more extensively than I can here. Following the publication of *The Next American Nation, Newsweek* did a cover story on the overclass (complete with a cartoon by *Doonesbury* creator Garry Trudeau). Since then, the word has become familiar, and for a very good reason: it describes a real and very important group in American society.

Though "overclass" is widely used, there is no consensus on its definition. Sometimes the term is used to refer to the affluent, sometimes to the skilled. I use the word "overclass" to refer not to the rich in general or the educated in general, but to a specific social group that is at once an elite and a quasi-hereditary social class. The overclass is the credentialed managerial-professional elite, consisting of Americans with advanced degrees (MBAs, JDs, PhDs, MDs) and their spouses and children. How big a group is it? Less than 10 percent of the U.S. population holds an advanced degree (and this includes advanced degrees from third- and fourth-rate universities). If we eliminate the holders of advanced degrees from diploma mills, and limit ourselves to graduates of professional or graduate programs at prestigious private schools or first-rate state universities, we discover that the overclass is very small indeed, no more than 5 to 10 percent of the American people (including children and spouses makes the number higher).

Tiny though this corps of highly educated managers, lawyers, professors, and doctors is, its members provide the overwhelming majority of leaders in the highest reaches of American business, politics, education, and journalism. There are differences among particular institutional elites—CEOs and federal judges tend to be more highly educated on average than members of Congress—but compared to the majority of Americans whose education ends with the acquisition of a high school diploma, these differences are minor.

The overclass, if I am correct, is—or is in the process of becoming—not merely an institutional elite, but a quasi-hereditary social elite.

Whether the overclass is a genuine social class, that is, a hereditary or quasi-hereditary elite, can be debated. If the overclass consists of random individuals from different backgrounds who just happen to acquire good degrees and good jobs, then the overclass is not a class at all, but a meritocratic elite, which can be expected to reconstitute itself with every generation. If, on the other hand, the members of the overclass tend to be born to overclass parents, then the overclass, in addition to being an elite, is a quasi-hereditary social class. Since the expansion of higher education after World War II, there has only been time for one generation to be born to a large stratum of college-educated parents. The question cannot be finally resolved, therefore, until 2025 or 2050.

In the meantime, the smart money should bet on the overclass turning into a self-perpetuating social stratum, instead of a completely open—and therefore completely unstable—meritocracy. The reason is what anthropologists call "assortative mating," that is, marriage between people of similar backgrounds. Now that coeducation has become the norm, college-educated members of the professional class increasingly marry other members of the college-educated professional class—often, the boyfriend or girlfriend they met in their first year of law school or business school. It is not a daring prediction that the children of two lawyers, or two MBAs, will be more likely to get a JD or an MBA than the children of parents whose education ended with the twelfth grade, or a BA.

Conservatives have attacked my account of the American overclass in two ways. Some have dismissed the overclass theory as "Marxism" (in fact, it owes its inspiration to non-Marxist sociological accounts of class, like those of Max Weber and Digby Baltzell). The conservative party line with respect to the subject of class in the United States holds that America is a classless society, or a two-class society, divided between the middle class (the 95 percent of the population that includes everyone from the working poor to the hereditary rich) and the underclass (the 5 percent or so made up of the nonworking hereditary poor). The absurdity of either view is self-evident, as is the utility, to the political faction that represents the wealthy, of a theory that persuades blue-collar workers that they really belong to the same class as Malcolm Forbes, Jr. or Pete DuPont or William F. Buckley, Jr. and share the same economic interests.

Another argument that conservatives use in their effort to prove that the United States is a classless, or two-class, society is the existence of a substantial degree of social mobility in America (as in other industrial democracies). The point is well taken—and irrelevant. The fact that there is a degree of mobility between classes does not mean that classes do not exist. For a thousand years, commoners have been joining the English aristocracy, while younger sons have been falling out of it. This turnover does not mean that there is no English aristocracy.

It is not my contention that the overclass is exclusively conservative. Most conservative politicians and intellectuals belong to the overclass. So do most left-liberal politicians and intellectuals. So do most neoliberal politicians and intellectuals. With the sole exception of their political views, overclass conservatives have more in common with overclass left-liberals and overclass neoliberals than they do with middle-class conservatives. They go to the same Ivy League schools and leading state universities, and send their children to the same private schools or good public schools; they have similar tastes in dress and dining and recreation; they have similar patterns of marriage and child rearing.

The latter is particularly significant. Consider this portrait of a typical overclass family. The parents of both the husband and wife were college-educated. Both husband and wife went to private schools or good public schools. Both husband and wife have advanced degrees and professional careers. Their children are raised by a maid or live-in servant, whom they need, because they are a two-professional family, and whom they can afford, because they are a two-professional family. The archetypal family pattern of the overclass is the "three-parent family"—husband, wife, and Latin American nanny.

Here, then, is a simple test of overclass status. Americans who do not have advanced degrees and cannot afford maids or nannies are middle class; Americans who have advanced degrees and can afford maids or nannies are overclass. It's as simple as that.

The "nanny question" shows the extent to which American public policy reflects the interests of the American overclass, in direct opposition to the desires of the American majority. Since the 1960s, according to every poll, a substantial majority of Americans has favored the restriction or ending of legal immigration. It is often said that middle-class opposition to immigration is a recent phenomenon that reflects frustration with stagnating wages. This is simply not true. Most Americans wanted immigration cut back in the booming sixties, just as most Americans want immigration restricted in the low-growth nineties. Recently, as a result of pressure from below, a faction of the Republican party led by Patrick Buchanan and Governor Pete Wilson of California has finally begun to support immigration restriction. Even so, the consensus position of the conservative establishment remains one favoring high, or even increased, immigration. The editors of the *Wall Street Journal* have gone so far as to call for a five-word constitutional amendment— "There shall be open borders"—that would permit hundreds of millions, perhaps billions of impoverished people from the Third World to resettle at will in the United States. Neoliberals like Bill Clinton support a policy of high immigration. So do many left-liberals. The political, intellectual, and journalistic elites of the United States are almost unanimously in favor of maintaining the present immigration regime in which there is a constant influx of low-wage labor from Latin America, the Caribbean, and Asia into the United States, at a rate of approximately a million legal immigrants a year.

Why is a high immigration policy opposed by most middle-class Americans but favored by almost all members of the overclass of all persuasions—left, right, and center? I discovered the answer after publishing a book in which I argued for reducing immigration levels in order to raise wages among unskilled workers in the United States. Friends and acquaintances of mine of various political viewpoints, all of them highly educated and affluent members of the overclass by my definition, found elements of my argument convincing. From both liberals and conservatives, however, I heard a similar complaint: "I don't agree with your idea about restricting immigration, though. We need our nanny!" In every case, it turned out that the objecting individual and his or her spouse paid a maid or nanny from Latin America or the Caribbean to look after their children while both parents worked at professional jobs. Take away the elaborate moral arguments of the overclass left for immigration, and the equally elaborate economic rationales of the overclass right, and what remains is the naked economic interest in maintaining a supply of poorly paid, nonunionized foreign women whose labor permits overclass parents of all political persuasions to enjoy a lifestyle like that of the aristocrats of the past with their nannies and governesses.

The continued access by affluent overclass families to poor Latin American and Caribbean domestic workers by means of a generous immigration policy is not the only issue that divides the overclass (left, right, and center) from the middle class (left, right, and center). Free trade is another. The right to unionize is another (supposedly "liberal" newspapers like the *Washington Post* and the *New York Times* are more liberal when the subject is a racial minority or an endangered species than in the case of unionized, blue-collar workers). The economic interests shared by the left, right, and center members of the overclass explain the fact that controversy about social issues, since the 1960s, has been accompanied by a curious consensus on economic issues among elites across the political spectrum.

The real social revolution of our time in the United States, then, is the rise of the overclass. This provides the answer to the right's rhetoric about "revolution." Conservative triumphalism does not end with the argument that there has been a Republican realignment (an argument which, I have tried to show, is half right, insofar as there has been a bipartisan conservative realignment). Conservatives also claim to be the champions of social and economic and technological revolution, as significant as the Industrial Revolution of the eighteenth and nineteenth centuries. According to Newt Gingrich, "the transformation we are experiencing is so large and historic that it can be compared with only two other great eras of human history—the Agricultural Revolution and the Industrial Revolution." If Gingrich is right, then those who oppose the Republican agenda are ignorant fools who do not realize they are opposing, not merely a party or a coalition of interests, but Progress with a capital P and History with a capital H.

The first observation that needs to be made about Gingrichian techno-conservatism is the fact that it clearly derives from Karl Marx (Gingrich derives his ideas from Alvin and Heidi Toffler, two thinkers who started on the left). It was Marx who taught that changes in politics and society could always be explained in terms of changes in "the means of production"; conservatives and liberals denied that there was any direct or necessary connection between different political systems and given structures of technology and economy. There have been republics, dictatorships, and monarchies (constitutional and autocratic) in both the agrarian and industrial ages; communist North Korea, under Kim Il Sung and his son and successor Kim Il Jong, has been a hereditary, autocratic monarchy of the ancient sort and, at the same time, an urban, industrial state. It is ironic that, at the very moment most thinkers in the former communist world were abandoning crude economic determinism in politics, conservatives, or pseudoconservatives, in the United States should have made it a central part of their ideology.

Let us ignore the Marxist origins of conservative Republican technological determinism, though, and examine the theory on its merits. If trends like the rise in inequality and the stagnation of middle-class incomes are really the result of a global technological revolution, a "third wave" or "information revolution," then those trends should be similar in all industrial democracies. A single cause, operating simultaneously on a group of similar societies, should produce roughly similar results. If, on the other hand, these trends are unique, or most intense, in the United States, then the causes are probably domestic and political as much as, or instead of, global and economic.

What do the data show? A cross-national comparison demonstrates that inequality and middle-class decline in the United States cannot be blamed primarily on trends in the world economy (though such trends may have played a minor part). Here are a few relevant figures: When it comes to poverty, according to the most thorough study of the OECD countries, the United States has not only a higher rate than other industrial democracies, it has twice the average rate. The ratio of income of the richest 20 percent of American households to the poorest 20 percent is *eleven times greater* than in all of the other industrial democracies. Nor is inequality growing at comparable rates in other industrial democracies, as the theory that blames American inequality on the global economy would suggest. In the 1980s and 1990s—which, not coincidentally, have been the highwater marks of conservative government since the 1920s—poverty in the United States grew much more rapidly than in comparable industrial countries.[10]

No doubt automation, competition with other industrial nations, and the expatriation of industry to Third World sweatshops have had significant effects on some American workers, as they have on comparable workers in similar countries. But those effects are concentrated in the industrial, blue-collar sector of the economy. The "global economy" cannot explain the economic troubles of the majority of Americans who work in "nontraded" sectors, just as automation cannot explain the stagnation or decline of wages of Americans whose jobs are not threatened by automation (for example, janitors and nurses). The fact that white-collar and pink-collar workers receive lower wages and fewer government benefits than their counterparts in most other industrial democracies has nothing to do with either the global economy or the technological revolution and everything to do with the bias of American government toward the well-to-do. American overclass elites use their control of both the neoliberal Democrats and the conservative Republicans deliberately to weaken unions, slash entitlements, and raise taxes on working Americans—and then, when their victims notice what is going on, they blame the results of pro-overclass policies on "historical forces" which are usefully vague and even more usefully un-stoppable. The world economy, like the information revolution, is not an explanation, it is an alibi. "Don't blame me," the bipartisan neolib-eral/conservative American overclass says to the middle class its pre-ferred economic policies have harmed. "The Information Age made me do it!" How convenient, that the policies that promote Historical Progress should also, by coincidence, be those that promote the short-term interests of the business elites that subsidize the Republican party, and the minority of Americans who belong to the overclass.

An extended discussion of the influence of the overclass on American politics would take me too far from the subject of the book. The discus-sion so far is sufficient, though, to permit us to return to, and elaborate upon, the map of American political viewpoints.

The fourfold map of political ideologies offered above, in Figure 1, is too simple (though it is an improvement over the twofold division of Americans into liberals and conservatives). If that fourfold schema is mapped onto the division of the electorate between the overclass and the middle class (the underclass does not vote), the result is the diagram in Figure 2.

Although in theory there are eight distinct political positions, in practice in the present-day United States only five are represented by substantial groups in the majority or the elite. Missing from the level of the middle-class majority are two positions: left-wing populism and a

Political Philosophy (left to right)

Overclass	Left Liberalism		Neoliberalism	Libertarian Conservatism
Middle Class		National Liberalism (the Radical Center)		Populist Conservatism (the Far Right)

FIGURE 2

grass-roots version of center-right neoliberalism. The attempt of former Texas Agriculture Commissioner Jim Hightower and others to promulgate a left-wing populism to counter the far-right populism stoked by talk-radio has been a miserable failure. And the very idea of working-class, corner-bar neoliberals angrily demanding new market-oriented approaches to public administration is enough to educe a smile.

The two political factions with the deepest resonance among wage-earning Americans are "the radical center" and "the far right." The term "radical center" was coined by sociologist Donald I. Warren in his 1976 book *The Radical Center: Middle Americans and the Politics of Alienation*. Warren's portrait of the "Middle American Radicals" (MARs) remains valid today. In the 1990s, as in the 1970s, the "extremists of the center" have tended to be high school educated, blue collar, and to be in the low-to-middle income category. According to Warren, Middle American radicals were more likely to be Catholic "white ethnics" than Protestants (the largest ethnic group in the radical center consisted of Italian-Americans). Many white southerners also fit Warren's definition; according to Warren, members of the radical center were twice as common in the South as in the north-central states. These alienated former members of the New Deal–vital center Democratic coalition shared a conviction that they were being squeezed by both the top and the bottom: "If there is one single summation of the MAR perspective, it is reflected in a statement which was read to respondents: *The rich give in to the demands of the poor, and the middle income people have to pay the bill.*"[11]

The radical center and the far right are often lumped together as "populists." The differences between these two popular political perspectives, however, are significant. The radical center is disproportionately made up of white Catholic "ethnics," while the far right is closely identified with white southerners and westerners from regions settled by southerners. The gun culture, a legacy of the Scots-Irish Highland South which has become central to the paranoid ideology of the far right, is alien to the radical center, few of whose members are tempted to join private paramilitary militias in order to fight the impending takeover of the United States by the United Nations and the international bankers. Many of the obsessions of far-right southern evangelical Protestantism and its offshoots around the country are also foreign to the Catholic members of the radical center, although the Catholic hierarchy joins the Protestant right in opposing legal abortion. The radical center does not share the far right's Jeffersonian and Jacksonian hatred of government as such. The radical center, it might be said, rejects the national elite but not necessarily the national government, whereas the far right rejects both.

The radical center and the far right, then, each represent large, nonelite constituencies of a kind that are lacking in the case of left liberalism and neoliberalism. At the elite level, yet another possible position is missing: the center left, by which is meant a contemporary version of the mainstream Progressive–New Deal–vital center liberal tradition. The center left would be to the right of the liberal left on social and cultural issues, and to the left of the center right with respect to economics. The center left would favor race-neutral antidiscrimination law, and oppose affirmative action and multiculturalism; at the same time, the center left would support generous big-government social programs and oppose massive tax cuts for the rich. A center-left faction in the overclass would be the elite ally of the radical center, in the way that libertarian conservatism is the elite ally of far-right popular conservatism. Merely to describe this viewpoint is to realize that there is not a single politician in national life who will defend such old-fashioned, pre-multicultural liberalism in public (though some defend it in private).

The yawning void where the center left should be is one of the major reasons the Democratic party is in trouble. For the disappearance of the center left has meant the two wings of the Democratic party are left-liberals and neoliberals (who are really moderate conservatives). It might make sense for the center left and left-liberals to team up to form a broad coalition to the left of center. It might also make sense for the center left and neoliberals to form a coalition of the center against the extremes of left-wing and right-wing radicalism. But left-liberals and neoliberals really should not be in the same party. Neoliberal Democrats have more in common with elite economic conservatives (if not with the populist far right) than they do with left-liberal Democrats.

The map in Figure 2 also helps explain why American politics is so consistently skewed to the right. For the moment, the right is where the elites and the masses are. Things might be different if there were a left-wing grass-roots movement with as much clout as the Christian Coalition has today, or as the unions once had. Things might also be different if there were a dynamic political-intellectual elite of the center left that could contest the left-liberals to one side and the neoliberals and economic conservatives to the other. Until a populism of the left or a new center-left elite, or both, materialize, however, the center of gravity of the American political order will continue to be not only to the right of center but in an upscale neighborhood.

The room for a center-left elite is the most intriguing possibility that American politics presents. Note that in this new pattern of five groups three are associated with the overclass (left liberals, the moderate middle, and the economic conservatives). One of the two genuine nonelite groups, the far right, is securely allied with the economic conservatives. That leaves the radical center as a nonelite group without allies or champions in the American elite. Lacking reputable representatives in politics and spokesmen in the press, members of the radical center turn to charismatic outsiders like Ross Perot and Patrick Buchanan (who has sought to synthesize the rather different but equally populist perspectives of the radical center and the far right).

In many ways, the three-way election of 1992 gave American voters a clearer choice between three opposing ideologies than any election since the four-way race of 1948. The race pitted representatives of overclass conservatism (George Bush) and overclass neoliberalism (Bill Clinton) against a champion of middle-class national liberalism (Ross Perot). (There was no representative of overclass left-liberalism in the race.) Half-baked though it was, Perot's program of economic nationalism and reform of campaign finance and lobbying offered a clear alternative to the conservative free-market orthodoxy shared by Clinton and Bush. By teaming up with Republican economic conservatives in opposition to his own party during the NAFTA debate, Clinton alienated Perot voters whom Patrick Buchanan, in his quest for the 1996 presidential nomination, has sought to bring into the GOP.

To sum up, my argument is that the United States is undergoing both a realignment and a revolution, albeit not the ones that conservatives claim to perceive. The realignment is a bipartisan conservative political realignment, which has rewarded neoliberal Democrats like Jimmy Carter and Bill Clinton as well as conservative Republicans at the expense of left-liberal Democrats like George McGovern and Michael Dukakis. The causes of the conservative political realignment are to be sought, not in vague social transformations like the globalization of the economy or the post-industrial information age, but in something much simpler: the destruction of Progressive–New Deal–vital center national liberalism as a force in the Democratic party by culturally radical left liberalism in the 1960s and 1970s. The social revolution in the contemporary United States, the growth in the relative wealth, power, and prestige of the overclass, is not directly responsible for the conservative political realignment. Rather, the effect of the over-class revolution is to strengthen the elite elements against the popular elements in *all* political factions. The overclass revolution strengthens cultural radicals on the left against middle- and working-class trade-union liberals, at the same time that it increases the clout of Wall Street conservatives at the expense of Main Street conservatives on the right.

It was not inevitable that conservatism in the United States should serve the interests of the overclass at the expense of the middle class. Not once but twice since World War II a more inclusive conception of conservatism has been defeated by proponents of a conservative move-ment employing imitation-populist rhetoric in the service of the rich and the business elite. In the next chapter, I examine the repeated defeat of one-nation conservatism by one-class conservatism in America.

Chapter 2

The Center Cannot Hold

The Defeat of One-Nation Conservatism in America

The history of modern American conservatism is a tale, as farcical as it is tragic, of missed opportunities. Twice in the past half century, there has been a fleeting opportunity to establish in the United States what in Britain is called "one-nation conservatism"—a political philosophy that sees the purpose of the conservative elite as reconciling the interests of all classes, labor as well as management, instead of identifying the good of society with the business class. Twice in the past half century the possibility of one-nation conservatism has been aborted. In both cases the proponents of one-nation conservatism went down to defeat at the hands of a coalition of Jacksonian populists and ex-communists who had not shed their radical and apocalyptic approach to politics.

In this chapter, I tell the story of the two great struggles that have shaped the course of modern conservatism. In the first battle, which occurred in the early 1950s, the McCarthyites led by the young William F. Buckley, Jr.—a band of old-fashioned anti-eastern populists and recent defectors from the radical left—wrested the conservative title from the post–World War II "new conservatives," conservative liberals like Arthur Schlesinger, Jr. and liberal conservatives like Peter Viereck. Unlike the new conservatives, the McCarthyite radicals who formed the nucleus of what is now known as the Old Right rejected the New Deal and viewed not only liberalism but Eisenhower conservatism as evils different in degree but not in kind from communism. The Old Right led the Republican party into disaster by nominating Barry Goldwater for pres-

45

ident. And the Old Right led the GOP to disgrace by converting the party of Lincoln into the party that fought the extension of civil rights to black Americans.

The second opportunity for an inclusive, one-nation conservatism came in the late 1970s and early 1980s, when the "neoconservatives"— heirs of the vital-center liberals and new conservatives of the early 1950s—sought a new home in the Republican party. The Republican neoconservatives engaged in several bitter debates with the Old Right in the 1980s and at the beginning of the 1990s. By 1992, however, the neoconservatives who had remained in the Republican party had abandoned all of the positions, like support for a strong federal government, New Deal social market capitalism, and commitment to secular, scientific modernity, that had distinguished them from the Old Right. Instead of taking over the Republican party, the neoconservative converts were taken over by the Republican party. What is more, in one of the most bizarre episodes in American political history, many of these former Democratic national liberals allied themselves not with their natural allies in the GOP, moderate Republicans, but with the Protestant fundamentalist far right.

The capitulation of the neoconservatives in the 1990s, following the defeat of the new conservatives in the 1950s, has doomed the enterprise of an intelligent, moderate, centrist conservatism in the United States. This was a project to which I was committed, for a decade. The story of the failure of one-nation conservatism is, in a small way, my own story.

The term "one-nation" conservatism comes from British politics. In British conservatism there have been two rival traditions: one-nation Toryism and classical liberalism. The patron saint of one-nation Toryism is the nineteenth-century British prime minister Benjamin Disraeli, who adumbrated a vision of class harmony as an alternative to the division of British society into "two nations" by industrial capitalism (the phrase "two nations" comes from Disraeli's political novel *Coningsby*). In the twentieth century Winston Churchill practiced a recognizable sort of one-nation conservatism. Conservatives in this tradition collaborated with socialists in establishing universal health insurance and other welfare-state measures designed to cushion citizens against market forces beyond their control. The enemies of the one-nation conservatives on the British right have been classical liberals like former prime minister Margaret Thatcher. For Thatcher, there was no such thing as "society," merely a collection of individuals pursuing economic gain. Thatcher, like members of the American radical right, considered one-nation conservatives as nothing more than deluded left-wing collectivists in disguise.

Versions of one-nation conservatism can be found today in other western democracies. In Germany, the Christian Democrats, inspired by the center-right strand of twentieth-century Catholic social thought, have promoted a conception of "the social market" that avoids the extremes of socialism and ruthless laissez-faire capitalism. The Gaullist tradition in France is an even better example of one-nation conservatism. Though Charles de Gaulle was clearly on the right, he rejected nostalgic conservatism and was willing to work with the left in order to modernize the French economy and provide economic security and opportunity for all French citizens. Nothing could be further from Gaullist thought than the American conservative sentiment expressed by former secretary of the interior James Watt: "There aren't liberals and conservatives. There are only liberals and Americans." De Gaulle was French first and conservative second. While Nixon considered liberal journalists as innocuous as Daniel Schorr enemies of the state who had to be harassed and silenced, de Gaulle refused to consider action against Sartre, even when that misguided philosopher was testing the limits of freedom of speech: "One does not arrest Voltaire."

If today's plutocratic and pseudopopulist version of conservatism were defeated, there might be a space in American politics for a constructive and inclusive conservatism in the twenty-first century—of the kind that might have been, during the past forty years. It need hardly be said that an American "one-nation" conservatism of the Disraelian, Christian Democratic, or Gaullist sort would differ radically from today's one-class, one-race, one-religion, one-opinion conservatism.

A one-nation conservatism in America would not be a vehicle for white resentment. Even as they repealed affirmative action and racial labeling as offensive to the ideal of a common citizenship, conservatives with a one-nation philosophy would propose new, race-neutral measures by which the government together with business and communities would seek to help the disproportionately nonwhite poor. A new one-nation conservatism would adumbrate a vision of the American nation far more inclusive than the contemporary right's parochial vision of a white Christian or Judeo-Christian nation. Blacks and Hispanics and Asian-Americans, and the growing number of mixed-race Americans, would not feel uncomfortable and out of place in a one-nation conservative movement—as they do on today's lily-white right.

One-nation conservatism would reflect the moral values of the American majority, not the eccentric obsessions of a reactionary Protestant fundamentalist minority in the South and West. With the great majority of Republican voters, one-nation conservatives would agree that abortion should be discouraged but legal and available. One-nation conservatives would reject the more radical proposals of gay liberationism, while supporting laws protecting gay and lesbian Americans from discrimination in employment and renting. The leaders of a one-nation conservatism in America would seek to make it easier for parents to protect children from the seamier aspects of the entertainment industry—but by means which minimized crude, coercive censorship. The deliberate and cynical provocation by political operatives of irrational "moral panics" over feminism, homosexuality, sex education, or satanism would play no part in either the intellectual discourse or electoral campaigns of principled one-nation conservatives. The electoral process itself would be reformed by one-nation conservatives in collaboration with liberals, in order to reduce the influence of big-spending special interests. Unlike today's conservative politicians, one-nation conservatives would be confident enough in the appeal of their positions that they would not feel the need for accumulating vast financial war chests to fund manipulative attack ads.

Like conservatives of all persuasions in every generation, one-nation conservatives in the United States would reject state socialism, and they would be cautious about expanding the role of government in the economy. However, they would take a pragmatic rather than a doctrinaire approach to economic matters. They would take for granted the need for a permanent and major role for the government in the provision of pensions, health insurance, and education at all levels. Unlike today's corporate-controlled right, tomorrow's one-nation conservatives would not oppose every measure to strengthen the rights of workers or to increase wages and benefits for ordinary Americans as "socialism" or as "crippling regulation" which will "destroy jobs." Shocking though the idea may seem to today's radical right, one-nation conservatives, in the tradition of Burke and Disraeli, of Lincoln and Theodore Roosevelt, would sometimes take the side of labor and consumers against big business. One-nation conservatives would reject the contemporary conservative dogma that what is good for employers and investors in the short term is always and necessarily identical with the long-term good of the nation. They would not confuse the part—the white overclass—with the whole—the American people.

In matters of international trade, one-nation conservatives would support policies that maximized the security of the defense industrial base and the wages of American workers, at the expense, if necessary, of profits for American corporations and investors acquired by exploiting the poverty and powerlessness of foreign workers. The defense policy of a one-nation conservative party would be inspired by the hardheaded national-interest realism of Washington, Hamilton, Lincoln, Seward, Hay, and Theodore Roosevelt. One-nation conservatives would favor a strong and flexible defense—but not the swollen Pentagon establishment of today, which serves the economic interests of Republican districts and Republican contractors better than it serves the country. Seeking to build and preserve a nonpartisan foreign policy consensus, one-nation conservatives, unlike today's right-wingers, would not opportunistically try to portray their opponents as incompetents or moral traitors in every case of disagreement over tactics or strategy.

After World War II, the United States was ready for a sophisticated one-nation conservative movement of this kind that wedded the respect of traditional conservatives for tradition and their skepticism about utopian social schemes with the soundest innovations of twentieth-century liberalism in the area of social welfare and civil rights. The United States that had just become the dominant world power and the leader of the nations of the West needed a mature and metropolitan conservatism comparable to the one-nation conservatisms of Churchill, Adenauer, and de Gaulle.

Immediately after World War II, a group of intellectuals including the poet and historian Peter Viereck, the historian Arthur M. Schlesinger, Jr. and the philosopher Reinhold Niebuhr were dubbed "the new conservatives." By today's standards, most of these thinkers would be considered liberals. But their liberalism, chastened by the experiences of the Depression, world war, and totalitarianism, was of a more measured and realistic kind than that of many of their idealistic and utopian Progressive predecessors. What Schlesinger christened as the liberalism of the vital center was not far from conservatism as it was envisioned by Viereck, who called for a "Manhattan classicism," an American Toryism at home in the modern world and free from the parochialism and nostalgia of the anti-New Deal, isolationist right.

Of the new conservatives, Schlesinger was perhaps the most closely identified with New Deal liberalism. In his 1949 polemic *The Vital Center,* Schlesinger explained how the liberalism of his generation differed from that of their New Deal and Progressive predecessors. For Americans who had reached maturity during the tenure of Franklin Roosevelt, "American liberalism has had a positive and confident ring. It has stood for responsibility and for achievement, not for frustration and sentimentalism; it has been the instrument of social change, not private neurosis."[1] In addition, Schlesinger wrote of his generation, "history had spared us any emotional involvement in the Soviet mirage. . . . The Soviet experience, on top of the rise of fascism, reminded my generation rather forcibly that man was, indeed, imperfect, and that the corruptions of power could unleash great evil in the world."[2] Schlesinger concluded: "Mid-twentieth century liberalism, I believe, has . . . been fundamentally reshaped by the hope of the New Deal, by the exposure of the Soviet Union, and by the deepening of our knowledge of man."[3] Though these could be described as conservative sentiments, the postwar American right was incapable of providing either political or intellectual leadership to the United States: "Terrified of change, lacking confidence and resolution, subject to spasms of panic and hysteria, the extreme right-wing elements keep the American business community in far too irresponsible a condition to work steadily for the national interest, at home or abroad."[4] Schlesinger noted that conservative Senator Robert A. Taft's "own not very enthusiastic attempts to mitigate hardship and poverty have won him a reputation for 'socialism' in the neanderthal circles of the Republican Party."[5] (Almost half a century later in Washington, I would hear conservative Republicans revile George Bush as a "liberal.")

While Schlesinger was concerned with stripping New Deal liberalism of the sentimental illusions that still beguiled the supporters of Henry Wallace on the left, Peter Viereck audaciously sought to work out a conservative philosophy suitable for the second half of the twentieth century in the United States and the West. Viereck, who recently retired after a long career as a professor of Russian history at Mount Holyoke, is one of the most accomplished, and unjustly neglected, American thinkers of the twentieth century. A polymath of remarkable erudition and diverse abilities, the Harvard- and Oxford-educated Viereck is the only American ever to have won Guggenheim fellowships both for history and for poetry (his first collection, *Terror and Decorum,* won the Pulitzer in 1949). His poetry and criticism alone, including his magisterial 1984 cycle *Archer in the Marrow,* his translations of the German poet Stefan George, and his theoretical writings about the art of verse, constitute a major contribution to American literature. Viereck has been ignored by the American literary intelligentsia because he was "politically incorrect" long before the term was coined. At a time when the most influential poets were abandoning form for shapeless and self-indulgent free verse, Viereck was renovating and extending the possibilities of rhyme. And Viereck's politics, though to the left of the right, were far enough to the right of the left-liberalism of the American literati to make him an "un-person." Viereck's harsh, and completely justified, criticism of the award of the prestigious Bollingen prize in 1949 to the pro-Nazi traitor Ezra Pound alienated him from much of the literary establishment. In recent years, Viereck the poet has begun to receive the attention and admiration he was long denied; the introduction to his most recent collection, *Tide and Continuities* (1994) was written (in rhyming verse) by one of his admirers, the late Russian-American poet and Nobel Prize winner Joseph Brodsky.

Viereck's contribution to American political thought and commentary is as substantial as his bequests to literature. Viereck's first book, *Meta-Politics: From the Romantics to Hitler* (1941), was a damning critique of Romantic irrationalism and its disastrous manifestation in politics. In a world of murderous ideologies and radio demagogues, Viereck sought to reconstruct, in a series of brilliant (and often savagely funny) books, a conservatism based upon the values of Greco-Roman classical humanism: reason, measure, discrimination.[6] Viereck anticipated the legitimate critiques by conservatives of left-liberal fallacies by making cruel fun of a mythical figure, "Babbitt Jr.," the trendy left-liberal son of Sinclair Lewis's archetypical small-town conservative. But for Viereck, "The new conservatism—meaning: a creative traditionalism—never admires the past passively in sterile escapism."[7]

Viereck's ambitious attempt to redefine the trans-Atlantic conservative tradition can be criticized; it can be argued, for example, that in overreacting to the excesses of illiberal nationalism in the twentieth century, he gives too much credit to the nineteenth-century opponents of liberal nationalism like Metternich. Nevertheless, Viereck's restatement of conservative philosophy is among the most impressive of the twentieth century; though it lacks the scholarly rigor, it also lacks the English parochialism of the work of conservative philosopher Michael Oakeshott. Unfortunately for the United States, Viereck's "new conservatism" was destined to have little influence.

In the *New York Times* of November 4, 1951, Peter Viereck reviewed the young William F. Buckley's *God and Man at Yale: The Surrender of "Academic Freedom."* "As gadfly against the smug Comrade Blimps of the left," Viereck wrote, "this important, symptomatic, and widely hailed book is a necessary counterbalance." Buckley's "Old Guard antithesis to the outworn Marxist thesis," however, left a great deal to be desired:

> Is there no "selfish materialism" at all among the National Association of Manufacturers as well as among the "New Deal collectivists" here denounced? Is it not humorless, or else blasphemous, for the eloquent advocate of Christianity, an unworldly and anti-economic religion, to enshrine jointly as equally sacrosanct: "Adam Smith and Ricardo, Jesus and Saint Paul?" And why is this veritable Eagle Scout of moral sternness silent on the moral implications of McCarthyism in his own camp?

The "Eagle Scout" Buckley shortly provided an answer, by writing a book with his Yale roommate Brent Bozell in defense of McCarthy, *McCarthy and His Enemies.* In vain Viereck tried to mobilize "traditional conservatives" like Russell Kirk against the demagogic senator from Wisconsin. In vain, too, Viereck pointed out that McCarthy, a rabble-rousing populist trying to discredit the most elitist institutions of society—the military, the universities—had all the hallmarks of a radical leftist in the Jacobin, Bolshevik, and Populist traditions. McCarthy, Viereck told the American Historical Association in 1954, is "not the Fascist type but the type of the Left-wing anarchist agitator" with a hatred for "everything venerable and patrician."

Viereck and his fellow "new conservatives" failed to launch a political movement and thus lost the struggle to define American conservatism to the circle around William F. Buckley, Jr.'s *National Review,* founded in 1955 by the young Yale graduate who had become famous by attacking his alma mater for the kind of "leftism" represented by the teaching of Keynesian economics. Although Buckley, the English-educated son of a Texas oil man, had the manner and lifestyle of a patrician, the conservative orthodoxy he and his followers promoted in domestic matters, hostile to the New Deal and civil rights, differed from that of the older right only in the substitution of militant anticommunism for isolationism (the young Buckley, like many rightists, had flirted with the America First Committee). Viereck, whose loathing for communism was joined by a detestation of McCarthy's "thought-control nationalism," retreated from polemics to a long and productive career as a scholar and poet.*

Buckley and other intellectual allies of McCarthy became the nucleus of the conservative movement that is usually dated to the founding, in 1955, of the *National Review.* (That date is used, one suspects, in order to avoid admitting that modern American conservatism really begins with McCarthy a few years earlier.) The Buckley conservatives— known today, rather inaptly, as the Old Right—found their con- stituency among veterans of the far right of the 1930s and 1940s (former isolationists, midwestern populists, business-class opponents of the New Deal, southern racists, and former fans of the pro-Fascist radio priest Father Charles Coughlin). Their intellectual leaders, however, tended to be ex-communists, like Trotsky's former lieutenant and Co- lumbia philosophy professor James Burnham (a founding editor of *National Review*) and Willi Schlamm (like many of the anticommunist conservatives not only an ex-leftist but an emigre). Most important of all, in terms of influence, may have been Whittaker Chambers, the ex- communist who exposed Alger Hiss. The coalition of right-wing pop- ulists, who tended to be anti-intellectual and xenophobic, and ex-leftist professors, many of them with European accents, may seem peculiar, but in fact it made a certain sense. The absurd conviction of ex-com- munists like Burnham and Schlamm that the United States was on the verge of defeat by the Soviet Union (a belief that more sensible liberal anticommunists like Arthur Schlesinger, Jr. and Dean Acheson did not share) gave conservative anticommunist writings a paranoiac tone that fitted in easily with the hysteria of the old Populist tradition. It was only necessary to substitute "communists" and "liberals" for the traditional enemies of right-wing populism, such as Catholics, Freemasons, Jews, and international financiers.

The Buckleyites, having rejected conservative welfare capitalism of the kind Viereck advocated, needed a philosophy. One was concocted in due course by *National Review* editor Frank Meyer, an ex-leftist who dubbed the grand philosophical synthesis "fusionism." The ingredients that were allegedly "fused" were laissez-faire capitalism and High

---

* Viereck was ex-communicated from the conservative movement by one of the editors of *National Review,* Frank Meyer, in a review of Viereck's 1956 book *Conservatism from Adams to Churchill.* See Frank S. Meyer, "Counterfeit at a Popular Price," *National Review,* August 11, 1956 (reprinted in Frank S. Meyer, *The Conservative Mainstream,* New Rochelle, 1969, pp. 67–70).

Church Burkean moral traditionalism (southern Protestant fundamentalism did not yet define "social conservatism"). Meyer persuaded most of the libertarian conservatives to agree that capitalism could only flourish in a society informed by conservative moral traditionalism. He could never quite get the traditionalist conservatives to agree to the converse—namely, that laissez-faire industrial capitalism was a prerequisite for a morally conservative traditional society. (Russell Kirk, the leading traditionalist, went to his grave believing that traditional conservatives had more in common with socialists than with libertarians.) With the dissent of the traditionalists noted, and the protests of radical libertarians like followers of Ayn Rand dismissed, fusionism became the formula for the developing Old Right.

As it turned out, the debate over fusionism was not the beginning of a flourishing intellectual tradition but the end of significant philosophical debate within the Old Right. The glaring contradiction between social conservatism and radical, destabilizing capitalism had not been resolved—but conservatives pretended it had been. Once Frank Meyer had perfected "fusionism," members of the Old Right, liberated from further deep thought about first principles, were free to devote all of their energy to calling for sterner measures against world communism ("rollback" instead of containment), making cutting remarks about liberals, and living their version of the lifestyle of English swells. The Old Right's attitude toward basic questions of political theory and economics, in the era of the fusionist consensus, was rather like that of the English gentleman who is supposed to have said, "I read a book once. It was so damnably good I've never read another."

The very lack of intellectual seriousness of the Old Right was a virtue of a sort. It prevented Old Right conservatives from becoming humorless zealots, and permitted heresies that a more disciplined movement would never have tolerated. However, the same intellectual frivolity that prevented the Old Right from degenerating into a sect caused it to degenerate into a club. The defeat of Viereck and like-minded new conservatives by Buckley and his fellow McCarthyites killed the chance for a postwar American Toryism in the United States as an alternative to the rejectionist right that opposed the New Deal and supported segregation. Even so, the circle around *National Review* created a half-Toryism, wedding the sprightly style of the patrician, Anglophile East Coast with the crude substance of midwestern anti–New Deal conservatism. The result was a sort of Frankenstein's monster, with the brain of a Knickerbocker and the heart of a Rotarian. *National Review* and its imitation, R. Emmett Tyrell's *American Spectator,* affected an anachronistic Edwardian coyness and fussiness. The *Spectator* not only borrowed its title from the London *Spectator* but also littered its pages with quaint Victorian and Edwardian woodcuts. Tory affectations were taken a step further in the 1980s, when young conservatives like the group around the *Dartmouth Review* made a cult of the *Masterpiece Theater* dramatization of Evelyn Waugh's *Brideshead Revisited.* They were triply pathetic, emulating not only a nation but a class and a generation not their own. Their version of conservatism was irrelevant to the challenges facing the United States. But then, it always had been.

In the 1950s, the opportunity for a one-nation conservatism in the United States was lost when conservatism became identified with the inverted, counterrevolutionary radicalism of the populists and ex-leftists who formed the McCarthy-Buckley-Goldwater Old Right. Between the late 1970s and the early 1990s, a similar coalition of right-wing populists and ex-leftist converts to the far right would prevent the establishment of an inclusive and intelligent right in the United States for a second time.

The second chance for American conservatism came in the 1970s with the alienation from left-liberalism of the liberals who came to be known as "neoconservatives" like Daniel Patrick Moynihan, Henry M. "Scoop" Jackson, Irving Kristol, Jeane Kirkpatrick, Norman Podhoretz, Daniel Bell, Nathan Glazer, and others. Most of the neoconservatives were former liberal Democrats (some of them former socialists or communists). They tended to be natives of New York, from Jewish or other European immigrant backgrounds. Most had careers in the academy or publishing; few had any acquaintance with the disciplines of greatest concern in politics, like law, economics, administration, or the minutiae of diplomacy and military science (their ignorance did not prevent these literati from issuing pronouncements on such matters).

The neoconservatives began their drift toward the right when the vital-center liberalism of the 1950s came under attack in the 1960s from the radical wing of the civil rights movement and the campus-based New Left. The eclipse of color-blind integrationism by black-power nationalism and affirmative action alarmed many liberals, especially Jews, who wondered whether they had succeeded in dismantling anti-Jewish quotas that protected WASPs only to be confronted with a new quota system protecting nonwhite Americans from Jewish competition.

Although the New Left sought its heroes in Castro, Ho Chi Minh, or Mao rather than in Khrushchev or Brezhnev, its often strident anti-Americanism repelled liberals who thought of the United States as a relatively just society in a struggle with communist totalitarianism. The 1968 Democratic party convention in Chicago revealed a deep fissure between the embattled vital-center liberals loyal to Johnson and Humphrey, and an increasingly influential left wing of antiwar activists, black-power militants and radical feminists. The fears of the moderate liberals were confirmed when the nomination and defeat of George McGovern inaugurated an era of Republican hegemony, based in large part on an identification of the party of FDR, Truman, and Johnson with the radical counterculture, an identification that continues to exist to this day.

The story of neoconservatism has two episodes. In the first, the neoconservatives attempted to take back the Democratic party—and failed. In the second episode, a group of neoconservatives attempted to take over the Republican party—and failed. When they failed, the Republican neoconservatives abandoned their former convictions and declared that the Old Right had been correct and the anticommunist New Deal liberals wrong all along.

Since the victory of the New Politics/New Left movement in 1972, there have been two major attempts to move the Democratic party back toward the center. Even before McGovern was defeated (he carried only one state—Massachusetts), supporters of Hubert Humphrey and Henry M. "Scoop" Jackson had formed the Coalition for a Democratic Majority (CDM). The CDM roster sounds like a roll call of the leaders of what would later be called neoconservatism: Ben Wattenberg, Jeane Kirkpatrick, Max Kampelman, Penn Kemble, Norman Podhoretz, Daniel Bell, Michael Novak, Nathan Glazer, Seymour Martin Lipset, and Albert Shanker. The goal of CDM, according to an ad the organization published in the *New York Times* on December 7, 1972, was to encourage "the Democratic party to return to the great tradition through which it had come to represent the wishes and hopes of a majority of the American people—the tradition of Franklin D. Roosevelt, Harry S Truman, Adlai Stevenson, John F. Kennedy, Lyndon B. Johnson and Hubert Humphrey." Long on brainpower and short on muscle, the organization failed to prevent the party, at a midterm convention in December 1974, from ratifying the McGovern-Fraser reforms of delegate selection and institutionalizing the power of New Politics Democrats.

The CDM, having served as a halfway house for many neoconservatives, who converted to the Republican right, faded away in the early 1980s. The most important vehicle for Democratic moderates became the Democratic Leadership Council (DLC). Like the CDM, the DLC was organized in the aftermath of a disastrous presidential election—in this case, the defeat of Walter Mondale in 1984. Republican congressional, gubernatorial, and statehouse gains in the South particularly alarmed Southern Democrats like senators Charles Robb (Virginia), Sam Nunn (Georgia), and Lawton Chiles (Florida), who joined with others to form the DLC with Richard Gephardt as chairman and Al From as executive director. (From had worked for Louisiana representative Gillis Long, whose House Democratic Caucus Committee on Party Effectiveness had served as a precursor to the DLC before Long's death in January 1985.)

Unlike the CDM, which had been organized by scholars and journalists, the DLC had been founded by elected politicians more interested in projecting an image of moderation than in hammering out a coherent ideological alternative to McGovernite liberalism and Reagan Republicanism. The DLC spun off a think tank, the Progressive Policy Institute (PPI), and published a magazine called the *New Democrat*. The predominance of corporations and professional and trade associations in financing the DLC and allied organizations led disgruntled liberal Democrats to joke about "Democrats Looking for Cash."

The DLC appeared to have been vindicated in 1992, when the organization's agenda at its annual conference became the foundation for the party platform, and when Bill Clinton, who had become chair of the DLC in 1990, received the nomination. In office, Clinton tried to implement DLC ideas about welfare reform, crime, reinventing government, national service, and the earned income tax credit. His New Democrat allies, however, were hostile to Clinton's health care reform and budget plans. Even worse, founding DLC member Sam Nunn helped orchestrate opposition to Clinton's attempt to reform the unjust treatment of homosexual soldiers—helping conservatives in their quest to identify Clinton in the public mind with the cultural left.

The 1994 Republican congressional landslide swept away many of the southern Democrats who supported the DLC. The most notable casualty was Clinton's successor as leader of the DLC, Oklahoma representative Dave McCurdy. While moderate and conservative Democrats were decimated, many northern liberals with safe districts survived the storm untouched. New Democrats and their supporters might argue that the debacle might not have occurred if the party had followed the DLC line more closely during its two years of control of White House, House, and Senate. A more convincing argument, however, can be made that the entire enterprise of the DLC was misconceived from the beginning. The New Democrats, by the 1990s, had come to look suspiciously like old-fashioned Republicans. By accepting the Republican critiques of big government and welfare, New Democrats inadvertently legitimized Republican prescriptions far more radical than their own. They offered an echo, not a choice. The New Democrats who called for "reinventing welfare as we know it" did not have the abolition of the federal guarantee of basic welfare in mind, or a vicious race-to-the-bottom among states competing to roll back help to destitute Americans. The New Democrats wanted something more moderate than that. But all of their talk of "moderation" was directed at distancing themselves from the liberals in their party, and not from extremists on the right. Now it is too late; the former "moderate" position of the New Democrats has now become the "liberal" position in a Congress in which Jesse Helms is the right and Bob Dole is the center. Having spent the past decade adapting right-wing arguments with only minor reservations, the New Democrats today are in no position to refute right-wing ideology.

In retrospect, the debate between the New Politics liberals and the New Democrats looks very much like a debate *within* the overclass elite that seized control of the Democratic party in the late 1960s. Many of the leading New Democrats, like Bill Clinton, had started out in the McGovern wing of the party and have managed to move slightly rightward, on military matters and economics, without moving *downward,* that is, reaching out to the dispossessed white working class. None of the neoliberals has attacked the New Politics/New Left orthodoxy of racial and gender preferences with anything like the fervor of Mario Proccacino and other old-fashioned white New Dealers. Indeed, it can be argued that for many New Democrats neoliberalism was simply the highest stage of left liberalism. The "yippies" of the 1960s matured into the "yuppies" of the 1970s and 1980s; while retaining many of the attitudes of the student counterculture about sex and authority, many became more conservative on economic matters as they became taxpayers in elite professions. For affluent neoliberals based in the private sector to argue that the party was too dependent on organized labor, or that entitlements that chiefly benefited working-class Americans were too high, was a choice that involved no economic sacrifice for them or their families. In the vocabulary of New Democrats, "labor" was a "special interest," but not business or finance. The NAFTA debate—in which Clinton and Gore broke not only with organized labor but with the congressional Democratic majority to side with the Republicans and the *Fortune* 500—was the most striking example of the extent to which New Democrats would go to prove their soundness to the business and financial communities. Al From, the director of the DLC, even registered as a lobbyist in order to lobby for the passage of NAFTA. The American business community repaid the efforts of New Democrats like Clinton and From to distance themselves from organized labor in the NAFTA debate by helping the Republicans defeat health care reform and pouring an unprecedented amount of money into GOP coffers in the weeks leading up to the 1994 election.

If the New Democrats had succeeded in ejecting the old, the United States would have had two pro-business, anti-labor parties—in effect, two Republican parties. Clinton himself recognized this, when he reportedly complained to his aides: "We're Eisenhower Republicans here, and we are fighting with Reagan Republicans. We stand for lower deficits and free trade and the bond market. Isn't that great?"[8] The New Democrats, like the Coalition for a Democratic Majority, fundamentally misdiagnosed the problem with the post-1972 Democratic party. The answer was not to find some "center" of respectable opinion in a classless America, but to reconnect the Democrats with the substantial number of white working-class voters alienated from both parties. To do so, however, the Democrats would have to support measures that would be opposed by the corporate interests that many of the New Democrats like Clinton have been assiduously courting.

Recent history shows that when Democratic presidential candidates have borrowed themes from the radical center, they can do well. Carter and Clinton won election by emphasizing national-populist themes later to be synthesized in Perot's 1992 campaign: Carter by running against a corrupt Washington insider culture of immorality and waste, Clinton by promising government action to relieve the economic distress of working-class and middle-class Americans. Mondale and Dukakis, by contrast, embodied the spirit of post-1972 New Politics liberalism (though Mondale was an heir of New Deal liberalism, he made no effort to distance himself from the party's dominant interest groups). Dukakis was the paradigm of the New Politics Democrat; despite his Greek ethnic background, he was an upper-middle-class reformer whose enemies in Massachusetts had been old-fashioned ethnic machine politicians. Both Carter and Clinton, having campaigned as national liberals, were forced, once in office, to move left to accommodate the interest groups that dominated the congressional Democratic party. The reason is simple: despite the importance of radical centrists to Democratic victories, there is no organized national liberal wing of the Democratic party, capable of supplying votes in Congress and appointees to the executive branch.

Neither of the established wings of the Democratic party can make its peace with the nationalism and populism that is destabilizing American politics. The New Politics wing is uncomfortable with the idea of American nationalism, even in its most inclusive forms; the New Democrat wing rejects the idea of aggressive government activism to arrest and reverse the economic decline of the working class, and has been indifferent to populist critiques of foreign lobbying and corporate domination of campaign finance. It is not too much to suggest that the "Old Democrats" and "New Democrats" are little more than factions within the affluent post-McGovern Democratic elite. The Old Democrats stress the cultural values of affluent liberal professionals, the New Democrats their economic interests. Bill Clinton, who staked his presidency on a Republican free-trade treaty and then, after careful review, came out in favor of affirmative action for minority-group members and women and free public education for illegal immigrants, has achieved a sort of synthesis of cultural liberalism and economic conservatism—at the price of appearing to be the alienated working-class white voter's ultimate nightmare.

While Democratic "centrism" has meant unsuccessfully courting business-class voters in the moderate middle, the Republican party has engaged in repeated efforts to woo the alienated working-class populists of the radical center, beginning with Nixon's successful attempt to win the Wallace vote in 1972. The purpose of Republican "culture war" politics is to divert the anger of working-class whites from corporations, lobbyists, and the Republican party toward the federal government, the mass media, nonwhites, and the Democrats. By concentrating on race-and-gender identity politics instead of lunch-bucket liberalism, the Democrats since McGovern have created their nemesis in the form of an identity politics of the right reaffirming the identity of the white and Christian majority.

The neoconservative Democrats, then, failed to revive New

Deal–vital center liberalism as a force within the Democratic party. The right wing of the Democratic party today is not neoconservative in the older sense, that is, culturally conservative and pro-labor, but rather neoliberal—culturally liberal, pro-business, and indifferent or hostile to organized labor.

The failure of the neoconservatives in the Democratic party has been accomplished by a failure of neoconservatives in the Republican party—a failure that at the same time has been a betrayal. Many of the neoconservatives supported Jimmy Carter, who ran as a conservative Democrat. Neoconservatives like Jeane Kirkpatrick and Norman Podhoretz soon turned against Carter, though, chiefly because of what they considered his weak and vacillating foreign policy, and with varying degrees of reluctance supported Ronald Reagan in 1980.*

The election of Ronald Reagan, the hero of the far right wing of the Republican party, divided the neoconservatives into two camps. The more impressive neoconservative intellectuals, including Daniel Patrick Moynihan and Daniel Bell, remained true to their older Democratic liberalism. Irving Kristol, Normal Podhoretz, Jeane Kirkpatrick, and others formed a faction of Republican converts or fellow travelers. At first, the Republican neocons like Kirkpatrick claimed that they agreed with Reagan's foreign policy but remained committed to the welfare state of FDR, Truman, and Johnson and to the civil rights tradition of Martin Luther King, Jr. By the 1990s, however, most of the neoconservatives had jettisoned their liberalism in economic and civil rights measures, and had converted, or had pretended to convert, to the views of the older Republican right, for whom former neoconservative heroes like Henry M. "Scoop" Jackson and Hubert Humphrey were sinister "socialists," "statists," "collectivists," "moral relativists," and "secular humanists."

---

* Some of the more apocalyptic pronouncements of neoconservatives at the time make amusing reading today, in light of what we now know about the deterioration of the Soviet Union by the late 1970s. In a strident book called *The Present Danger* (New York: Touchstone Books, 1980), Norman Podhoretz warned of the imminent "Finlandization of America, the political and economic subordination of the United States to superior Soviet power" and wondered whether the United States had reached a stage in its rivalry with the Soviet Union at which "surrender or war are the only remaining choices. One finds it easy to think this, and one finds it easy to despair." However, one can find equally fatuous comments by commentators of the time who wrongly minimized Soviet power and communist oppression. In foreign policy, there is less harm in exaggerating a genuine threat than in minimizing it.

At the beginning of this decade, so-called "paleoconservatives" or veterans of the Old Right like Patrick Buchanan warned that the neo-conservatives were taking over the Republican party. They need not have worried; the Republican party has taken over the neocons. Within the Republican party, neoconservatism has died, leaving a deposit of personnel, but scarcely a trace of distinctive neoconservative ideology. The Republican combination of anti-New Deal radicalism, in the interests of the business class, with Protestant fundamentalism could not be more remote from the vital center liberalism of the 1940s and 1950s. That the Republican neoconservatives, who were influenced in their youth by Reinhold Niebuhr, should end their careers as apologists for a quite different kind of Protestant pastor, Pat Robertson, suggests that their liberalism was never as deep as their ambition.

The abandonment of old-fashioned neoconservatism by the leaders of the Republican neoconservatives has produced an exodus by the leading younger intellectuals formerly associated with the neoconservative right, including Bruce Bawer, Jeffrey Herf, and Jacob Heilbrunn. Genuine neoconservatism, in its original form as the continuation of New Deal and vital center liberalism, is dead on the right. It is impossible to imagine Hubert Humphrey or Scoop Jackson, much less that neoconservative icon Harry S Truman, supporting Newt Gingrich, Dick Armey, or Phil Gramm in their efforts to enact the anti-regulatory and anti-labor agenda of corporate America, or joining in causes like the criminalization of abortion, the promotion in public schools of school prayer and "creation science," and the dismantling of the New Deal. The claim of the Republican neoconservatives that they have remained true to the liberal principles of their past is belied by their contribution to the defeat of universal health care, a key element of the reform programs of both Truman and Johnson. Former *New Republic* senior editor Mickey Kaus's proposal for replacing welfare with work-fare is more plausibly viewed as a continuation of the tradition of FDR, Truman, and Johnson than Charles Murray's proposal for the abolition of welfare, which will be discussed at length in a later chapter. Indeed, Murray, who bases his radical proposals on sweeping, controversial theories, symbolizes the union of political hubris with social science that the original neoconservatives criticized on the left in the 1960s and 1970s. The harmful influence on public policy of hubristic intellectuals like Charles Murray is the disease for which neoconservatism once promised to be the cure.

My own political journey led me to become a neoconservative at the very moment that neoconservatism was being abandoned by the intellectuals and politicians I had once identified with, like Jeane Kirkpatrick, Norman Podhoretz, and Irving Kristol. The political tradition I was born into was that of old-fashioned New Deal liberalism, the liberalism of FDR and Harry Truman, of Lyndon Johnson and Martin Luther King, Jr. In the first election I can remember, that of 1968, I rooted for Hubert Humphrey and jeered Richard Nixon. In college, I was a moderate Democrat. While I opposed the multicultural identity politics and reflexive anti-military stance of the left-liberal Democrats who had taken over the national party in the McGovern campaign, I distrusted the Republican party, and conservatism in general, which I associated with the educational backwardness and appalling poverty rates of my native Texas. Texan conservatism was symbolized in the 1970s by an alliance between the governor, a rich oil man named Bill Clements, and a fundamentalist leader, Brother Lester Roloff. My distrust of the Republicans deepened when I worked as an aide for a Democratic state senator in the Texas legislature. At the time the Republican party was collaborating with black activists to promote black-majority districts that would undermine the biracial districts of white moderates and liberals.

Texas, though, is such a conservative state that even Texan liberals seem like right-wingers to outsiders. When I went to graduate school at Yale, I encountered left-liberalism in all of its folly and fury. My Humphrey-Johnson Democratic liberalism earned me a reputation as a "Republican" and a "conservative" on the Yale campus, where the political spectrum among graduate students and faculty tended to run from pink to infrared to ultraviolet. At the time, the mid-1980s, the Republican party under Reagan appeared to be mellowing and moving toward the center. At the same time, the hold on the Democratic party of the left-liberals and "the groups" (racial minorities, feminists, unions) appeared to be cemented by the defeat of Gary Hart, a candidate I liked, by Walter Mondale (who despite his New Deal liberal origins ran as a candidate of the post-McGovern liberal left). Along with many others at the time, I concluded that "the vital center" of American politics was more likely to be restored by the center-right than by the center-left. At the time, I considered becoming a registered Republican, but I was dissuaded by an essay by Jeane Kirkpatrick, "Why I am a Democrat." The

Democrats, according to Kirkpatrick, were the party of the ordinary American, the Republicans the party of the rich. And in the great battles of the twentieth century—the New Deal, the civil rights revolution—the Republicans had consistently been on the wrong side. Though Kirkpatrick later became a Republican, her essay persuaded me to remain a dissident Democrat.

After obtaining a law degree at the University of Texas, I spent the late 1980s in Washington, D.C., within the conservative network—as a fellow at the Heritage Foundation and a research assistant to William F. Buckley, Jr., who helped me to obtain a grant from Russell Kirk's Historical Research Foundation to write a never-completed book on political theory. I expected the movement of the mainstream conservative movement away from the far right toward the political center, evident in the late 1980s, to continue throughout the 1990s. One encouraging sign, I thought, was Buckley's endorsement of the idea of national service (I helped him research his book on that subject, *Gratitude*). Around that time Fred Barnes wrote a piece in the *New Republic* announcing the rise of "big-government conservatism," exemplified by Jack Kemp. The religious right appeared to be losing influence, as a result of scandals involving Jim and Tammy Faye Bakker and Jimmy Swaggart. Jerry Falwell dissolved the Moral Majority. In the late 1980s, the neoconservatives—former New Deal Democrats—appeared to be in the ascendant, not only to me but to "paleoconservatives" like Patrick Buchanan and the editors of the magazine *Chronicles of Culture,* who launched a bitter attack on the alleged neocon takeover of the right. At a lunch around 1990, a former colleague from the Heritage Foundation confidently predicated that by the mid-1990s the Republican party would have dropped its crusade to outlaw abortion and move toward the moderate mainstream on other social issues.

Despite my friendship with Buckley, who is one of the most charming and magnanimous individuals in American public life, I had always felt more at ease with the views of the neocons. As the 1990s began, I hoped that Buchanan's darkest fears about the takeover of the right by the neocons would be confirmed. There have been three phases of American liberalism, each making greater compromises with American business and the American constitutional structure than the last. The New Deal liberals were more conservative than the Progressives; the vital center liberals were more conservative than the New Dealers. Given this trend, it was not unreasonable to believe that neoconservatism, slightly more conservative than vital center liberalism, would mark the natural next stage of liberal evolution. Neoconservatism, in other words, would represent the fourth stage of twentieth-century liberalism. The historical sequence would not be McCarthyism–segregationism–conservatism but rather Progressivism–New Deal liberalism–vital center liberalism–neoconservatism. The leading neoconservatives themselves encouraged this view. In 1979, Norman Podhoretz wrote, " 'Neo-liberal' would perhaps have been a more accurate label for the entire group than neo-conservative, except for the fact that its liberalism was old and not new—that is, it derived from the New Deal and not from the New Politics."[9] In 1983, Irving Kristol observed: "In economic and social policy, [neoconservatism] feels no lingering hostility to the welfare state, nor does it accept it resignedly, as a necessary evil."[10]

My belief that the heirs of FDR-Truman-Johnson liberalism had displaced the far right as the dominant influence on American conservatism was not unreasonable, then, in the late 1980s. The first time I became aware that the encouraging movement of the right toward the center was being checked and reversed came during the 1990 budget debate. I could not understand why the conservatives were pouring derision on President Bush for his decision to cooperate with Congress in raising taxes to reduce the deficit. By that time, after all, it should have been clear to any intelligent person that "Reaganomics" had been discredited. Much to my astonishment, supply-side economics not only rose from the dead but became the orthodoxy once again on the right.

My second thoughts about the conservative movement thus began with the budget debate in 1990. Though their hysterical reaction to Bush's tax increase led me to silently dismiss Buckley's associates as zealots, I still had hopes for the neoconservatives, many of whom had started out as old-fashioned Democrats like me. It was with some relief that, after a brief stint at the State Department's Foreign Service Institute, I entered neoconservative circles when I took a job as executive editor of the *National Interest,* edited by Owen Harries and published by Irving Kristol, who has been described as "the godfather of the neoconservatives." The *National Interest* was not a partisan conservative magazine at all, but one representing the "realist" strain of foreign policy thought; indeed, it has frequently been attacked by conservative ideologues. While I enjoyed working with Owen Harries, a former Australian diplomat, I was perturbed when Kristol invoked his prerogative as publisher to print in the *National Interest* in 1993 an essay entitled "My Cold War," which argued that the true enemy of America all along had been, not communism, but liberalism: Truman and Johnson, it seems, had been greater threats than Stalin and Castro.

I continued to visit Bill Buckley once or twice a year, discussing music and literature more often than politics, and I attended conservative functions in cases where a refusal would have been undiplomatic, given my position. Still, I found myself increasingly estranged by the economic policies of the right. I remember being shocked when President Bush vetoed legislation that would have required business to provide *unpaid* maternity leave, on the grounds that it would somehow cripple American industry (the same argument made by opponents of child labor laws around World War I). I was just as disturbed by the silence of neoconservatives in the face of Republican assaults on the New Deal/vital center tradition. Where were the "Scoop Jackson Democrats," where were the champions of Hubert Humphrey liberalism, where were the friends of anticommunist labor unions, when the Republicans were savaging labor and the middle class? My grumblings aroused such hostility from acquaintances—one mentor accused me of being a "Fabian socialist" when I commented that I found the idea of private toll roads replacing free streets objectionable—that I kept quiet, a practice that no doubt caused people to conclude from my affiliations that I was much more conservative than I actually was.

By 1992, the reversal of the earlier course of the conservative movement toward the center was unmistakable. Not only had supply-side economics been revived, but the religious right had risen from the ashes of the Moral Majority, in the form of the Christian Coalition, which rapidly became the most powerful grass-roots force in the GOP. Friends of mine who were active in Republican party politics told me how, in precinct after precinct, "Bible-believing Christians" were seizing control of the party from "the liberals"—by which they meant Reagan-Bush Republicans.

Though I had voted for Bush in 1988 and had supported his budget compromise as a method of reducing Reagan's disastrous deficit, his desperate pandering to the far right repelled me. I returned to my moderate Democratic roots and supported Bill Clinton. Along with other neoconservative Democrats with expertise in foreign policy, including Zbigniew Brzezinski, Samuel Huntington, Joshua Muravchik, and Martin Peretz, I was asked to sign my name to an endorsement of Bill

Clinton that appeared in the *New York Times.* To do so, however, would have been to publicly break with my employer, Irving Kristol, so I chose not to. As it happens, the public break was soon provided by Patrick Buchanan.

Like most Americans, I was appalled by Buchanan's call at the 1992 Republican Convention in Houston for "cultural war" and "religious war." When President Bush invited Pat Robertson to join him in the presidential box, I experienced an epiphany of sorts, recalling the alliance of another Texas oil man, Texas governor Bill Clements, and another southern fundamentalist preacher, Brother Lester Roloff. Clements and Roloff, Bush and Robertson—the pattern was unmistakable. There, on the national level, was the alliance of callous plutocracy and crackpot fundamentalism that was the basis of the classical Texan and Southern conservatism that I had grown up despising—an alliance which I had hoped that a more centrist, inclusive national conservative movement had forever left behind.

I attacked Buchanan in the lead op-ed of the *New York Times* on the day of Bush's renomination. In doing so, I believed I was following the example of Bill Buckley in driving the zealots of the John Birch Society out of the mainstream conservative movement in the 1960s. I assumed that the right would be divided into factions over the Buchanan-Robertson extremists, with the center-right ultimately prevailing. Indeed, something like this debate began within the Republican party after Buchanan won the New Hampshire primary in 1996.

By that time it was too late. When I repudiated Buchanan and Robertson in 1992, I found myself isolated. Bill Buckley praised Buchanan's disastrous Houston convention speech, and Irving Kristol wrote favorably of the Protestant fundamentalist right. The opportunistic "no enemies to the right" policy of the mainstream conservatives did not end with the campaign. After Clinton was elected, the journalists and leaders of mainstream conservatism cynically played to the fears and prejudices of the Buchanan-Robertson far right. The *Wall Street Journal,* the *American Spectator* and the Rush Limbaugh program helped disseminate far-right conspiracy theories about the death of White House aide Vincent Foster. Gay-baiting, which had hitherto been a specialty of the far right, was adopted by the mainstream conservatives, cynically trying to capitalize on the controversy about President Clinton's ill-fated attempt to treat gay and lesbian soldiers as equal citizens. Not content to join the far right in sounding the alarm about alleged murders committed by the Clintons and warning of the imaginary homosexual threat to the republic, the mainstream conservative movement joined the lunatic fringe in sympathetically describing criminals like David Koresh and Randy Weaver as martyrs of resistance to big government.

By this time I had lost any hope that the conservative movement could be redeemed, though I still hoped that there might be a resurgence of moderate Republicanism. Although I continued to work indirectly for Irving Kristol as the executive editor of the *National Interest,* the "no enemies to the right" policy that became the conservative party line in the fall of 1992 and the spring of 1993, and the successful effort of the conservatives to deny every American guaranteed health care coverage turned my disenchantment with the right into disgust. After witnessing Bill Buckley act as Pat Robertson's debating partner on a *Firing Line* television special about the religious right, I ended my fraying friendship with Buckley. In early 1995, after I had moved to New York to join *Harper's Magazine* as a senior editor, I made my three-year-old disenchantment with the conservatives public by exposing Pat Robertson's theories about Jewish high finance in the *New York Review of Books* and publishing an essay in *Dissent* entitled "The Death of Intellectual Conservatism." These controversial articles led many observers to conclude, reasonably but quite wrongly, that alarm at the religious right had made me leave conservatism for the left. In fact, as I have noted, I had begun moving away from conservatism five years earlier, not over social issues (on which my views are mostly moderate to conservative), but rather over economics—specifically, over the post-1990 resurrection of supply-side economics and free-market radicalism. The critical issue in my gradual estrangement from conservatism was not the New Right but the New Deal. Nor, despite the attempts of some conservative writers like Richard Brookhiser and James Bowman to smear me as a "socialist" or a "Marxist," did I join the left, which I attacked in my subsequent book as vigorously as I criticized the right. A critic in the *Nation,* Ellen Willis, claimed that I was really nothing but an old-fashioned neoconservative of the Daniel Bell variety. This was not far from the mark.

The truth is that my political journey has been far less dramatic than a switch from left to right. At most, I have wobbled slightly around the vital center. I have gone from the right wing of liberalism to the left wing of conservatism and back. I was a paleoliberal in the 1970s, a neoconservative in the 1980s, and a neo-paleoliberal in the 1990s. My political views have scarcely changed since college. For me the three sacred dates in twentieth-century American history are 1932 (the beginning of the New Deal), 1948 (the victory of Harry Truman over the leftism of Henry Wallace and the segregationism of Strom Thurmond), and 1964 (the Civil Rights Act). My goal has been to support the forces— whether in the Democratic or the Republican parties—which seemed most likely to return to the tradition of the great age of midcentury liberalism of 1932–68. I spent only around six years, or about a third of my adult life, thinking of myself as a member of a conservative movement, and then only during the brief period in the second Reagan administration and the early Bush administration when it appeared that conservatism henceforth would build upon the colossal achievements of Franklin Delano Roosevelt, Harry Truman, Lyndon Johnson, and Martin Luther King, Jr., and not repudiate them.

As neoconservatism disintegrated around me, I often found myself wondering why the Republican neocons had gone so far to the right while the neoconservatives who stayed in the Democratic party, like Daniel Patrick Moynihan, had remained true to their commitment to a third way between left-liberalism and far-right radicalism. Opportunism was a factor, of course, for neoconservatives who discovered that maintaining their New Deal liberal convictions would prevent them from rising within the ranks of the Republican party in Washington. I suspect, however, that another factor was just as important: inverted radicalism.

I have already noted the central role played in the formation of McCarthy-Buckley-Goldwater Old Right conservatism by ex-communists and other ex-radicals like James Burnham, Frank Meyer, Whittaker Chambers, Willi Schlamm, and Willmoore Kendall. It is surely significant that the neoconservatives who have gone furthest to the radical right—Kristol, Podhoretz, Novak—were the ones who started out on, or dallied with, the radical left. Kristol's introduction to politics was Trotskyite communism; Podhoretz dabbled with the counterculture in the 1960s and opposed the war in Vietnam; Novak was part of the student left; Eugene Genovese, a Stalinist supporter of Ho Chi Minh in the 1960s, is now a scourge of feminism and a fellow traveler of southern conservatism. Neoconservatives like Moynihan and the late Henry M. Jackson who began as New Deal liberals continued to be New Deal liberals; having never swung to the far left in their youth, they had no need to overcompensate by swinging to the far right in their maturity.

Irving Kristol, in his essay "My Cold War," has told us that his real enemy, all along, has been not communism but liberalism. There is every reason to believe him. As a young communist, he fought liberalism from the left; as a fellow traveler of the far right, he now fights liberalism from the right. In a recent public debate with *National Interest* editor Owen Harries (a genuine conservative of the British school), Kristol's wife, the historian Gertrude Himmelfarb, claimed that what the United States needs today is not conservatism but counterrevolution. Much is explained by the thesis that the major Republican neoconservatives have not gone from being liberals to conservatives at all. They have gone from being illiberal radicals of the left to being illiberal radicals of the right.

For the foreseeable future, as for the past half century, the honorable name of conservatism is likely to remain the property, in the United States, of shifting coalitions of libertarians, racists, medievalists, Protestant fundamentalists, supply-siders, flat-taxers, isolationists, gun fanatics, anti-Semites, and eugenics theorists. The United States is the only western democracy in which conservatives seek to outlaw abortion (as it is the only western democracy in which abortion clinics are frequently vandalized and bombed by right-wing extremists). In no other western democracy has the economic program of the right been centered almost entirely on reforms chiefly of benefit to the rich, like capital gains tax cuts and the proposed flat tax. No other conservative movement in the West is hostile to government controls on the private ownership and sale of machine guns. American conservatism, compared with British conservatism, German Christian Democracy, and French Gaullism, seems like a bizarre blend of Calvinist moral authoritarianism, social Darwinist economics, and paramilitary radicalism.

The contemporary American right is alien not only to conservatisms elsewhere in the democratic world, but to the major conservative traditions of the past. The conservatism of the United States at the end of the twentieth century bears almost no connection to either the Burkean conservative tradition in Britain or the Federalist-Whig-Republican tradition, Daniel Webster's "national conservatism," in the United States. Indeed, by the standards of today's conservatives, Edmund Burke was a cultural relativist (he defended the dignity of Hindu culture in the face of the chauvinism of his fellow Britons) and an enemy of "Judeo-

Christian family values" (as a member of Parliament, he used his authority on several occasions to seek leniency for individuals convicted under the sort of repressive laws against homosexuality which the American right approves of). The other great figures of British conservatism would fare no better in an evaluation by the contemporary American right. David Hume was an atheist, and Father Richard John Neuhaus recently told an audience at the American Enterprise Institute that an atheist cannot be a good citizen. Samuel Taylor Coleridge believed in the importance of an intellectual "clerisy"—a "cultural elite" of the sort former vice president Dan Quayle has denounced to much applause from the contemporary American right. Benjamin Disraeli, the father of "one-nation conservatism" in Britain, dared to criticize business for exploiting workers; even worse, Disraeli thought little of low-church Protestant sects of the sort that dictates the positions of today's Republican party. Churchill had doubts about free trade.

Like the greatest British conservatives, the great conservative nationalists in the older American tradition flunk the test of contemporary right-wing orthodoxy. George Washington, Alexander Hamilton, and Daniel Webster were economic nationalists who believed in a strong central government with an industrial policy; ergo, they were "socialists" and "collectivists" and "statists." So were Abraham Lincoln, who did not have sufficient respect for states' rights, and Theodore Roosevelt, whose enthusiasm for federal regulation of big business no doubt marks him as a "liberal." From a contemporary conservative perspective, H. L. Mencken has to be identified as a member of "the liberal media elite," in light of his mocking attacks on populist politicians and Biblical literalists (who tended to be Democrats in his day, and who tend to be Republicans in ours). If the American pantheon were cleared of the effigies of statesmen and thinkers who would be defined as "liberals," "cultural elitists," and "secular humanists" by the standards of today's right, hardly any statues would be left except for those of Andrew Jackson and William Jennings Bryan.

The defeat of one-nation conservatism is, among other things, a defeat for American Catholicism. After World War II, it can be argued, the United States might have had its own version of the center-right, predominantly Catholic Christian Democratic parties of Germany and Italy. The Christian Democrats drew on a century of Catholic social teaching which held up a moderate, humane version of capitalism, respecting the rights of labor as well as the privileges of businesses, as an alternative to the extremes of collectivism and free-market radicalism. Because of the transnational nature of Catholicism, Catholic anticommunism tended to be immunized against perversion into nativism (like the sort of conservative anticommunism that was simply a displacement of earlier Protestant anti-Catholicism). Finally, the institutionalized and hierarchical nature of the Catholic church has made it inhospitable to the kind of charismatic populism so characteristic of the Protestant southern right in the United States.

If the chief element in postwar American conservatism had been an Americanized version of Catholic Christian Democracy, the right today might have been dramatically different. Its center of political gravity might have been found among the "white ethnic" working class of the industrial Midwest and Northeast, not among small-town and suburban white Protestants in the South and West. The Catholic-influenced economic theory of American Christian Democrats might have placed the interests of members of trade unions as high as, or higher than, the interests of investment bankers, professionals, and the heirs of great fortunes. The universalism of the Catholic tradition might have been brought to bear to combat the deeply rooted racism and nativism of American folk culture. Catholic conservative intellectuals might have contested left-liberal ideologues without lapsing into the crude anti-intellectualism that both the Old Right and the neoconservatives have engaged in. In foreign policy, a flourishing Catholic conservative intelligentsia might have been able to contribute insights from the church's traditional just-war theory.

It was not to be. Although many of the Old Right intellectuals were Catholics, they had little contact with the mainstream of European Christian Democratic thinking of the mid-twentieth century. Notwithstanding the importance of the labor movement for white working-class Catholics, William F. Buckley, Jr. and his Catholic associates were resolutely anti-union. The prominent Catholic conservative intellectuals of recent years, like Richard John Neuhaus (a former left-wing Lutheran pastor) and Michael Novak, have contributed little or nothing that is specifically Catholic to the worldview of the intellectual right. For the most part they and other Catholic thinkers on the right have been content to serve as junior partners to Protestant fundamentalists and business-class conservatives, aiding the cause by coming up with what purport to be "Catholic" reasons to support the teaching of creationism or capital gains tax cuts. They are token Catholics in a movement dominated by Pat Robertson and the *Wall Street Journal*.

The greatest influence of modern Catholic social thought has been on twentieth-century American liberalism, not twentieth-century American conservatism. In a speech during the presidential campaign of 1932 entitled "The Philosophy of Social Justice Through Social Action," Franklin D. Roosevelt alluded to two papal encyclicals, *Quadragesimo Anno* (1931) and *Rerum Novarum* (1891), which had sought to promote a "third way" between laissez-faire capitalism and socialism. FDR contrasted two philosophies: "One of these old philosophies is the philosophy of those who would 'let things alone.' The other is the philosophy that strives for something new—something which I believe the human race can and will attain—social justice through social action."[11] For decades, pro-labor liberalism (though not cultural liberalism) enjoyed the support of the American Catholic hierarchy. Today, however, in the absence of an American counterpart of European Christian Democracy, many Catholics in the United States find themselves alienated from a political system in which their combination of moral traditionalism and economic liberalism is not represented. If the far right in the United States is disproportionately southern and western and Protestant, the radical center is disproportionately made up of white ethnics in the industrial regions of the country. Many of the southern whites who formed one half of the Jefferson-to-LBJ coalition have found a new home on the Republican right. The other half of the old Democratic coalition, the largely Catholic descendants of European immigrants in the North, have been estranged from both parties for a quarter of a century. At different times, Wallace, Reagan, Perot, and Buchanan have attracted their votes. Their alienation, and the destabilizing effect it has on American politics as a whole, is one of the major consequences of the failure of one-nation conservatism in the United States.

The southernized right of today, the alliance of the national and multinational business elite with a Republican party dominated by white southern politicians and voters and counterrevolutionary intellectuals, is not conservative at all, in the older sense of the term. Its populist radicalism is a fraud; its capitalist radicalism is genuine. It cannot be redeemed; it has to be defeated, if the United States is to avoid a decline as long and turbulent as that of Argentina. To paraphrase Ronald Reagan, "Conservatism is not part of the solution. It is the problem."

In the next chapter, I describe how the American right operates, before turning, in the chapter that follows, to a recent instance of the conservative propaganda machine in action: the Pat Robertson scandal.

Chapter 3

The Triangular Trade

How the Conservative Movement Works

The failure of Peter Viereck and the "new conservatives" in the 1950s, and of the moderate neoconservatives in the 1980s, to establish a centrist, one-nation conservatism in the United States has meant that conservatism in America has become a synonym for right-wing radicalism. Today's conservatives claim they are revolutionaries, and they are almost correct. They are counterrevolutionaries; and counterrevolutionaries have always had more in common with radicals than with genuine conservatives or for that matter genuine liberals.

A friend of mine who is a veteran of the conservative movement summed up modern conservatism in a single sentence: "Conservatism consists of midwestern foundations paying Jewish and Catholic intellectuals in the Northeast to tell Southern Baptists why they should vote for Sunbelt politicians" (Nixon, Reagan, Bush). One might speak of the interaction of money, ideas, and activists on the right as a "triangular trade," like the eighteenth-century cycle of rum-slaves-molasses described in American elementary school history texts. In this chapter, I will describe the triangular trade in some detail, explaining how the various components of the right-wing political and intellectual machine, from activists and intellectuals to special-interest donors, work together to promote their agenda of pro-business radicalism.

"Gaul is divided into three parts," is the famous beginning of Julius Caesar's memoir of his Gallic campaign. Like Caesar's Gaul, the conservative movement has three parts: the grass-roots right, the corporate right, and the brain trust right.

The grass-roots right is by far the oldest element of the conservative movement. Many of the leaders of the grass-roots right are veterans of the Goldwater campaign, which in turn emerged from the activism of both the post-1955 *National Review* conservatives and far-right organizations like the John Birch Society. The ideology of the grass-roots right has hardly changed since the 1950s—it is anti-civil rights laws, anti-New Deal, anti-foreign aid, anti-federal government, anti-secular, anti-gay, anti-modern art, anti-public education—in a word, just plain anti-liberal. It would be tedious, and irrelevant to the discussion, to list the various institutional forms the grass-roots right has taken, from the Young Americans for Freedom in the 1950s and 1960s to the Christian Coalition of the 1990s. The front organizations of the grass-roots right appear and vanish with startling rapidity, while a few professional activists—conservative anti-feminist Phyllis Schlafly and far-right organizers Paul Weyrich and Howard Phillips—endure at the center of grass-roots conservatism.

Despite the many continuities with the Goldwaterites and the Birchers, there have been two major changes in the grass-roots right over the past forty years. The first was the adoption of direct mail as a fund-raising technique (pioneered by conservative activist Richard Viguerie, himself a veteran of the 1964 Goldwater campaign). Since the 1970s, grass-roots conservative activists have mastered the technique of raising funds and mobilizing voters by means of highly inflammatory direct-mail missives targeted at susceptible voters whose names are listed in computer banks and traded among Republican party activists, conservative institutions, and businesses. (I made ends meet for a few weeks in the early 1990s by working part-time for a Republican direct-mail firm that bought and sold "lists" of names with the efficiency of the Big Brother government that direct-mail conservatives purport to fear.) The grass-roots right is really an "astroturf" right—it consists mostly of a few careerists who have lived in Washington for decades and whose contact with the masses is mediated by computer technology.

The other difference between the contemporary conservative grass-roots right and the Goldwater-Bircher activists is the prominence of the religious right. Today's religious right, far from being a spontaneous rebellion on the part of "people of faith" as Christian Coalition leaders Pat Robertson and Ralph Reed would have it, was engineered from above by Howard Phillips, a Jew, Richard Viguerie, a Catholic, and other grass-roots activists in the 1970s. These veterans of right-wing Republican campaigns saw the potential of white southern Protestants and northern white Catholics as allies of the New Right (as the grass-roots right became known in the 1970s). They helped to inspire Jerry Falwell's Moral Majority and lent their expertise to what has since become a sizable cadre of religious-right activists.[1]

Like the Moral Majority, which folded in the 1980s, Pat Robertson's Christian Coalition is the product of politics from above, not below. It was started with the help of seed money from the Republican party, and its basis was the direct-mail list of voters who supported Robertson during his 1988 campaign for the Republican presidential nomination. The Christian Coalition's public face is now that of its executive director Ralph Reed, a former college Republican leader whose chief accomplishment has been to make the Christian Coalition less of a religious pressure group and more of a movement supporting conventional economic-conservative causes like tax cuts.

The populist conservatives of the grass-roots right are, then, neither populist nor conservative. Their remote-controlled, computer-based targeting of voters who might respond to their propaganda has less to do with genuine community-based politics than with the advertising techniques of Madison Avenue. The content of their populism is curiously selective—while they play upon the patriotism of ordinary working Americans (the Panama Canal is being given away by the liberals!) and their prejudices and anxieties (the homosexuals are brainwashing your children!), the grass-roots right has nothing to say about the economic issues of greatest concern to ordinary wage-earners. On issues like the minimum wage, protection against arbitrary firing and discrimination in the workplace, maternity leave, and leave to take care of sick children or elderly parents, the grass-roots right is either silent or endorses the conventional overclass-conservative economic agenda of lowering taxes on the rich and corporations while cutting back benefits and lowering wages for working Americans. Their silence about these issues is striking, considering that William Jennings Bryan, their major turn-of-the-century predecessor, united his populist critique of modern culture with support for legislation protecting workers and government regulation of the trusts and railroads. The closest equivalent to "the Boy Orator of the Platte" today is Rush Limbaugh, a "populist" who never criticizes the rich or the business elite, and whose corporate-sponsored show is produced by veteran Republican spin doctor Roger Ailes.

If the grass-roots right is not genuinely populist, neither is it conservative, in any way that Edmund Burke or John Adams would have recognized. The grass-roots activists are radical demagogues, of the worst kind. They are demagogues, not only by choice but by necessity—they make their living by frightening the wits out of gullible people. In order to keep the contributions flowing in, they must employ wild exaggeration and lurid imagery in the direct-mail solicitations they are constantly sending out. The next election, the next vote in Congress, may be the one that forever decides the contest between the forces of faith and freedom and the sinister powers of secular humanism and godless communism—so send that check today. That television evangelists like Jerry Falwell and Pat Robertson should have taken so easily to the grass-roots right is no coincidence. Both TV preachers and direct-mail conservatives specialize in claiming that Armageddon is almost at hand—but enough contributions might stave off the Last Judgment just a little bit longer.

The corporate right, as an organized force, is a more recent phenomenon than the grass-roots right. Whereas the grass-roots right dates back to the McCarthy era and the Goldwater campaign, the modern corporate right coalesced during the 1970s and 1980s. Two factors in the emergence of the corporate right were critical. The first was the formation in the 1970s of the Business Roundtable, consisting of the CEOs of the one hundred largest U.S. corporations. While business has always had a predominant influence in American politics, the Business Roundtable provided the corporate elite with its own pressure group far more powerful than earlier pro-business organizations like the National Association of Manufacturers.

Also in the 1970s, the business elite acquired its own intelligentsia, in the form of the libertarians. Strictly speaking, libertarians are not conservatives at all, but classical liberals or even radicals. The patron saints of libertarians are enemies of the state like Ayn Rand, Friedrich Hayek, and Thomas Paine. Their consistent antistatism leads them to favor the legalization of drugs and the reduction of the U.S. military to a minimum force, as well as free trade, deregulation, and the abolition of all welfare entitlements, for poor, middle class, and rich alike.

Libertarians have had a running feud with the conservative movement since it crystallized under the leadership of William F. Buckley, Jr. in the 1950s. The libertarians approved of the pro-market ideology of the *National Review* conservatives, but rejected the movement right's crusading anticommunism, its law-and-order stance, and its support of censorship and organized religion. During the Vietnam war, disputes between the conventional conservatives and the antiwar libertarians wrecked the grass-roots organization Buckley had founded, the Young Americans for Freedom. Exiting from organized conservatism, the libertarians sought to establish themselves as a separate force. Like many splinter groups, they succumbed to the disease of factionalism, disintegrating further into warring sects. The Libertarian party, which has run candidates for president as well as for other federal and state and local offices, has remained insignificant, in part as a result of factional strife.

The only libertarian organization of any importance in American politics is the Cato Institute, founded in 1977 in San Francisco by Ed Crane. From modest origins, the Cato Institute, now based in Washington, D.C., has grown into a significant public-policy think tank. The secret of its success (or so more radical libertarians complain) is that Cato plays down the controversial, unconservative views of its intellectuals on drug policy, gay rights and abortion, and foreign policy, and concentrates on the libertarian economic agenda of deregulation, free trade, and tax cuts. The pro-market agenda of the libertarians is by no means identical with the pro-business agenda of the Republicans. Libertarian ideologues, true to their classical-liberal principles, wish to abolish government subsidies to corporations and government favors for the wealthy, as well as entitlements for working and poor Americans. In practice, however, this poses no problem for the Republican party. Republicans simply adopt the pro-market libertarian reforms that benefit business, and ignore the pro-market libertarian reforms that might hurt business. The body of libertarian thought is raided selectively by Republican strategists for ways to reduce government programs that benefit wage earners and the poor, while leaving the interests of the rich and U.S. corporations unscathed.

Are the libertarians part of the conservative movement, or not? The answer is obvious. The economic program of Newt Gingrich's Republicans, when it has not been written by business lobbyists, has been drafted by experts from the libertarian network, such as Stephen Moore of the Cato Institute (Moore suggested to the House congressional leadership that they start charging citizens for admission to the United States Capitol to reduce wear and tear). Whether they admit it or not, the libertarians play an assigned, and subordinate, role in the conservative Republican coalition. Their support for the decriminalization of marijuana and gay marriage is tolerated and indulged by the Republican elite because the libertarian policy analysts are so useful in providing the business community with what it wants.

The populist, or pseudo-populist, grass-roots right and the libertarian corporate right might as well be in different parties—indeed, on different planets. For a grass-roots conservative who distrusts big business and opposes free trade, a libertarian supporter of free trade and free love is as horrifying as a liberal. For their part, pro-business libertarians look on grass-roots conservatives as little more than fascists.

The strategy of the modern Republican party is based on a division of labor, with the grass-roots right serving as an electoral coalition, and the libertarian right as a governing elite. To be elected, Republican conservatives need the mailing lists and phone banks of the grass-roots right; once elected, they have to rely on the Washington-based libertarian policy experts to draft legislation that will please the corporations and rich individuals who subsidize their campaigns. What this means, in practice, is that grass-roots conservatives repeatedly feel they have been betrayed, by candidates who run as populists and then govern as country club elitists. In order to convince the grass-roots activists and the economic libertarians that they really are part of the same great political movement, an umbrella ideology, manufactured and disseminated by a group of generalist intellectuals, is necessary.

In the 1950s and 1960s, that umbrella ideology was known as "fusionism." What fusionism allegedly "fused" was economic libertarianism and social conservatism. Conservatives favored freedom in the marketplace, but not in the bedroom. As I have noted, the more ardent libertarians rejected this compromise between libertarianism and statism, but as an umbrella philosophy it was more coherent and flexible than anything that left liberalism has had to offer. Fusionism was hammered out in the pages of *National Review* and Russell Kirk's quarterly *Modern Age,* in books published by the conservative publishing house Alfred A. Regnery, and at meetings of a conservative intellectual group called the Philadelphia Society.

This Old Right intellectual network declined in influence in the 1970s and 1980s. The modern conservative brain trust originated in a scheme hatched in the 1970s by William E. Simon, Irving Kristol, and others. Like so many of the leaders of the American right, including Malcolm Forbes, Jr., Pete DuPont, and William F. Buckley, Jr., William E. Simon was a very rich man. In the 1980s, Simon made the *Forbes* list of the four hundred richest Americans, with a worth estimated at more than $300 million. According to Donald L. Bartlett and James B. Steele, Simon acquired this vast fortune chiefly "by taking advantage of the tax deduction for corporate debt" as a Wall Street corporate raider taking over companies with money borrowed in leveraged buyout deals.[2]

Simon, who had been treasury secretary under Nixon and Ford, became president of the John M. Olin Foundation in 1976. His goal was to lead an effort to direct the financial resources of the American business community toward conservative propagandists: "the only thing that can save the Republican Party . . . is a counterintelligentsia." According to Simon, it was necessary for American business and Wall Street finance to "funnel desperately needed funds to scholars, social scientists, writers and journalists who understand the relationship between political and economic liberty . . . [and whose work would] dissent from a dominant socialist-statist-collectivist orthodoxy which prevails in much of the media, in most of our large universities, among many of our politicians, and, tragically, among not a few of our top business executives. . . ." In the 1950s, Kristol had been a co-editor with Stephen Spender of the Anglo-American journal *Encounter,* which was revealed in the 1960s to have been funded through a front—as it happens, a foundation—by the CIA, as part of a network of anticommunist intellectual institutions, including the Congress for Cultural Freedom, set up in the late 1940s and early 1950s. Kristol denied, and continues to deny, any knowledge of the CIA connection to *Encounter.* Nevertheless, as Sidney Blumenthal and others have pointed out, the conservative intellectual network set up in the 1970s and persisting today bears a striking resemblance to the CIA-orchestrated network of cultural fronts in the United States and Europe of the early years of the cold war. The foundations, the little magazines, the little institutes and think tanks—all represent the application, in U.S. domestic politics, on behalf of big business and international finance, of techniques earlier used by the CIA to influence opinion abroad. The CIA, in turn, learned these techniques from the front organizations of the Soviet Union and pro-Soviet communist parties. (The wit who suggested that American conservatism is the highest stage of American communism was on to something.)[3]

Among the "scholars, social scientists, writers and journalists" who were soon being funded by the new conservative foundation network orchestrated by Simon, the Wall Street corporate raider, and Kristol, the ex-communist apparatchik, were Charles Murray and Dinesh D'Souza. Murray has spent much of the last decade and a half living on the largesse of the conservative foundations, with offices formerly at the Manhattan Institute and now at the American Enterprise Institute. D'Souza first came to the attention of the leaders of the conservative movement as a writer at the *Dartmouth Review,* a scurrilous campus tabloid that became the model for many campus conservative journals funded by the Institute for Educational Affairs (renamed the Madison Center for Educational Affairs in 1990).[4] The Institute for Educational Affairs, not coincidentally, was founded in 1978 by William Simon and Irving Kristol. D'Souza, whose higher education ended with his undergraduate degree, has spent most of his adult life being subsidized by the major right-wing foundations; like Murray, he is now on the staff of AEI.

The success of Murray and D'Souza in mastering the system of post-1970s conservative foundation grantsmanship gives the lie to their claims that they are lonely scholars, persecuted Galileos. Murray and D'Souza and other conservative publicists are the heavily subsidized conservative publicists that William E. Simon called for in 1976. If this seems too harsh a judgment, suppose that Murray's research had convinced him that in fact Head Start programs did work, and needed to be substantially expanded—and that to do so he recommended higher income taxes on the rich. One need not be a complete cynic to think that he might have trouble getting grants in the future from conservative foundations, or renewing his stay at AEI.

The picture of the intellectual conservative movement needs to be rounded out by mention of two important groups: "minicons" and "immicons." The "minicons" (the term was popularized by Charlotte Hays, a conservative journalist who has broken with the right) are the highly placed children of leading conservative intellectuals and journalists. The chief minicons are Christopher Buckley (the son of William F. Buckley, Jr.), William Kristol (the son of Irving Kristol and Gertrude Himmelfarb), and John Podhoretz (son of Norman Podhoretz and Midge Decter). While the younger Buckley, the author of two successful comic novels set in Washington, *The White House Mess* and *Thank You For Smoking,* has kept his distance from the conservative movement, the younger Kristol and the younger Podhoretz have spent their entire adult careers within the movement their parents dominated. William Kristol worked for one of his father's proteges, William Bennett, at the National Endowment for the Humanities, before becoming Dan

Quayle's chief of staff (Bush kept neocons off his personal staff, preferring old friends and country club Republicans). John Podhoretz has had a series of minor jobs in and out of government, ranging from a brief stint as a speechwriter at the White House to serving as an editor and movie reviewer within the *Washington Times* media empire. In 1995, Kristol and Podhoretz talked Australian media mogul Rupert Murdoch into giving them millions of dollars to start a new conservative weekly, the *Weekly Standard,* intended to be the conservative equivalent of the *New Republic.* The success of the minicons in manipulating their parents' connections to advance their careers suggests that Old Right conservatives like Patrick Buchanan and the editors of *Chronicles* are not exaggerating very much when they complain about the takeover of Washington intellectual conservatism by a "mafia" of well-connected former New York Jewish intellectuals.

The minicons are joined by "immicons"—my own coinage for the strikingly large number of conservative intellectuals who are immigrants from Britain, Canada, or continental Europe. These include John O'Sullivan, the English journalist whose lack of American citizenship did not prevent William F. Buckley, Jr. from making him editor of *National Review*; Stuart Butler, another English immigrant who has been the major domestic policy expert at the Heritage Foundation for more than a decade; and journalist David Frum, a vigorous opponent of entitlements for wage-earning American citizens who happens to be the child of one of Canada's richest families. The most exotic of the "immicons" is undoubtedly Arianna Stassinopoulos Huffington, a Greek emigre who made a great splash in political and journalistic circles in Britain, before making her way to the United States. Here she joined the cult of a West Coast guru named "John-Roger," married Michael Huffington, the heir to a Texas oil fortune and failed candidate for one of California's U.S. Senate seats, and became part of Newt Gingrich's group of intellectual advisors along with pop intellectuals Alvin and Heidi Toffler. In addition to contributing disproportionately to the ranks of Washington conservatism, foreigners and immigrants have played a major role in funding the journalists of the right. Rupert Murdoch, as I have noted, is the "angel" behind William Kristol's and John Podhoretz's *Weekly Standard* (the very name of which sounds more English than American). Even more important is the Reverend Sun Myung Moon, the head of a cult based in South Korea, the Unification Church. The cult led by Moon, who has served time in prison in the

United States for tax evasion, owns the conservative daily, the *Washington Times,* the flagship of a media empire that includes two magazines, *Insight* and *The World and I.* One can easily imagine what conservatives might say if much of the liberal intelligentsia wrote or worked either for a foreign media mogul who introduced sleazy tabloid television to the United States or for an East Asian cult leader and ex-convict.

The irony that a movement pretending to represent one-hundred-percent Americanism is disproportionately staffed by immigrants and subsidized by foreign interests is not new. The Old Right of William F. Buckley, Jr. and the other McCarthyite intellectuals drew even more heavily on emigre activists like Willi Schlamm and emigre intellectuals like Eric Voegelin and Leo Strauss. Columnist Samuel Francis, an Old Rightist and critic of the New York–Washington conservative establishment, notes that "the Old Right intellectuals had few links with the 'grass roots,' the populist, middle-class, and WASP nucleus of traditional American culture. *National Review* itself was not only Manhattanite but also Ivy League and Roman Catholic in its orientation, as well as ex-communist and ethnic in its editorial composition." One need not share Francis's views in order to agree that it is peculiar that "of the twenty-five conservative intellectuals whose photographs appeared on the dust jacket of George H. Nash's *The Conservative Intellectual Movement in America Since 1945,* published in 1976, four are Roman Catholic, seven are Jewish, another seven (including three Jews) are foreign-born, two are southern or western in origin, and only five are in any respect representative of the historically dominant Anglo-Saxon (or at least Anglo-Celtic) Protestant strain in American history and culture (three of the five later converted to Roman Catholicism)."[5]

The alliance on the right between evangelical Protestants in the South and West and an intelligentsia that is disproportionately made up of Jewish and Catholic Americans and European immigrants is not unprecedented. Indeed, it is the contemporary version of the alliance of white southerners and westerners with northeastern ethnics and immigrants within the Democratic party, from Thomas Jefferson to Lyndon Johnson. The constituencies that fled the Democratic party, when it was captured by a mainline Protestant-Jewish-black alliance in the 1960s, are being regrouped in the Republican party. The "class war" of southerners, westerners, and white ethnics against the northeastern WASP establishment has been replaced by the "culture war" which attempts to mobilize the same constituencies against the same northeastern elites—

with one exception. This time the enemy is supposed to be "big government" and "the cultural elite," not "big business" or "international finance." Indeed, according to the contemporary conservative intelligentsia created by William E. Simon, Irving Kristol, and others, Wall Street and the City of London are not the natural enemies of southern and white ethnic populists, but their friends and allies in the greatest struggle of our times—the battle to win a few English departments from a few middle-aged hippies with tenure.

By the early 1990s, thanks to the success of the Simon-Kristol initiative, almost all major conservative magazines, think tanks, and even individual scholars had become dependent on money from a small number of conservative foundations. The chief among these have been the John M. Olin Foundation, Lynde and Harry Bradley Foundation, J. Howard Pew Freedom Trust/Pew Charitable Trusts, Smith-Richardson Foundation, and Sarah Scaife Foundation. The *American Spectator, Commentary, Policy Review,* the *Public Interest,* the *National Interest,* the *New Criterion*—all are funded, in whole or in part, by a few foundations, and frequently feature the work of foundation-funded authors. The far-right magazine *Chronicles* was expelled from the network, and *National Review* maintained a certain independence. Increasingly, however, groups of writers and scholars on the right merged into a common pool of talent that wrote for the same magazines and received grants from the same program officers. Washington had come to resemble Hollywood, with the foundations playing the role of the big studios, the program officers acting as producers, editors playing directors, and the talent—policy wonks, publicists—divided between a few well-paid superstars and legions of poorly paid wannabes. The behind-the-scenes coordination of the intellectual right, by foundation program officers, editors, and think-tank executives, has done more to suppress dissent and debate on the right than any other single factor. It was not so much a matter of external censorship as of reflexive self-censorship. Conservative intellectuals did not dare to criticize other conservative intellectuals sharing the same financial patrons; conservative thinkers, it was understood, were on the same team. Good team players would advance, from grant to grant, in the manner of superstars Charles Murray and Dinesh D'Souza; troublemakers would suffer the fate of the fractious editors at *Chronicles,* and have their funding cut off.

If the Old Right intellectual movement had been organized like a stuffy and rather disorganized gentlemen's club, the neoconservative network orchestrated by the foundations resembled an old-fashioned political patronage machine, or perhaps one of the party writers' or scholars' guilds in communist countries. The purpose of intellectuals was to write essays and op-eds attacking liberals and supporting official Republican party positions. Where the official position of the Republican party was not yet decided, debate was permitted. But once the party line had been adopted, any conservative scholar who questioned the new dogma in print would find himself the victim of a whisper campaign about his "liberalism." The party line tended to be adopted at periodic "conservative summits," private meetings once a year or so between conservative editors like Kristol, Podhoretz, and Buckley, occasional journalists like Charles Krauthammer, Republican politicians, and foundation executives. It is as though George McGovern, Dan Rather, and Jesse Jackson met periodically to decide what the party line of "liberalism" would be, and then issued marching orders to their subalterns in the Democratic party and the media.

Another "summit" on the right, which is possibly more influential, is the annual meeting of the Council on National Policy (CNP). The membership roster of this secretive organization, which does not allow the press to attend their meetings, shows the degree to which mainstream Republicanism now blends imperceptibly into far-right extremism. At CNP meetings, Republican congressional leaders like the House majority leader, Dick Armey, and House majority whip Tom DeLay, and religious-right paladins like Ralph Reed, Pat Robertson, and Paul Weyrich mingle with far-right radicals like Larry Pratt, the leader of Gun Owners of America, whose attendance at conclaves of the white-supremacist right caused a scandal in February 1996 over his status as co-chairman of Patrick Buchanan's presidential campaign.[6]

The communication between the Republican party and the conservative editors and journalists, through summits and less formal means, has tended to be one-way. That is to say, Republican politicians would adopt a position, in response to pressure from this or that constituency—corporations seeking bigger depreciation allowances, the anti-abortion movement, the NRA—and the intellectuals would undertake to provide scholarly sounding rationalizations for the conservative Republican line. There was never any debate, among conservative intellectuals, on the adoption of a strict anti-abortion position as the "conservative" position. That position was dictated by the religious right to the Republican party, which in turn dictated it to conservative scholars and journalists, via a few editors and program officers. Similarly, the official conservative opposition to the most moderate and sensible gun control measures—even the Brady Bill, named for Ronald Reagan's press secretary, who was crippled for life by a maniac with a handgun—was not adopted because it was the consensus among conservative intellectuals who had carefully considered the issue on the merits and engaged in an unconstrained public debate. If there had been free and open debate on the subject, within a genuine conservative intellectual movement, it is quite possible that the intellectuals would have reasoned themselves to a position similar to that of conservatives in every other western democracy, for whom strict gun control laws are an essential element of a conservative approach to law and order. For that very reason, perhaps, the matter was never put to a vote among conservative thinkers. On this subject, the magazines of the right will publish only arguments that will supply intellectual ammunition to an important Republican constituency, the National Rifle Association.

Chiefly because of the *Gleichshaltung* (coordination) carried out in the past several decades by the conservative foundations and a few well-placed fixers like Irving Kristol and his son William, there is no longer an independent conservative intellectual movement in the United States. What passes for intellectual conservatism is little more than the subsidized propaganda wing of the Republican party. Public dissent on matters of concern to the U.S. business elite—most notably, on matters of taxation and public spending—is not tolerated. If a neoconservative art critic, say, announced that he agreed with other aspects of the Republican agenda, but that he believed in universal health care and denounced the GOP for opposing it, then his funding by conservative foundations would almost certainly be endangered—even though he wrote mainly about aesthetic concerns, not public policy issues. Ironically, the neoconservatives, with the zeal of converts, have proven to be far more dogmatic in their newfound right-wing radicalism than the eclectic and eccentric thinkers of the Old Right like Russell Kirk and Willmoore Kendall. In a very short time, the neoconservatives—at least those who followed Kristol and Podhoretz into the Republican camp—have subordinated themselves far more slavishly to the GOP than Old Right intellectuals ever did.

In 1954, Lionel Trilling expressed astonishment at the absence of a significant conservative intelligentsia in the United States. "In the United States at this time," Trilling wrote, "liberalism is not only the dominant, but even the sole intellectual tradition. For it is the plain fact that nowadays there are no conservative or reactionary ideas in general circulation." At most, there were conservative impulses that did not express themselves "in ideas, but only in action or in irritable mental gestures that resemble ideas."[7] Today's conservatives often quote Trilling with relish, pointing out that a year later, in 1955, the modern conservative intellectual movement began, with the founding of William F. Buckley, Jr.'s *National Review.* Four decades after Trilling wrote, conservative ideas had driven liberal ideas from the field—or so conservatives like to believe.

They are wrong, of course. The conservatism that has triumphed in politics, if only for the time being, is a conservatism of "action" and "irritable mental gestures that resemble ideas." Conservative "intellectuals" have two purposes: to discredit the political adversaries of pro-Republican pressure groups like the Christian Coalition and the National Rifle Association, and to rationalize the reduction of taxes on the rich and of regulation on business.

If conservative thought is considered to be something more than Republican party propaganda, then its vitality cannot be measured by counting electoral successes in national or state elections. Unlike the political electorate, the intellectual electorate (if I may coin a phrase) is heavily weighted in favor of the well-informed. By its very nature, the republic of letters is an oligarchic republic, an aristocratic republic. The judgment of the educated minority, not of the easily manipulated mass public, is the test of a philosophical or artistic movement. It is a test that post-1945 American conservatism fails.

In the last fifty years, American intellectual conservatism has been extraordinarily sterile. The magnitude of the failure of the conservative intellectual movement, after almost a half-century, is striking, by contrast with the right's political successes. That failure is put into even more striking relief when modern American conservatism is compared to political-intellectual movements that had a far more lasting effect on American intellectual and cultural life in far less time and with far fewer political successes. Think, for example, of the profound influence on subsequent generations of the New England transcendentalists, or in this century of the Southern Agrarians. Both movements were initially as much political as they were literary or artistic. Long after the political causes of the transcendentalists and agrarians—opposition to the Mexican War, opposition to industrial capitalism—were forgotten, the themes of their leading spirits continued to resonate for Americans, their best works had become classics in the American canon.

The conservative movement has had half a century to incubate a similar efflorescence; its leaders have had vast financial resources and public attention at their disposal. What is the result of the conservative intellectual renaissance of late twentieth-century America? A few position papers from think tanks subsidized by the aerospace and tobacco industries; a few public-policy potboilers slapped together by second-rate social scientists or former student journalists subsidized by pro-business foundations; a few collections of op-eds by right-wing syndicated columnists. Not one philosopher of world rank, not one great political or constitutional theorist, not one world-class novelist or poet has been enrolled in the ranks of late twentieth-century conservative intellectuals, or had anything more than fleeting association with them. It is not just that the postwar conservative intelligentsia has failed to produce equivalents of Aristotle or Petrarch or Shakespeare or Kant. It has not even lived up to the standards of previous American intelligentsias. No Emerson, no Hawthorne, no Melville, no Robert Penn Warren or Allen Tate has emerged from the amply subsidized groves of the American conservative Parnassus. It is safe to predict that the works of Progressive intellectuals like Walter Lippmann and Herbert Croly will occupy more space on library shelves of the future than all of the remnants of half a century of American conservatism.

Conservatives cannot point to economic thinkers like Milton Friedman and Friedrich von Hayek—for all their influence on Republican economic policy, they have refused the label conservative, calling themselves, accurately enough, libertarians or classical liberals. One might have expected that in the area of political and constitutional theory, at least, the intellectual right would have produced at least one thinker of the stature of Oliver Wendell Holmes, Jr., or John C. Calhoun, or Joseph Storey. For half a century, after all, conservatives have debated ideas about federalism, the relationship of the individual to society, the separation of powers, and checks and balances—and to what end? Where is the great conservative constitutional treatise, where is the jurist who will be read generations from now? I do not think that I am being unfair to the leading jurist of the contemporary right, Judge Robert Bork, when I express doubt that the constitutional scholars of the twenty-first and twenty-second centuries will rank him with the select company of great American constitutional thinkers.

Perhaps, however, my statement of the problem is mistaken. The question was, "Why have there been no world-class American conservative intellectuals?" when it should have been, "Why are there so few American conservative intellectuals?" By intellectuals I do not mean propagandists or casuists, who provide the party faithful with the party line on subjects of the day. I mean independent thinkers, who may be "conservative" or "liberal" or "libertarian" or "socialist" in terms of their basic principles, but who are free to draw their own conclusions without looking over their shoulders and fearing punishment for heterodoxy. A conservative intellectual, thus defined, might agree with the political right 80 percent of the time, or 60 percent, or as little as 51 percent; but he would freely and boldly side with liberals, or even socialists, when he thought the conservatives were wrong on a particular issue. At his best, William F. Buckley, Jr. occasionally demonstrated this kind of independence of mind; it is a quality completely lacking, however, in most of the prominent members of today's subsidized conservative intelligentsia.

The crudely instrumental attitude of the foundation-centered right toward ideas was revealed at a speech given by Michael S. Joyce at a *National Review*-sponsored conference in Washington. Though Joyce's name is unfamiliar to the general public, as the president of the Lynde and Harry Bradley Foundation he is one of the most influential behind-the-scenes leaders of the foundation-funded right (I never had any dealings with him, although the Bradley Foundation indirectly paid a portion of my salary during my three years as executive editor of the *National Interest*).

In his speech at the *National Review* conference, Joyce argued that the tradition of Progressive and New Deal economic reform, and practically all reform since the Gilded Age of the robber barons, has been a terrible mistake. The sinister Progressive–New Deal reformers were helped by muckraking novelists and dramatists, who vilified big business, as Upton Sinclair did in his novel about the horrors of the meat-packing industry, *The Jungle*.

Far from being the province of average citizens, these so-called muckrakers suggested the American public was in fact in utterly subservient position, submissive to corrupt, entrenched, self-serving special interests; the big corporations, the railroads, the utilities, the political parties, city hall itself. In cheap mass-circulation magazines, in pulp novels, in clever editorial cartoons, in early silent films the muckrakers embellished and broadcast this lurid vision of American life. . . . Then, and only then, only after the artists had been recruited to the cause, only after the public imagination had been stirred by its power, could the concrete political programs of liberalism make headway, coming ultimately to dominate 20th century American life.

Joyce's history is confused. The corruption of turn-of-the-century city halls and political parties, and the abuses of powerful economic interests, were exposed by the muckrakers, but they were not invented by them. What is more, it is simply not accurate to say that the muckrakers were the artistic branch of the Progressive movement. Many of the Progressives like Theodore Roosevelt and Herbert Croly believed that large business combinations were more efficient than small businesses, and wanted only to regulate them. The chief hostility to trusts came from old-fashioned populists and classical liberals—the intellectual ancestors of today's social conservatives and libertarians— not from the Progressives who inspired twentieth-century "corporate liberalism."[8]

Joyce is even less convincing when he gives Ida Tarbell, Upton Sinclair, and other "muckrakers" a central role in the promotion of the major economic and political reforms of the twentieth-century United States. Every modern industrial democracy, whether it had "muckrakers" or not, has adopted a similar set of food and drug regulations, social insurance, and environmental protections, as a response to the genuine evils incident to modern industrial capitalism, an efficient economic system which is more beneficial in a refined rather than a raw form. Reforms of the kind identified with the progressive-liberal tradition in the United States have been undertaken by conservatives in much of Europe and East Asia in the twentieth century.

Joyce's argument is significant not so much for its skewed account of history as for its practical implications for the conservative intellectuals whom he and other program officers subsidize with foundation money. It is not enough, Joyce argues, for conservative revolutionaries to roll back the reforms of the twentieth century and return America to the laissez-faire capitalism of the late nineteenth century. The hearts and minds of the American people might be won over, by novelists, playwrights, screenwriters, and artists who use their talents to provide illustrations for conservative arguments:

. . . Perhaps then we will be able to attract to our ranks great numbers of those possessing creative and artistic talents. For all about us are dramatic, compelling tales and pictures begging to be written, filmed and painted, of courageous individuals struggling to run their own lives according to their own lights and yet who are ignored or abused by powerful social structures jealous of their own prerogatives; the impoverished mother, who struggles against the public school bureaucracy to put her child into a private school where discipline and values prevail; the street vendor who battles licensing and zoning boards in order to make an honest living; the middle-class family that braves the ridicule of the social-service professionals in order to challenge the distribution of condoms to their children in school; the public-housing tenant who seeks only to govern his own project, in spite of an enervating maze of regulations. Let us make their stories our stories. And in the fertile soil of these timeless human dramas, these quintessential American tales of oppression, of rebellion, and of restored citizenship, let us cultivate a new generation of Upton Sinclair's and Ida Tarbell's, of Jack London's, Finley Peter Dunne's, Booth Tarkington's, and Jacob Riis [*sic*].

If further proof is needed for my contention that much of today's conservative political theory is merely Marxism with the substitution of "bourgeois" for "proletariat" and "culture" for "class," it can be found in Joyce's call for enlisting art and literature in the service of Republican conservatism, a program that is indistinguishable, except in its content, from the aesthetic orthodoxy of American communists during the 1920s and 1930s. As left-wing writers in the 1930s were expected to turn out propaganda novels glorifying labor and vilifying business, so today's conservative writers, if Joyce had his way, would crank out novels and plays and movies pitting heroic capitalists against villainous union leaders. The literary and artistic techniques used by communists and fascists alike would be adopted to disseminate conservative ideology.

To my knowledge, no budding novelists or playwrights on the right have taken Joyce up on his offer. (Perhaps they are awaiting the announcement of Bradley or Olin Foundation grants in conservative novel writing, or a William E. Simon chair in pro-market poetry.) For the time being, it seems, Americans interested in fiction with a right-wing perspective will have to be content with the work of conservative public policy intellectuals.

It remains to be seen whether Patrick Buchanan's insurgency permanently divides the grass-roots right from the corporate and intellectual right. For now, the conservative movement remains a lavishly funded, centralized, highly coordinated, Washington-based network which combines Jacksonian populist activists and ex-Marxist intellectuals with corporate and foundation funds to promote an agenda favoring the rich and the corporate elite that has been drafted by libertarian public policy experts. Just how efficient and well-coordinated this machine is was recently demonstrated by the right's response to the most embarrassing conservative scandal of the 1990s—the revelation that the leader of the religious right, Pat Robertson, was a purveyor of anti-Semitic conspiracy theories. The Pat Robertson scandal, and what it revealed about the intellectual and moral integrity of contemporary American conservatism, is the subject of the next chapter.

All of this raises the question of the distinction between intellectuals and ideologues. The tendency of conservative writers to lump centrists, liberals, and radical leftists together as a monolithic entity called "the left" obscures the enormous differences among, say, establishment liberals, black nationalists, social democrats, radical environmentalists, tiny sectarian Marxist groups, and so on. This very disunity, though it may weaken the left politically, is a source of intellectual vitality; a liberal and leftist intellectual today finds it relatively easy to challenge this or that popular liberal or leftist idea or public policy without being drummed out of the "movement" as a "closet conservative." Next to the centralized, dogmatic church militant of contemporary Washington–New York conservatism, the left looks less like a denomination than like a dozen squabbling sects.

On the broadly defined right as well, there are political intellectuals who are not mere ideologues supplying rationalizations for policies favored by Republican pressure groups. Most of the principled intellectuals who remain on the right are members of the libertarian movement, which as I have noted earlier is an ally of the conservative movement rather than a subordinate branch of it. Libertarianism, in my view, is based on erroneous premises about the nature of human beings and society; nevertheless, one must admire libertarian intellectuals for their integrity in refusing to make themselves more useful to the Republican coalition by sacrificing their unconservative views on social policy in matters like drug decriminalization and support for legal abortion. The fact that libertarianism is a loose intellectual movement gives libertarian intellectuals the independence to criticize not only the Republican party but also one another.

Why do American conservative intellectuals lack the same license to disagree on matters of public policy—on abortion, for instance, or gun control—that intellectuals on the left, and even intellectuals on the right outside the conservative movement, take for granted? The chief factor, as I have argued, is the financial dependence of the new conservative intelligentsia on the foundations which, in consultation with Republican electoral strategists, set the contemporary conservative party line. Conservative intellectuals who publicly dissent from the party line on important issues will have their foundation funds cut off. But there is more to the matter than the old saying, "Who buys my bread, his song I sing." The influence of twentieth-century American Marxism on the rigid dogmatism of the American conservative elite cannot be exaggerated.

From its beginnings, the conservatism of Joe McCarthy, William F. Buckley, Jr., Irving Kristol, and Norman Podhoretz was not just anti-communist or noncommunist (as any conservatism of any kind would be) but countercommunist. The key figures on the intellectual right, from Whittaker Chambers and James Burnham to Irving Kristol, were mostly ex-communists who thought that old-fashioned Burkean traditionalism was too feeble and genteel to withstand the assault of the cunning and well-organized communist conspiracy. The conservative movement these ex-radicals crafted was therefore one that adopted the characteristic institutions and strategies of communism while purveying an anticommunist (not merely a noncommunist) message. The conservative "movement" took the place of the Communist Party. The Popular Front strategy of allying the communist vanguard with American liberals was replicated in the "no enemies to the right" policy of allying conservative intellectuals and activists with the religious right and the paramilitary right. The myth of the struggle of the heroic proletariat against the evil bourgeoisie became the structurally identical myth of the struggle of "entrepreneurs" or (more broadly) "producers" or (more broadly still) "middle Americans" against a sinister new class of bureaucrats and intellectuals. Even the historical vision of dialectical materialism was taken over from communism, although "the end of history" was redefined from the worldwide triumph of socialism to the worldwide triumph of "democratic capitalism."

American conservatism, then, is a countercommunism that replicates, down to rather precise details of organization and theory, the communism that it opposes. In the way that it mirrors the very threat it claims to be neutralizing, the modern American conservative movement of the 1950s–1990s has resembled nothing so much as the anti-Catholic Native American or "Know-Nothing" movement of the decades preceding the Civil War. The common use of the term "know-nothing" to refer to ignorant and bigoted populists is based on a misunderstanding of the origins of the term. The original nativists, far from being lower-class or rural illiterates, tended to be solid members of the Anglo-American middle class and elite. They were honestly convinced that the absolutist Catholic monarchies of Europe, which had entered into a "holy alliance" to crush the spread of liberal and democratic ideas, were seeking to undermine the Protestant and republican United States by means of Catholic immigrants—chiefly Irish—and the American Catholic hierarchy. The only way to combat a secret international conspiracy, the nativists concluded, was to organize a secret national counterconspiracy. Thus the nativist movement, before it led to the formation of a political party, the American party, took the form of covert cells limited to white Protestants. Members were supposed to say, if asked if they knew anything about the movement, "I know nothing."

The parallel between the antebellum nativists and the cold war conservatives can be taken one step further. While the nativists and the conservative countercommunists grossly exaggerated the power and conspiratorial gifts of their enemies, the threats they thought they perceived had some basis in fact. There really were nineteenth-century Catholic authoritarians in Europe and Catholic clerics in the United States who rejected American-style liberalism and republicanism as monstrous heresies, just as there really was an international communist movement directed by Moscow that worked to undermine U.S. foreign policy by means of traitors and fellow travelers. In both cases, the legitimate defense of American liberalism and republicanism against premodern Catholic antiliberalism and communist totalitarianism degenerated, not only into a style of politics as conspiratorial and authoritarian as the original threat, but also into an excuse for vilifying other opponents in domestic politics—the slave-owning southern Democratic allies of northern Catholics, in the case of the nativists, and anticommunist liberals and social democrats and civil rights activists, in the case of cold war conservatives.

In the three chapters that follow, I will detail some of the consequences that flow from the peculiar nature of modern American conservatism as a countercommunism. The next two chapters, on Pat Robertson and on the American white South, explore the conse-

quences of the contemporary conservative movement's recent "no enemies to the right" policy—a policy reminiscent of the Popular Front
strategy that led American communists in the 1930s to support the
labor liberals and democratic socialists that they had previously opposed.
In Chapter Six, I turn from conservative coalition-building to ideology
in order to discuss the conservative myth of the "new class": a notion
providing a convenient bridge between the inverted Marxism of the establishment conservative intelligentsia and the paranoid populism of the
rising far right which seems destined to replace the cold war conservative movement as the dominant force on the American right.

Chapter 4

No Enemies to the Right

The Pat Robertson Scandal and What It Means

The grass-roots insurgency led by Patrick Buchanan has created a split in Republican ranks, but not within the conservative elite. Indeed, the conservative establishment today is more unified than it has been in decades—largely because of the unilateral surrender of the neoconservatives who converted the Republican party to the economic and social orthodoxy of the extreme right. By 1992, most of the neoconservative intellectuals who had joined the Republican party had completely repudiated their earlier centrist liberal views. As recently as 1990, in their pamphlet war with Patrick Buchanan and the paleoconservatives, the neocons had sought to defend a distinct position on the right as defenders of the legacy of mainstream New Deal liberalism. Now they simply abandoned all of their earlier criticisms of other conservatives, in the interests of a "no enemies to the right" policy. The final episode in the decade-long surrender of the Republican neoconservatives to the Republican far right contributed to one of the most bizarre chapters in recent American political history—the Pat Robertson scandal.

In the late 1980s and early 1990s, the political power of the religious right gave every indication of being in steep and permanent decline. Jerry Falwell dissolved the Moral Majority. A number of prominent televangelists, including Jim and Tammy Faye Bakker and Jimmy Swaggart, had been discredited by sexual and financial scandals. A Republican president who promised a "kinder, gentler" America was in the White House. On the right, the dominant force seemed to be secular and centrist neoconservatives, and mainstream conservatives like

William F. Buckley, Jr. who had distanced themselves from the extreme right.

In only a few years the scene had changed almost beyond recognition. The religious right was back, in the form of the Christian Coalition, founded in 1989 by the Reverend Marion "Pat" Robertson. Republican presidential candidates like Bob Dole and Phil Gramm, and conservative publicists like William Bennett and William Kristol were making pilgrimages to the Christian Coalition's "Road to Victory" Conferences to win the blessing of Robertson and his followers. The neoconservatives, who only a few years before had been denouncing the far-right conservatism of "the fever swamps" (Midge Decter's term), had caught a bad case of far-right fever themselves. In the pages of *Commentary,* the *New Criterion,* and other journals, neoconservatives, many of them Jewish, claimed that Protestant fundamentalists in particular, and Christians in general, were a persecuted minority in an America tyrannized by radical anticlericalists. Irving Kristol's wife Gertrude Himmelfarb, a widely respected historian, went so far as to declare that a model of higher education could be found in Baylor, a Baptist university in Waco, Texas, that until 1996 had banned dancing as immoral.

What was going on? There were no upheavals in American society between 1991 and 1993 that might explain the sudden sharp starboard course correction of the former center-right. The election of a Democratic president in 1992 was a factor—but the result of the 1992 campaign, it can be argued, had less of an influence on the strategy of the conservative leadership than the campaign itself. For the campaign to reelect George Bush revealed the extent to which the Christian Coalition was the dominant—in much of the country, the only—grass-roots political force within the GOP. Elite conservatives in Washington and New York were as slow as the media to realize that even as the religious-right network of Falwell, Swaggart, and the rest had been cracking up between 1988 and 1992, a new, more effective and perhaps more durable vehicle of the religious right had been forged by Pat Robertson from the mailing lists generated in the course of his 1988 campaign for the Republican nomination. Slowly it dawned on the elite conservative intellectuals and operatives that the road to power in the Republican party, in the 1990s, ran through Robertson's headquarters in Virginia Beach, Virginia. The conservative leadership revised its rhetoric and its priorities accordingly.

Today Pat Robertson is the single most important kingmaker in the

Republican party. Without the support of his Christian Coalition, it is unlikely that any Republican can win the nomination for the presidency. It is all the more disturbing, then, that Robertson is the single most important purveyor of crackpot conspiracy theories in the history of American politics. The scandal over Robertson's recycling of anti-Semitic ideology, and the conservative response, are significant in two respects. To begin with, they show the extent to which the conservative intellectual movement, thanks to its coordination by foundation officers, publishers, editors, and think tank executives, is a unified force, devoted to the short-term electoral interests of the Republican party and intolerant of dissenters in its ranks. The Robertson affair is even more important in showing the growing power of the religious right—which, as it happens, is also more or less identical with the southern and western right.

I had never paid much attention to either Robertson or the religious right when I picked up a copy of *The New World Order* in 1991. I expected to be amused by the promised explanation of world events like the Gulf War (during which I held a minor position in the State Department). Instead, I was shocked to discover that Robertson, whom I had assumed was a conventional evangelical like Jerry Falwell, had accused President Bush (for whom I had voted, and for whose administration I had briefly worked) and the Council on Foreign Relations (which I had joined after being nominated by William F. Buckley, Jr.) of being part of a Judeo-Masonic-Satanic conspiracy. When Robertson, instead of fading away like the other TV evangelists, became a power broker in the 1992 election, I remembered his crazy book and immediately tried to sound the alarm.

My first public criticism of Robertson's conspiracy theories was "The Exorcism," an essay in the December 14, 1992 issue of the *New Republic*. At the time I was still the executive editor of the *National Interest,* the foreign policy quarterly published by Irving Kristol. I still hoped that mainstream conservatives might repudiate the disastrous "no enemies to the right" strategy. In the months that followed, however, to my astonishment and dismay, mainstream conservatives and neoconservatives closed ranks with the religious right. William F. Buckley, Jr. even organized a *Firing Line* debate on the religious right in which his debating partner was Pat Robertson. Buckley, a member of the Council on Foreign Relations, had successfully nominated me to membership—

and here he was, acting as an ally and apologist for a conspiracy theorist who had accused the Council of being a front movement for Lucifer. After seeing Buckley on TV with Robertson, I severed my ties with him and the conservative movement once and for all.

As the religious right mobilized to help the Republican party take over Congress in the fall of 1994, I drew attention to *The New World Order* once again in an article in the Outlook Section of the *Washington Post* of October 16, 1994 entitled "Calling All Crackpots." Like my earlier mention of Robertson's theories, this drew little attention. Not until the *New York Review of Books* put my full-length expose, "Pat Robertson's Great Conspiracy Theory," on the cover of its February 2, 1995 issue did *The New World Order* become the subject of a national controversy. No doubt the intervening election of a Republican Congress was partly responsible for the increased attention: Robertson was no longer a fringe leader of a minority party, but the kingmaker of the new majority party.

Although the scandal broke in 1994, the story begins four years earlier. In 1991, Pat Robertson, who had written a number of previous books ranging from prophecy to economics, published the now-infamous *The New World Order*. The central theme of this rambling diatribe is the existence of a two-hundred-year-old, worldwide conspiracy that explains many of the events in American and world history. The adoption of Masonic imagery in the Great Seal of the United States in 1782, the publication of the *Communist Manifesto* in 1848, the call for a new world order by Woodrow Wilson in 1917, and a similar statement by Nelson Rockefeller in 1968—all have been part of the same conspiracy:

> Can it be that the phrase the new world order means something entirely different to the inner circle of a secret society than it does to the ordinary person . . .
>
> Indeed, it may well be that men of goodwill like Woodrow Wilson, Jimmy Carter, and George Bush, who sincerely want a larger community of nations living at peace in our world, are in reality unknowingly and unwittingly carrying out the mission and mouthing the phrases of a tightly knit cabal whose goal is nothing less than a new order for the human race under the domination of Lucifer and his followers.[1]

The basis of this conspiracy is a secret alliance between Jews and Freemasons. According to Robertson, the conspiracy all began on May

1, 1776, when "a Bavarian professor named Adam Weishaupt launched a small secret society called the Order of the Illuminati." With funding from Jewish bankers in Frankfurt—"a center controlled by the Rothschild family"—the Illuminati unleashed the Reign of Terror during the French Revolution and the European revolutions of 1848. "Although Illuminism had been banned in Germany and was discredited in France, it surfaced again in the 1800s through revolutionary societies holding to the basic tenets of Illuminism. Operating in France and Germany, these societies commissioned the writing of a militant manifesto"—the *Communist Manifesto*. The intermediary between the Illuminati and the communists, if Robertson is to be believed, was a Jew: "The precise connecting link between the German Illuminati and the beginning of world communism was furnished by a German radical named Moses Hess."[2] (Throughout *The New World Order*, as I shall show in further detail below, Robertson uses "German" or "European" where his anti-Semitic sources have "Jewish".) Just as the Rothschilds presided over the marriage of Illuminism and Freemasonry, so Moses Hess, the secret Illuminist, turns out to be the true father of world communism. Hess, of course, was one of the founders of modern Zionism. Thus Robertson gives his readers a version of one of the most venerable conspiracy theories on the far right, which holds that Jewish Zionist conspirators are behind Freemasonry and Communism alike.

The members of the Judeo-Masonic conspiracy, having organized world communism, next decided to bring down the American republic:

> Later the European powers [i.e., bankers like the Rothschilds] began to see the wealth of North America as a great treasure, and some of them still wanted to get their tentacles into America's economy [note the "octopus" metaphor, a staple of anti-Semitic and anti-capitalist rhetoric]. They eventually did so not by force, but by investing their money here, by sending people [i.e., Jewish bankers like Paul Warburg and Jacob Schiff], and by buying land. Europe could not defeat the United States by military force, but the European financiers knew that they could control the United States economy if they could saddle us with an American equivalent of the German Bundesbank or the Bank of England.[3]

The nefarious schemes of international high finance, however, were thwarted by two great American leaders. "The so-called Bank of the United States (1816-36) was abolished by President Andrew Jackson. . . ."[4] While Jackson lived to savor his victory, another president who foiled international finance was not so lucky:

> Lincoln's plan to print interest-free currency, called "greenbacks," during the Civil War—instead of issuing bonds at interest in exchange for bank loans—was so revolutionary that it would have destroyed the monopoly that European bankers exercised over the nation's money. There is no hard evidence to prove it, but it is my belief that John Wilkes Booth, the man who assassinated Lincoln, was in the employ of the European bankers who wanted to nip this American populist experiment in the bud.[5]

Defeated by Jackson and Lincoln, the "European bankers" like the Rothschilds got their way during the Wilson administration with the founding of the Federal Reserve, an evil deed that Robertson attributes to bankers who turn out—guess what?—to be Jewish. "Their efforts failed until 1913, when a German banker, Paul Warburg, succeeded in establishing the Federal Reserve Board, America's privately owned central bank."[6] What was the goal of these international bankers, who themselves were puppets of the Illuminated Freemasons (who in turn answered to "Lucifer and his followers")? Robertson's answer comes close to repeating one of the most vicious anti-Semitic libels of all—the claim that wealthy, cosmopolitan Jews consciously incite wars so that they can make money as war profiteers.

Robertson's version of this blood libel begins with his ruminations on usury. "The companion secret to wealth building is compound interest, called by Baron Rothschild 'the eighth wonder of the world.' "[7] Robertson goes on:

> In fact, no individual has the resources to sustain long-term compounding of interest. Only a sovereign government, armed with the enforcement mechanism of an income tax, can sustain the long-term compounding of debt.
>
> The money barons of Europe, who had established privately owned central banks like the Bank of England, found in war the excuse to make large loans to sovereign nations from money that they created out of nothing to be repaid by taxes from the people of the borrowing nations. The object of the lenders was to stimulate government deficit spending and subsequent borrowing. War served that purpose nicely, but from 1945 to 1990 the full mobilization for the Cold War and the resultant massive national borrowings accompanied the result just as well without a full-scale shooting war.[8]

Believe it or not, in this passage the leader of the Christian Coalition is arguing that the "money barons of Europe" like the Rothschilds have been enriched by compound interest payments on government deficit spending on the military—including Ronald Reagan's military buildup. It is easy to imagine what conservatives would have said about a leftist who suggested in print that the cold war may have been a hoax designed to channel money from hardworking taxpayers to international bankers by means of the budget deficit:

> Military preparation for the Cold War during the last forty-five years kept the economy on such a wartime footing that our government will owe an amount approaching $4 trillion in direct debt at the end of the fiscal year. . . .
>
> During the Cold War and *detente,* we were told that the Soviet Union was an economic powerhouse. . . . Suddenly we learned that the awesome Soviet colossus is, in reality, a broken-down Third World country. . . .
>
> One of two things is certain: either the CIA and the foreign policy establishment deliberately misled the American people about the strength of the Soviet Union so that the United States would continue its Cold War levels of wasteful spending, or the communists (like the Gideonites of biblical times) have deliberately sabotaged the consumer economy for the purpose of lulling the West into letting down its military, intellectual, and spiritual guard. . . .[9]

Although Robertson protects himself by saying that "the latter alternative seems more likely," he has managed to insinuate the suggestion that the cold war was a hoax by the American government in the minds of his readers. Elsewhere in *The New World Order* the most powerful leader of the grass-roots right in the United States hints that the cold war really was a hoax:

> We were told that behind the Iron Curtain—and later the Bamboo Curtain—lived the enemy. The Cold War required constant massive expenditures for arms, maintaining large numbers of United States ground forces in Europe and Asia, and stockpiling an ever-growing arsenal of thermonuclear weapons. . . .
>
> After we had spent the money developing our weapons, our leaders then negotiated with the Soviets to limit or destroy them.[10]

The key to such bizarre behavior by "our leaders" is found in the mystery of "compound interest." By pretending that the communist bloc was much more powerful than it really was, the American elite could justify spending the taxes of ordinary Americans to repay government loans from international bankers. Robertson even hints that the conspiracy extended to "planned obsolescence" in the arms race. If the leader of the Christian Coalition is to be believed, not only American taxpayers but the Russian people may have suffered for generations in order to enrich a small number of New York moneylenders:

> In fact, is there not a possibility that the Wall Street bankers, who have so enthusiastically financed Bolshevism in the Soviet Union since 1917, did so not for the purpose of promoting world communism but for the purpose of saddling the Soviet Union with a totally wasteful and inefficient system that in turn would force the Soviet government to be dependent on Western bankers for its survival?[11]

The cold war was not the first great-power conflict that might have been "a setup" by a secret behind-the-scenes global elite of Rothschilds and Illuminati, according to Robertson:

> After [World War I], the Prussian Kaiser was gone, the Ottoman Empire was gone, the Hapsburg Empire was gone, and the Tsarist empire was gone. The result was so profound and the excuse for war so flimsy, that casual observers would have reason to suspect that someone had planned the whole thing.
>
> Before the war, monarchies held sway. After the war, socialism and high finance held sway. Was it planned that way or was it merely an "accident" of history?[12]

Robertson does not go so far as to suggest that World War II was a Judeo-Masonic plot. However, he does hint that the Gulf War was arranged by the international conspiracy: "Is it possible that the Gulf War was, in fact, a setup?"[13] He raises the possibility that the Bush administration deliberately provoked Saddam Hussein into starting an unnecessary war in order to promote the two-century-old Judeo-Masonic scheme for a "new world order": "Could it have been that the wrong signals were sent to Saddam because powerful people wanted a situation that was so obviously dangerous to the entire world that all nations would join together to deal with it?"[14]

The vision of a worldwide conspiracy of Jewish bankers, Illuminati, and Freemasons to enrich themselves by promoting communism and world wars, while secretly guiding mankind toward a "new order for the human race under the domination of Lucifer and his followers" is not original with Pat Robertson. *The New World Order* draws together themes from two centuries of far-right extremist literature in Europe and North America. As Jacob Heilbrunn has pointed out, the most important sources for *The New World Order* are two books by Nesta H. Webster, an English historian of the 1920s—*World Revolution: The Plot Against Civilization* and *Secret Societies and Subversive Movements*—and a book by a contemporary American conservative writer, Eustace Mullins, entitled *Secrets of the Federal Reserve: The London Connection.* Both books are blatantly anti-Semitic; indeed, their theories about Jewish machinations are difficult to distinguish from those of Hitler and contemporary neo-Nazis.[15]

In *The New World Order,* Robertson lifts whole passages from Webster and Mullins almost word for word—while being careful to reword them to eliminate overt anti-Semitism. In his discussion of the origins of the Illuminati, for example, Robertson follows Webster almost verbatim. Webster writes that the Bavarian Adam Weishaupt was "indoctrinated into Egyptian occultism by a certain merchant of unknown origin from Jutland, named Kolmer, who was travelling about Europe during the year 1771 in search of adepts. Weishaupt . . . spent no less than five years thinking out a plan by which all these ideas could be reduced to a system. . . ."[16] In Robertson's book, this becomes: "Weishaupt had been indoctrinated into Egyptian occultism in 1771 by a merchant of unknown origin named Kolmer, who had been seeking European converts. It was said that for five years Weishaupt formulated a plan by which all occultic systems could be reduced to a single powerful organization."[17] Robertson is careful, however, not to paraphrase this passage from Webster: "I do not see in Illuminism a Jewish conspiracy to destroy Christianity, but rather a movement . . . aided and abetted perhaps by Jews who saw in it a system that might be turned to their advantage." Nor does Robertson paraphrase Webster when she writes, "Either Freemasonry is the cover under which the Jews, like the Illuminati, prefer to work, so that where cover is not available they are obliged to come out more into the open, or that Grand Orient Masonry is the directing power which employs Jews as agents in those countries where it cannot work on its own account."[18] The fact that Robertson drops passages like these, while paraphrasing others, almost to the point of plagiarism, suggests that he is aware of the anti-Semitism of this source and determined to camouflage it.

The most striking example of the care with which Robertson strikes out the most blatant anti-Jewish references in Webster, while preserving the substance of Webster's theory, is found in Robertson's redaction of Webster's discussion of the origins of the Judeo-Masonic conspiracy. Noting that "the years of 1781 and 1782 were remarkable for the growth of another movement which found expression at the Congres de Wilhelmsbad, namely, the emancipation of the Jews," Webster writes:

> A more immediate effect, however, was the resolution taken at the masonic congress of Wilhelmsbad—which was attended by [the Jewish philosopher] Lessing and a company of Jews—that henceforth Jews should no longer be excluded from the lodges. At the same time it was decided to remove the headquarters of illuminized Freemasonry to Frankfurt, which incidentally was the stronghold of Jewish finance, controlled at this date by such leading members of the race as Rothschild, Mayer Amschel—later to become Rothschild also—Oppenheimer, Wertheimer, Schuster, Speyer, Stern, and others. At this head lodge of Frankfurt, the gigantic plan of world revolution was carried forward, and it was there that at a large masonic congress in 1786 two French Freemasons afterwards declared the deaths of Louis XVI and Gustavus III of Sweden were definitely decreed.[19]

Robertson's version of Webster cuts out the epic catalog of Jewish names—"Oppenheimer, Wertheimer, Schuster, Speyer, Stern"—but retains the substance of Webster's account:

> That same year, 1782, the headquarters of Illuminated Freemasonry moved to Frankfurt, a center controlled by the Rothschild family. It is reported that in Frankfurt, Jews for the first time were admitted to the order of Freemasons. . . .
>
> New money suddenly poured into the Frankfurt lodge, and from there a well-funded plan for world revolution was carried forth. During a Masonic congress in 1786, the deaths of both Louis XVI and Gustavus III of Sweden were decreed.[20]

Robertson relies on Webster not only for his account of the French Revolution, but for his arguments that the Jewish-Illuminist conspiracy was behind the *Communist Manifesto* and the Bolshevik Revolution. According to Robertson, "British author Nesta Webster researched and wrote extensively on subversive movements. She described a group in Switzerland claiming direct descent from the founder of the Illuminati,

Adam Weishaupt. She says the same secret ring of Illuminati is believed to have been intimately connected with the organization of the Bolshevik Revolution. . . . None of the leading Bolsheviks are said to have been members of the innermost circle, which is understood to consist of men belonging to the highest intellectual and financial classes, whose names remain absolutely unknown."[21] Robertson does not tell readers of *The New World Order* that his source, Nesta Webster, speculates as to the identity of these "men belonging to the highest intellectual and financial classes." In the chapter of *Secret Societies* that Robertson is alluding to, Webster writes:

> There is another power at work, a power far older, that seeks to destroy all national spirit, all ordered government in every country, Germany included. What is this power? A large body of opinion replies: the Jewish power.[22]

Robertson's account of the alleged alliance between international Jewish bankers and the Federal Reserve derives largely from a contemporary American purveyor of far-right conspiracy theories, Eustace Mullins. According to a publisher's note in *Secrets of the Federal Reserve,* the book was originally commissioned by the poet Ezra Pound in 1949. At the time Pound was confined in a mental hospital, as an alternative to being tried for treason for his broadcasts on behalf of Hitler and Mussolini during World War II. Mullins writes in his foreword that his book was banned and burned in West Germany in 1955, presumably under the laws banning neo-Nazi propaganda.

The Federal Reserve—and government central banks in general—play a central role in conspiracy theories of the far right (and of the far left as well). The combination of secretive deliberations with great power over the economy makes central bankers a favorite subject of conspiracy-mongering cranks. In the United States, the easily exaggerated role of several Jewish bankers in the formation of the Federal Reserve gives anti-Semitic conspiracy theorists a field day.

According to the anti-Semitic account of the origins of the Federal Reserve, the key figures in modern central banking in the twentieth century were German-American Jews. Robertson writes:

> But the centers of European finance could not rest until they had brought the powerhouse of the New World into their orbit. In 1902, Paul Warburg, an associate of the Rothschilds and an expert on European central banking,

came to this country as a partner in the powerful Kuhn, Loeb and Company. He married the daughter of Solomon Loeb, one of the founders of the firm. The head of Kuhn, Loeb, was Jacob Schiff, whose gift of $20 million in gold to the struggling Russian communists in 1917 no doubt saved their revolution.[23]

Robertson's statement about Jacob Schiff's alleged gift to the Bolsheviks is a blatant falsehood, which he evidently picked up in Mullins. In reality, according to historian Ron Chernow, Schiff loaned a million rubles to the liberal democratic government of Alexander Kerensky; he *lost* his money when the Bolsheviks came to power.

Robertson continues, "Warburg was to become the catalyst, when joined with the Rockefeller and Morgan banking interests, to bring about the creation of a central bank for the United States."[24] Robertson's source for this appears to be Mullins, who describes how Warburg allegedly imposed the Federal Reserve system on U.S. government officials and financiers at a 1910 meeting: "Warburg's thick alien accent grated on them, and constantly reminded them that they had to accept his presence if a central bank plan was to be devised which would guarantee them their future profits."[25]

The accounts of Warburg's role by Robertson and Mullins are strikingly similar to a passage in *Pawns in the Game,* a 1955 exoneration of Hitler by the Canadian writer William Guy Carr published in Toronto by the "National Federation of Christian Laymen," a group that sounds surprisingly similar to the Christian Coalition:

> Since the Great War the International Bankers had set up twenty-six central banks. They were modelled after the Federal Reserve Banks in the United States, which had been established in 1913 according to the theories of Mr. Paul Warburg, the German who had gone to America in 1907 and become a partner in Kuhn-Loeb & Co. of New York.
>
> Mr. Paul Warburg's creation of 1913 had been steadily attempting to set up a "Central Banking Organization" which would acknowledge no authority on this planet above it. *Hitler knew that if Warburg and his associates had their way, the Bank of International Settlements would become as autocratic in regard to international affairs, as the Bank of England is in regard to British National Affairs and Foreign Policy.* (Emphasis added.)[26]

By far the most important predecessor of Robertson as a politically influential purveyor of anti-Semitic conspiracy theory in the twentieth-century United States was Father Charles Coughlin (1891–1979), who like Robertson combined the offices of Christian cleric and political agitator. Largely forgotten today, this "radio priest" of the 1930s pioneered both the electronic evangelism of Pat Robertson and the talk-radio conservatism of Rush Limbaugh. Like Robertson, who runs a media empire from his Christian Broadcasting Network (CBN) headquartered in Virginia Beach, Virginia, Coughlin had his own radio and publishing empire, based in his Shrine of the Little Flower in Royal Oak, Michigan. Robertson's Christian Coalition is similar to the political organizations Coughlin founded, the National Union for Social Justice and, later, the Christian Front. Like Robertson and other modern religious right activists, Coughlin played on anxieties about government control of church schools.[27] Though Coughlin's pro-fascist Catholic corporatism differs from the small-government conservatism of Robertson, Coughlin's paranoid theories about world conspiracies in the 1930s and 1940s portray an uncanny similarity to Robertson's views in the 1980s and 1990s.

Like Robertson in *The New World Order,* Coughlin in his radio addresses claimed that Jewish international bankers were supporting a world revolution against Christianity and capitalism. The Rothschilds played as big a role in Coughlin's theories as in Robertson's: "Under the flag of their leadership, there assembled the international bankers of the world. . . . The horrible, hated word spelled W-A-R was the secret of their success."[28] (Recall Robertson's hints that international bankers profited from arms races and wars.) Robertson's speculations that U.S. presidents have been pawns of a secret Masonic conspiracy were anticipated by Coughlin as well: "Word comes to me from France, from England, from every State in our Union that Masonry—Free Masonry—From Presidents Polk and Buchanan down to Presidents Wilson and Roosevelt, is behind the scenes playing its hand to tear down the Catholic Church and destroy the Christian religion."[29] Most of the details of Robertson's 1991 conspiracy theory are present in Coughlin's radio broadcasts, from the origins of communism in Adam Weishaupt's Illuminati (the subject of a Coughlin address in 1930) to the power over the destinies of nations that was supposed to "rest in the hands of the Morgans and Kuhn-Loebs and central banks and Rothschilds who have grown fat by the billions at the expense of the millions of oppressed people" (1933).[30]

My 1995 article in the *New York Review of Books* drew so much attention to Robertson's crackpot theories that the leaders of the conservative movement had to respond. Although I had broken with my former conservative allies over their appeasement of the far right (including the racist right and the paramilitary right, as well as the religious right), I had thought that, confronted with the truth about Robertson's worldview, they would have no choice but to distance themselves from the Christian Coalition leader. The situation, after all, was not unprecedented. In the early 1960s, the most powerful grass-roots movement on the right—a predecessor of the Christian Coalition—was the John Birch Society (named after a Baptist army chaplain killed in China by Chinese communists shortly after World War II). Like Robertson, the founder of the John Birch Society, Robert H. W. Welch, revived old notions of a Masonic conspiracy: "In 1964, for example," writes historian David H. Bennett, "he returned to John Robinson's 'expose' of the Bavarian Illuminati, linking the Illuminati's alleged role in the making of the French Revolution to the contemporary communist conspiracy, suggesting that only the John Birch Society could prevent 'collectivists . . . perpetrating repetitions of [this] tragic history.' "[31] Robert Welch went too far, though, when he published a book called *The Politician,* which asserted that President Eisenhower was either "a mere stooge" for communism or "has been consciously serving the communist conspiracy for all of his adult life."[32] William F. Buckley, Jr. denounced Welch's conspiracy theories, and Barry Goldwater—reluctantly, to be sure—distanced himself from the John Birch Society during the 1964 campaign. Pat Robertson's theories are far more bizarre and sinister than anything found in the writings of Robert Welch and his associates in the John Birch Society. Nevertheless, mainstream conservatives did not respond to the exposure of Robertson's views as they had to the John Birch Society. Instead, they did their best to kill the messenger.

The editors of *National Review* informed their readers that "the liberal establishment," upset by the November election results, got me "to do a hit on Pat Robertson." This was simply untrue; I had sent my piece without solicitations to the *New York Review* months before the November elections, at a time when it appeared that the Democrats would retain their majority. The editors of *National Review* excused Robertson as a harmless crank who was prejudiced against bankers, not Jews: "Paranoia about bankers runs deep in the American mind." Why Robertson, like his sources Webster and Mullins, should focus on Jewish bankers like Warburg, Schiff, Kuhn, and Loeb, when the higher reaches of banking for most of U.S. history have been reserved by the informal quotas for gentiles, is a mystery the editors of *National Review* did not explain. They went on to argue that "Robertson's writings have . . . gotten a free pass because they are not part of his political pitch. Robertson did not mention them on the hustings of Iowa" when he ran for president in 1988.[33] The obvious reply to this is that former Klan leader David Duke was careful to include only mainstream Republican issues like opposition to affirmative action and welfare in his campaigns for office as a Republican; this did not prevent the conservative leadership, including *National Review,* from denouncing him. Buckley absolved Robertson of the charge of anti-Semitism on the authority of Midge Decter. Decter, the wife of *Commentary* editor Norman Podhoretz, had published an attack on an Anti-Defamation League report of 1994 that accused Robertson and other religious right leaders of anti-Semitic tendencies. At the time she savaged the ADL report.

Other conservatives soon joined Buckley and *National Review* in defending Robertson and attacking me. James Bowman, in the neoconservative journal the *New Criterion* in March 1995, wrote that my expose of Robertson showed that I was "playing the Comintern game" (the reference is to the Communist International, which was dissolved in the 1940s, two decades before I was born). By his repeated references to my supposed "Marxian techniques," "the generally Marxist quality of the analysis," and "quasi-Marxian analysis," Bowman proved that, though communism is dead, red-baiting lives on.

For the conservative line on Robertson to be effective, however, all of the major conservative leaders needed to repeat it. The united conservative front crumbled when Norman Podhoretz published a lengthy essay in the August 1995 issue of *Commentary:* "In the Matter of Pat Robertson." Unlike all of the other conservatives who weighed in on the controversy, Podhoretz conceded that I and Jacob Heilbrunn, another former editor at the *National Interest* who clarified the connections between Robertson, Webster, and Mullins in a subsequent issue of the *New York Review* had been correct all along in alleging that Pat Robertson, if not an anti-Semite, is an energetic retailer of anti-Semitic libels: "The conclusion is thus inescapable that Robertson, whether knowingly or unknowingly, has subscribed to and purveyed ideas that have an old and well-established anti-Semitic pedigree." Podhoretz proceeded to reach the bizarre conclusion that Robertson, despite the manifest evidence of his anti-Semitism, should be supported by conservative Jews because he is pro-Israel.

"Four things were set up in the year 1913: . . . the Federal Reserve

Bank, the IRS, the FBI and the Anti-Defamation League of B'nai B'rith. All were set up in the same year. Is that a coincidence? Or is there a tie-in?" Though this sounds remarkably like Pat Robertson, these words are those of Nation of Islam leader Louis Farrakhan, in a speech of February 26, 1995. Podhoretz calls comparisons between Farrakhan and Robertson "intellectually absurd and morally dangerous. Farrakhan attacks Israel while Robertson defends it; and whereas Farrakhan calls Judaism 'a gutter religion,' Robertson speaks throughout *The New World Order* with the greatest respect of the faith of 'the God of Jacob.' "

For Podhoretz, it seems practically any lunacy can be forgiven the conspiracy-mongering leader of a mass movement, as long as he supports Israel. Podhoretz is not the only Jewish conservative who takes such a position. Writing in *Commentary* in 1984, Irving Kristol excused an evangelical Protestant leader who had remarked that God does not hear the prayers of Jews. Kristol wrote: "Why should Jews care about the theology of a fundamentalist preacher? . . . What do such theological abstractions matter as against the mundane fact that this same preacher is vigorously pro-Israel?" One can only speculate whether Podhoretz and Kristol would support Farrakhan, if the Nation of Islam supported Israel. At any rate, Robertson's pro-Israel statements and deeds, according to Podhoretz, outweigh his anti-Semitic propaganda, in light of the ancient rabbinical rule of *batel b'shishim:* "if the contaminant has slipped in accidentally or unintentionally, and is no more than one-sixtieth of the whole, it is neutralized and the food can be lawfully eaten." It seems that Reverend Robertson is kosher.[34]

Robertson's support for Israel appears to be far more contingent and equivocal than Podhoretz believes. Like other far-right fundamentalists (and unlike classic anti-Semites and neo-Nazis), Robertson supports the state of Israel, whose establishment he views as a fulfillment of prophecy. Lest Jews derive any great comfort from this, it should be pointed out that the same interpretation of Scripture that leads Protestant fundamentalists to support Israel also leads them to expect its annihilation in war in the relatively near future during the Last Days. In his book *The New Millennium,* published in 1990, Robertson writes: "That tiny little nation will find itself all alone in the world. Then according to the Bible, the Jews will cry out to the one they have so long rejected" and be converted to Christianity. This will not save them from being slaughtered in the Battle of Armageddon, but at least their souls will be saved.

As it happens, the arguments that Robertson has used to defend him-self against the charge of anti-Semitism are similar to those employed in the 1930s and early 1940s by Father Charles Coughlin, who claimed he was a "friend and champion of the Jewish people" even as he dissemi-nated the Protocols of the Elders of Zion and railed against international Jewish financiers.[35] Coughlin invoked what would nowadays be called the Judeo-Christian tradition: "Christ and the Apostles were Jews. And the first thirty-three popes were Jews. Among the last ten popes we've had, three were predominantly Jewish. I can't be anti-Jewish."[36] More-over, like Robertson, who has conservative Jewish allies, Coughlin was able to point to a number of Jewish leaders who initially supported the broad social and political reforms advocated by his movement. (Most of these broke with Coughlin, however, as he became more stridently anti-Semitic.)

Coughlin claimed that he was not opposed to Jews as such, but to "atheistic" or "apostate" Jews who were misleading what he called "good religious Jews." In the same way, Robertson has argued that his objection is not to the Jewish majority but to a sinister minority of lib-eral Jews. In a truly chilling parallel, Robertson, like Coughlin, has warned that all Jews may suffer from an anti-Semitic backlash that might be provoked by the actions of "cosmopolitan" or "liberal" Jews. In his book *The New Millennium,* Robertson predicts that one day the United States will acquiesce in the destruction of Israel: "One day a vote against Israel will come in the United Nations when the United States neither abstains or [sic] uses its veto in the Security Council to protect Israel." Why would the United States turn against Israel? Robertson suggests that American Christians will rise in misguided, irrational wrath pro-voked by the "cosmopolitan, liberal, secular Jews" who want "unre-stricted freedom for smut and pornography and the murder of the unborn." Elsewhere Robertson describes "the ongoing attempt of lib-eral Jews to undermine the public strength of Christianity" and warns of the possible consequences:

> The part that Jewish intellectuals and media activists have played in the as-sault on Christianity may very possibly prove to be a grave mistake. . . . For centuries, Christians have supported the dream of Zion, and they have supported the Jews in their dream of a national homeland. But American Jews invested great energy in attacking these very allies. That investment may pay a terrible dividend.[37]

Note how Robertson plays on the stereotype of the Jew as money changer with the metaphor of Jews "investing" in liberalism and gaining "a terrible dividend."

Robertson's warning that Israel may pay the price for "the assault on Christianity" by liberal American Jews echoes Coughlin's warnings in the 1930s that all Jews were in danger of being punished for the misdeeds of the international conspiracy by "communistic" and "atheistic" Jews: "The Jewish people are victimized by the Elders of Zion, [whose actions] . . . create the inevitable friction which causes such cruel persecution." After *Kristallnacht* of November 10, 1938—the nationwide pogrom in Germany organized by the Nazi government—Coughlin in a radio broadcast explained that the events were ultimately the fault of the "Jewish bankers, Kuhn Loeb & Company of New York, among those who helped finance the Russian Revolution and Communism." The role of Jewish bankers in financing communism had led the German people into the mistaken but understandable error of uniting a just hatred of communism with an indiscriminate attack on Jews. Coughlin urged his listeners not to let sympathy for the Jewish victims of *Kristallnacht* make them forget the "more than 20 million Christians" murdered by the supposed Jewish-financed communists of Soviet Russia. The treatment of Christians in the Soviet Union "by the atheistic Jews and gentile" was far worse, Coughlin argued, than the treatment of German Jews by Hitler: "By all means let us have the courage to compound our sympathy not only from the tears of Jews, but also from the blood of Christians—600,000 Jews whom no government official in Germany has yet sentenced to death."

In a passage that anticipates Robertson's warning to American Jews in *The New Millennium* about the coming backlash to be provoked by Jewish liberalism, Coughlin told "the good Jews of America" that they should avoid being "indulgent with the irreligious, atheistic Jews and gentiles. . . . Yes, be not lenient with your high financiers and politicians who assisted in the birth of the only political, social and economic system in all civilization that adopted atheism as its religion, internationalism as its patriotism, and slavery as its liberty."[38] In subsequent addresses, Coughlin repeated this theme, posing as a friend of "good" Jews who was seeking to protect them against a backlash that would take the form of a "holocaust": "Thus, for his collective safety, the American Jew must repudiate the atheistic Jew. . . . We are concerned, then, with extinguishing this fire before it consumes our inheritance and before the flames of hatred enfold themselves around the millions of innocent Jews and gentiles in a holocaust of persecution." Coughlin managed to anticipate all of Robertson's themes—the distinction between bad, "liberal" Jews and good, religious Jews, the new world order, and the threat of secular humanism: "According to the reformed or liberal Jews who have departed from the ancient hopes and aspirations of Judaism . . . the world is waiting for a Messianic Age which will be the result of Jewish national leadership—an age of naturalism which will have for its end the subjections of all nations to the naturalistic philosophy."[39]

The parallel between Coughlin and Robertson breaks down in one respect to be sure: Father Coughlin was soon silenced by the Catholic Church and politically disgraced. Robertson, after expressing almost indistinguishable views in almost identical language, continues to be defended by conservative intellectuals, including the leading Jewish conservatives, and is courted by Republican politicians like Bob Dole seeking his blessing.

Robertson is not alone among televangelists and religious right leaders in airing anti-Semitic theories and sentiments. According to the Reverend James Robison, who gave the opening prayer at the Republican Convention in 1984, an "anti-Semite is someone who hates Jews more than he's supposed to." Jimmy Swaggart once told an audience, "Don't bargain with Jesus. He's a Jew." Jerry Falwell evoked the same stereotype, telling an audience, "I know why you don't like the Jew. . . . He can make more money accidentally than you can on purpose."[40]

The Robertson affair took yet another bizarre turn on October 26, 1995. The Christian Coalition leader, who had been keeping a low profile since my expose, appeared on the New York talk show hosted by Charlie Rose to push yet another book—a novel entitled *The End of the Age*. Published by Word Publishing in Dallas (the same publisher responsible for *The New World Order*), Robertson's novel tells the story of a giant meteor plunging into the earth from outer space and inaugurating the series of events foretold in the Book of Revelation.

During the show, Rose pressed Robertson on the controversy raised by *The New World Order*. Robertson tried to dismiss the debate by describing me as someone who "has formerly been a conservative. Now he's turned liberal. And he was going to discredit those who, who were driving the train to change the Congress. And this was a political statement to hurt me, and that's all. I don't have an anti-Semitic bone in my body. I have done more for Jewish causes. I've come up here to this city [New York] to lobby against the sale of British fighters to Saudi Arabia. . . ."

But what about the reliance on Nesta Webster in *The New World Order?* Robertson blamed the offending passages on a research assistant: "And in that regard, my researcher misled me." The conspiracy is real, but the international financiers, it turns out, are mostly Scots and Englishmen:

> Number one, I was talking about the Bank of England. I've made it clear in a whole chapter that I was speaking about a Scotchman—I'm Scotch—whose name was Patterson, who started this bank. And the man named Thompson, who was the first president, said, "We will create—we will gain interest on money which we create out of nothing." And this was the beginning of central banking. We have had a history of Presidents—Andrew Jackson, particularly—who fought the concept of a central bank being imposed by the Bundesbank and by the Bank of England . . .[41]

Let us be charitable and pass in silence over Robertson's new claim that Andrew Jackson, who was president from 1828 to 1836, was engaged in a war not just with the Second Bank of the United States but with the Bundesbank (which was not even established until after Germany was united in 1870). A glance at *The New World Order* belies Robertson's exculpatory account. The book dwells on Warburg, Schiff, and the other villains of classic anti-Semitism, mentioning gentile bankers only in passing. Twice in *The New World Order,* Robertson attributes a remark about interest being "the eighth wonder of the world" to a "Baron Rothschild."

Not that there is any contradiction between anti-Semitic and anti-English conspiracy theories. In the writings of the turn-of-the-century American populist and monetary crank William H. "Coin" Harvey, to name only one example, the two conspiracies are blended. In his 1894 propaganda novel *A Tale of Two Nations,* two English financiers, one Jewish, the Baron Rothe (Rothschild), and another whose name sounds Jewish, Sir William T. Cline, hatch a plot to ruin America by demonetizing silver. According to Richard Hofstadter in his study of Harvey:

> Three years later the conspiracy brings to Washington the young nephew of the Baron, one Victor Rogasner, a darkly handsome cosmopolitan of sybaritic tendencies. . . . Rogasner is aided by a secretary, by two former

Scotland Yard men, whose business it is to work on congressmen, and by a passionate and beautiful Russian Jewess who will do anything to advance the projects or achieve the happiness of the man she loves.

It should be noted that Harvey was careful to publicly denounce anti-Semitism:

> You should not be prejudiced against any race as a race. . . . Among Jews, many became money changers; it seems to be natural with them, probably on account of their excessive shrewdness. They see that it has advantages not possessed by any other business.[42]

It would be pleasant to think that Robertson is merely a harmless monetary crank. But in September 1995, a month before his appearance on *The Charlie Rose Show*, Robertson declared, "The Christian Coalition . . . is dominant in the Republican parties in 18 states and substantial in 13 more. . . . But we are only a portion of the way there. We must complete the job in all 50 states."

This brings us back to the question raised earlier—why have the mainstream conservatives who broke with the conspiracy-mongering leader of the John Birch Society in the 1960s apologized for the even more extremist leader of the Christian Coalition in the 1990s? The difference, it seems, is numbers. The John Birch Society never had much more than sixty thousand members. The Christian Coalition claims millions. Perhaps if the John Birch Society had had millions of members, and had controlled the nomination of Republican presidents, Robert Welch would have been treated as respectfully as Pat Robertson has been.

Shortly after I published my first criticism of Robertson in the *New Republic* in 1992, when I was still a conservative in good standing, I received a call from a leading conservative editor with whom I was then on cordial terms. He wanted to know why I was so critical of the religious right. I told him that its leader was a crackpot who claimed that Jews and Freemasons were secretly running the world. What more reason did anybody need? The conservative editor replied: "Of course they're mad, but we need their votes." With a cynicism that astonished even me (a veteran of political work since college), this editor proceeded to explain that the 12 percent of the electorate who identified with the religious right had to be courted if the Republican party were to build "the natural conservative majority in this country."

If Robertson were just another televangelist, I suspect that the conservative movement would have denounced him long ago. Robertson's Christian Coalition, though, claims over a million members and 1.8 million households on its mailing list. According to People for the American Way, 60 percent of the six hundred candidates for national, state, and local offices backed by the religious right won election on November 8, 1994.

In the 1980s, members of a movement headed by another influential conspiracy theorist attempted to infiltrate the Democratic party by taking control of local precincts. Like Robertson, Lyndon LaRouche ran for president; like Robertson, LaRouche is a conspiracy theorist (indeed, in *The New World Order* Robertson gives, as one of his sources, LaRouche's book *Dope, Inc.,* an alleged expose of the role in international drug trafficking of Queen Elizabeth II of England). Suppose that the LaRouche movement were as large as the Robertson movement. Suppose that the LaRouche movement managed to replace the Christian Coalition as the most powerful grass-roots movement within the Republican party. Say that 40 percent of the delegates at Republican national conventions were LaRouchites. For the sake of argument, let us imagine the LaRouche movement taking over the conservative daily the *Washington Times,* along with its magazine *Insight* (at present, the *Washington Times* media empire is owned by another cult—the Unification Church, led by the Korean messiah Reverend Sun Myung Moon, who, like LaRouche, has served prison time in the United States). Lyndon LaRouche would then have a media empire comparable to that based on Pat Robertson's Christian Broadcasting Network (CBN).

What would conservative intellectuals and activists do if the LaRouche movement held the balance of power in the Republican party? It would be pleasant to believe that the conservative elite would expose LaRouche's crackpot conspiracy theories. From the precedent set by their response to Pat Robertson and the Christian Coalition, though, it seems likely that many leaders of the right would swallow their objections and begin to defend Lyndon LaRouche and his followers, stressing LaRouche's pro-growth economics and his ardent support during the Reagan years for the Strategic Defense Initiative. Nor is it difficult at all to envision conservative pundits savaging critics of the LaRouche wing of the Republican party as "moral relativists" and "Marxians" and welcoming LaRouche as an ally in "the culture war." After all, the neoconservative magazine *First Things* has printed a disingenuous attempt to partly exonerate David Koresh for ambushing and murdering federal law enforcement officers; from this, it would be no great leap to publish writers who complain that the description of the LaRouche movement as a "cult" is typical of the supposed liberal animus against religion in America. Republican presidential candidates, and would-be Republican executive branch appointees, can all too easily be imagined making pilgrimages to the headquarters of the LaRouche movement, where they would express agreement with LaRouchite goals in language sufficiently vague to distance themselves from LaRouchite lunacies. "Of course they're mad, but we need their votes." The cynical conservative editor who told me this was referring to the Christian Coalition, but he could just as well have been referring to the Lyndon LaRouche movement, if it had enough members, and enough political clout.[43]

Conservatives, and particularly neoconservatives, like to talk about "the treason of the intellectuals." But the *trahison des clercs* that Julien Benda, a left-wing French Jew, criticized in the 1920s was the abandonment of Enlightenment humanism by converts to the right among the French intelligentsia eager to participate wholeheartedly in political movements of national regeneration based on racism, integral nationalism, and religious revivalism. Many of the new rightists whom Benda criticized ended up as apologists for the Nazi-installed Vichy regime, whose leaders blamed the troubles of France for the previous few centuries on conspiracies by communists, liberals, and—not least—by Illuminati, Freemasons, and Jews.

The neoconservatives who volunteered to act as public-relations agents for Pat Robertson, a bizarre television evangelist from Virginia, were right about one thing: the southernization of the American right. In their search for influence and power, both the East Coast Old Right and the Republican neoconservatives turned to the ascendant force within the right wing of the Republican party—conservative ex-Democrats from Dixie. The haunted South was replacing the staid Midwest as the heartland of the American right.

The southernization of the American right is not limited to the conversion of white southerners, formerly conservative Democrats, to the Republican party. Just as important, perhaps more important in the long run, is the reshaping of national conservatism along lines long familiar in the South. The new, southern-style conservatism is much more radical than Taft's midwestern conservatism or Buckley's Manhattan conservatism or the Beltway conservatism of the neocons in the 1980s. Neo-southern conservatism unites intense hostility to the national government with ruthless, cutthroat capitalism. The politics of neo-southern conservatism is based upon the "culture war"—a euphemism for the old-fashioned southern demagogy that distracted poor white voters from the realities of their exploitation by the rich and the corporations by means of theatrical denunciations of blacks, Catholics, Jews, atheists, homosexuals, modern artists, Darwinian biologists, and various other supposed enemies of the people.

In the next chapter, I describe the southernization of the right in detail. In the chapters that follow, I try to demonstrate how the neo-southern national right uses the culture war, a revival of racism, and radical antigovernment rhetoric as part of its strategy of distracting voters from the hidden agenda of the right—shifting benefits upward and taxation downward.

Chapter 5

Whistling Dixie

The Southernization of the American Right

Contemporary American conservative ideology, as I have argued in the preceding chapters, is a bizarre blend of themes from American populism and American Marxism—a synthesis symbolized by the unlikely alliance between Pat Robertson and the ex-liberal and ex-leftist Republican neoconservatives. Although libertarians are responsible for the details of the economic agenda of the Republican party, the umbrella philosophy of the American conservative movement has largely been formulated by ex-leftists like James Burnham, Frank Meyer, and Irving Kristol, and its chief appeal has been to radical populists on the right, like the followers of Patrick Buchanan and Pat Robertson. Indeed, it is not too much of an exaggeration to say that the unacknowledged patron saints of post-1955 American conservatism have been William Jennings Bryan and Karl Marx.

While ex-leftists with a pro-business, "inverted Marxist" ideology are influential in the ranks of the New York and Washington conservative intellectual network, when it comes to elections the populist strain of contemporary conservatism is by far the most important. Populism, in the United States, has taken the form of the Anti-Federalist/Jeffersonian/Jacksonian tradition, which in different periods has been consistently opposed to the changing manifestations of the Federalist/Hamiltonian/Lincolnian nationalist tradition. Each of these rival traditions is "liberal" in the broad sense in which liberalism means support for private enterprise, constitutionalism, and some sort of democracy; Jefferson-Jackson liberalism unites liberalism with populism at the expense of nationalism, while Hamilton-Lincoln liberalism combines liberalism with national-ism, at the expense, if necessary, of populism.

The historic strongholds of Hamilton-Lincoln national liberalism have been New England, the parts of the Midwest and Pacific Coast settled by pioneers from New England, and the northern Plains states settled by Germans and Scandinavians who brought with them compat-ible nationalist and statist traditions. Jefferson-Jackson populist liberal-ism has predominantly been a phenomenon of the American South and of the parts of the Midwest like southern Missouri and Kansas settled by southerners. As national liberalism in the United States speaks with a Yankee accent, so populist liberalism speaks with a drawl.

The Republican party, from Lincoln to Theodore Roosevelt, was the national liberal party. Based on an alliance of the Northeast and the Midwest with the black minority in the South, it stood for a strong fed-eral government, an industrial capitalist economy, and (if only intermit-tently) for federally enforced civil rights for nonwhite Americans. The Democrats, from Thomas Jefferson to Woodrow Wilson, were the pop-ulist liberal party. Based on an alliance of the South and West with the European-Catholic minority in the North, the Democrats stood for states' rights, agrarian capitalism, and (if only intermittently) regulation of northern industry in the interests of southern and western farmers and northern workers. The battle in the late nineteenth-century South between Populists and conservative Democrats was a family squabble within the Jefferson-Jackson populist liberal tradition.

Between World War I and World War II this pattern was trans-formed. From Lincoln to Theodore Roosevelt, the Republican party had succeeded in modernizing the American economy in the interests of northern industry. Mostly-Republican Progressives like TR and Herbert Croly, the author of *The Promise of American Life* and the founder of the *New Republic,* believed that the time was ripe for a new version of Hamiltonian national liberalism that would extend the bene-fits of American growth to workers as well as capitalists. The business interests that controlled the Republican party, however, rejected this "democratic Hamiltonianism," and TR was forced to lead a valiant but doomed crusade as the 1912 presidential candidate of the short-lived Progressive party.

Theodore Roosevelt's failure to prevent the Republican party from being identified with the narrow interests of the business class created an opportunity for Democrats like Woodrow Wilson to position themselves as leaders of reform. However, it took the Great Depression and the political genius of Franklin Delano Roosevelt for the Democratic appropriation of national liberalism to be complete. Although Roosevelt was careful to pay homage to Thomas Jefferson and Andrew Jackson, it was clear to southern Democratic conservatives that he was steering the party into the path of those detested northerners Alexander Hamilton and Abraham Lincoln (if not, indeed, taking the party down the road to socialism or communism). FDR's failed attempt to purge southern conservative Democrats in 1938 effectively ended the New Deal, by cementing an alliance in Congress of right-wing southern Democrats with Republicans. The adoption by the Democrats under Truman of the traditionally Republican cause of civil rights led much of the South to bolt from the Democrats in 1948 and vote for the segregationist States' Rights party's candidate for president, Strom Thurmond.

Since the New Deal, and especially since the civil rights revolution, the exchange of constituencies between the two parties has accelerated. The Democrats—formerly the southern populist liberal party—are now a northern national liberal party. The Republicans—formerly the northern national liberal party—are now a southern populist liberal party. The most faithful Republican voters today are the kind of conservative white southerners who voted for Strom Thurmond in 1948. And the most faithful Democrats today are the constituencies that used to be the backbone of the Republican party—social liberals in the North and black southerners. The Democrats are now the party of Lincoln, and the Republicans have become the party of Thomas Jefferson, Andrew Jackson, and William Jennings Bryan—if not, indeed, of Jefferson Davis.

In this chapter I describe the southernization of the Republican right. The southernization of the right has meant more than the "southern strategy" devised by Goldwater and Nixon and perfected by Reagan and Bush—a strategy for luring white southerners away from the Democratic coalition. It means the adoption, by the leaders and the intellectuals of the American right, of a "culture-war" approach to politics that was perfected by southern conservative Democrats during the period of their one-party rule in the South from the end of Reconstruction until the civil rights revolution. It means, as well, the adoption by the Republican leadership of a "southern" rather than a "northern" vision of the future of American capitalism and American politics—a vision of the United States as a low-wage, low-tax, low-investment industrial society like the New South of 1875–1965, a kind of early-twentieth-century Mississippi or Alabama recreated on a continental scale. Just as the rhetoric of Jefferson-Jackson populism disguised the harsh realities of the economic exploitation by the white southern Bourbon ruling class of the white majority and the black minority in the New South, so the culture-war politics of the southernized GOP diverts attention from the class war of the small and prospering American overclass against the American middle-class majority.

After the Republicans gained control of both Houses of Congress in the 1994 midterm election, jubilant conservatives declared that the Republican party had converted America to its views. This was not quite right—most Americans disagree with conservative views on social issues and the economy, and defectors from the Democratic party have tended to swell the ranks of independents, not Republicans. Although 1994 probably did not signal a lasting Republican realignment, it was important for another momentous development: the Republican takeover of the South.

It might be more accurate to say the southern takeover of the Republican party. The key to understanding American politics at the end of the century is understanding that the dominant group in the dominant party today consists of white southerners. American conservatism today is southern conservatism, writ large. The obsessions and themes, the rhetoric and imagery, of today's national right are, with few modifications, those of yesterday's Dixie segregationists and demagogues.

The transformation of the Republicans into the vehicle of southern white reaction is the most remarkable paradox in American history. The Republicans, after all, were the first purely sectional party in the United States—a purely sectional *northern* party. In 1860, Republican presidential candidate Abraham Lincoln did not receive a single southern vote. The roots of the Republican party, moreover, were in the modernizing, nationalist tradition of the Northeast, the tradition of the Federalist and National Republican and Whig parties. This tradition was a version of conservatism, if conservatism is identified with emphasis on property, business, and leadership by members of a social establishment. But it had little to do with the reactionary rural conservatism found south of the Mason-Dixon line. Northern conservatives like Alexander Hamilton, Daniel Webster, and Abraham Lincoln favored a strong federal government with a tax base adequate for funding "internal improvements"—turnpikes, canals, railroads. Conservatives in the

Federalist-Whig-Republican tradition also favored what would nowadays be called "industrial policy"—the promotion of American industry by means of tariff protection, subsidies, and a first-rate system of public education. Alexander Hamilton and his mentor George Washington (a Virginia planter with "northern" or nationalist principles) even wanted to create a professional civil service elite to run the centralized nation-state they envisioned. The American mandarins would be trained for service in the federal bureaucracy at a national university that would be the civilian equivalent of West Point (Washington toyed with the idea of making Columbia University in New York the national university).

Southern conservatism was radically different. Southern conservatives like Thomas Jefferson and Andrew Jackson stressed states' rights (though not to the point of secession) and opposed the promotion of industry and finance by the federal government (Jackson destroyed the Second Bank of the United States). Whereas Washington freed his slaves, and Hamilton supported the earliest efforts to abolish slavery, Jefferson lent the weight of his prestige as a naturalist to the fallacious theory of black genetic inferiority in his *Notes on the State of Virginia;* in his old age, in retirement, he bitterly denounced northern abolitionists (in letters that are never discussed in civics classes). The greatest political thinker the South has produced, John C. Calhoun of South Carolina, devoted his life to the defense of slavery and the "compact theory" which views the United States as a federation of sovereign states rather than as a federal nation-state. By means of their vehicle, the Democratic party, the southern planters dominated the U.S. federal government from Jefferson's election in 1800 until Lincoln's election in 1860. When the success of the Republican party in 1860 made it clear that the white South could no longer dominate the Union, the leaders of the white South decided to destroy the Union.

After being defeated in the Civil War, the southern conservative ruling class reorganized itself as the so-called Bourbon oligarchy that dominated the South from the end of Reconstruction in 1875 until the civil rights revolution of the 1950s and 1960s. Throughout this period, as before the Civil War, the Democratic party was an alliance of white southerners with white workers, particularly Irish Catholic immigrants, in the cities of the North. The Solid South was created in the early twentieth century when southern Democrats effectively crushed the Republican and the Populist parties in their region and disfranchised not only blacks but much of the lower-income white population. The former Confederacy became a belt of one-party Democratic states, where small oligarchies of wealthy white families lorded it over an exploited majority of miserable whites and segregated and harassed blacks.

In 1932, Franklin Delano Roosevelt was elected as the northern leader of what was still a substantially southern party. In the congressional midterm elections of 1938, FDR's attempt to purge the most reactionary southern Democrats and replace them with New Deal liberals failed. Conservative Democrats joined with Republicans in "the conservative coalition," an effective majority in Congress that blocked most progressive legislation until the 1960s. The triumph of northern liberals like Hubert Humphrey in strengthening the civil rights platform of the Democratic party in 1948 inspired a rebellion among segregationist southern Democrats, who organized a short-lived "states' rights party" that nominated Strom Thurmond of South Carolina for president.

Many white Southerners voted for Eisenhower in 1952—beginning a two-generation pattern in which the white southern vote would be split between the Republicans in presidential elections and conservative Democrats in congressional and state and local elections. During the Eisenhower years, midwestern conservatives who supported Robert A. Taft and Joseph McCarthy and despised the "modern Republicanism" of Eisenhower and the moderate northeastern establishment wing of their party saw white southerners who were hostile to civil rights for blacks as potential allies. Nixon devised a "southern strategy" during his campaign for the presidency in 1960 (his refusal to call Coretta Scott King during Martin Luther King's imprisonment in a Birmingham jail led to a shift of black support toward Nixon's opponent, Senator John F. Kennedy of Massachusetts, who did make a phone call).

Barry Goldwater, one of eight senators to vote against the Civil Rights Act of 1964, was the first Republican presidential candidate since Lincoln to repudiate even a nominal commitment to the federal enforcement of civil rights for blacks. Ever since the Civil War, black southerners had tended to be loyal Republicans; Goldwater was willing to sacrifice black votes in order to get the white racist vote in the South. In 1963, baseball player Jackie Robinson wrote a prescient article for the *Saturday Evening Post* entitled "The GOP: For White Men Only."[1] He warned Goldwater against alienating blacks by following Nixon's 1960 southern strategy of writing off the black vote. Goldwater, though, dismissed the idea of reaching out to black voters, telling an Atlanta audience in 1961: "We're not going to get the negro vote as a block in 1964 and 1968, so we ought to go hunting where the ducks are."[2]

When the votes were counted, Goldwater had lost the entire country—except for the black belt. In 1964, the only states Goldwater carried, apart from his home state of Arizona, were five states in the Deep South—Alabama, Mississippi, Louisiana, Georgia, and South Carolina—four of which had not voted for a Republican president since Reconstruction. A comparison of the electoral votes for Thurmond in 1948, Goldwater in 1964, and Wallace in 1968 is instructive. Thurmond won South Carolina, Alabama, Mississippi, and Louisiana; Goldwater won South Carolina, Alabama, Mississippi, Louisiana, and Georgia, along with Arizona; Wallace won Georgia, Alabama, Mississippi, Louisiana, and Arkansas. The three candidates disagreed on many matters; indeed, in the realm of economic policy George Wallace, a populist and a statist who was somewhat to the left of Lyndon Johnson, could hardly have been further from Barry Goldwater. Thurmond, Goldwater, and Wallace won more or less the same set of Black Belt states because of the one policy they shared in common—opposition to federal enforcement of civil rights for black Americans. Despite the landslide of Lyndon Johnson, the Goldwater movement—as William Rusher, the former publisher of *National Review* and one of the architects of the Goldwater campaign, has noted—"turned the Republican party over—permanently, as matters turned out—to a new and basically conservative coalition based on the South, the Southwest and the West, ending the long hegemony of the relatively liberal East in the GOP's affairs." The party of Abraham Lincoln was well on its way to becoming the party of Jefferson Davis.

In his 1988 memoirs, Goldwater wrote that as a result of his candidacy in 1964 "conservatives come from all regions, every social class, every creed and color, all age groups."[3] The numbers tell a different story. Eisenhower managed to win 20 percent of the black vote in 1952 and 40 percent in 1956, after he sent troops into Little Rock to enforce school desegregation.[4] In 1960, Nixon, whose platform called for federal civil rights legislation, won 32 percent of the national black vote. Goldwater in 1964 won 6 percent. No Republican presidential candidate since then has recaptured Nixon's share of the black vote in 1960.[5]

The success of George Wallace in 1968 convinced Richard Nixon to emulate Wallace's demagogic populism in his 1972 campaign, by campaigning on "white backlash" issues like busing and "law and order" (understood to be a coded reference to black crime). "The whole secret of politics," said Kevin Phillips, one of the architects of Nixon's southern strategy, "is knowing who hates who." Phillips told the campaign, "Substantial Negro support is not necessary to national Republican victory. The GOP can build a winning coalition without Negro votes. Indeed, Negro-Democratic mutual identification was a major source of Democratic loss—and Republican or American Independent Party profit—in much of the country" in 1968. Phillips, an Irish-American from the Bronx educated at Harvard Law, argued for reconstituting the GOP as a southern and western party: "Who needs Manhattan when we can get the electoral votes of eleven Southern states? Put those together with the Farm Belt and the Rocky Mountains, and we don't need the big cities."[6]

Although he pandered to white racists, and shared their sentiments, Nixon was not a conservative of the Jefferson-Jackson school. Indeed, as his mercantilist trade policy and wage and price control policy showed, he was something of an economic nationalist in the Federalist-Whig-Republican tradition. Nixon, an admirer of Charles de Gaulle, intended to reshape the Republican party along Gaullist, nationalist lines, or, failing that, to establish a new party. His grandiose ambitions were wrecked by the revelations of his criminality during the Watergate investigations and his subsequent resignation.

Ironically, one of the consequences of Nixon's self-destruction was the delivery of the Republican party to a new right wing based in the South and the West. Ronald Reagan, the champion of the conservatives, narrowly missed wresting the presidential nomination in 1976 from Gerald Ford. During Reagan's two terms in the White House, the Republican party did not achieve a national realignment; but the long-term realignment of the South continued.

In the first congressional elections of the New Deal era in 1934, there were virtually no Republicans from the South or West. Ninety percent of the Republican members of the Seventy-fourth Congress came from the northern tier. As recently as 1946, the GOP gained control of the House thanks to votes from New England and the Atlantic, Great Lakes, and Plains regions. By 1984, however, more than 50 percent of the Republicans in the Senate were from the South and the West.

The southernization of the Republican party did not take place only at the federal level. Beginning in the 1960s, the Republican party has increasingly been able to elect governors, other state officials, and legislators in the South, although local and county machines still tend to be dominated by the Democrats. In November 1994, the gains were particularly striking, with large-scale conversions of conservative Democrats to the GOP following the election in southern states like Texas. (The defectors followed a path pioneered by "boll weevil" Democrats like Bob Stump, an Arizona congressman who joined the Republicans in 1982, and Phil Gramm, who converted in 1983 after he was thrown off the House Budget Committee by Democratic leaders.) This increasing local depth gives southern Republicans what they lacked until recently—a large pool of able, experienced politicians at lower levels who can be recruited to run for more important offices.

The results were on display in 1994. For the first time since President Rutherford B. Hayes pulled federal troops out of the former Confederacy and Republican puppet regimes in the southern states collapsed, the Republicans gained a majority of southern seats in the House (64 to 61) and the Senate (12 to 10). The passage of white southerners out of the Democratic party, underway for a generation, has not yet run its course. In the South, racial redistricting, by separating white and black voters, has tended to create secure districts for black Democrats and white Republicans, while devastating white Democrats who depend on biracial electorates. In 1994, while not one of the South's seventeen black Democratic members of Congress lost his safe, gerrymandered seat, sixteen seats held by white Democrats were lost to Republicans. The security of black Democratic seats in the South can only cement the equation between "black" and "Democratic" in the minds of white voters.

It remains to be seen whether the 1994 election signals a period of Republican hegemony in Congress matching the Republican domination of the White House (which Clinton may only have temporarily interrupted). One thing is certain: the Republican party now, and for the indefinite future, speaks with a Southern drawl. When the new Republican Congress was sworn in, the difference was one of regions as much as of parties. The defeated Democratic leadership had been almost exclusively from the Northeast, the Midwest, and the Pacific Northwest, with Speaker Tom Foley of Washington, Majority Leader Dick Gephardt of Missouri, and Majority Whip David Bonior of Michigan in the House, and, on the Senate side, Majority Leader George Mitchell from Maine. The only southerner in the Democratic congressional leadership was Senate Majority Whip Wendell Ford of Kentucky. By contrast, all but one of the new leaders of the Republican Congress hailed from a former state of the Confederacy. Speaker Newt Gingrich was a Georgian, House Majority Leader Dick Armey and Whip Tom DeLay were both Texans, and Senate Majority Whip Trent Lott was from Mississippi. In this crowd of southerners, only Senate Majority Leader Bob Dole was a fossil of the Lincoln-to-Eisenhower era when the GOP was a party of the Midwest and Northeast that seldom received a Southern vote. Strom Thurmond, the 1948 candidate of the segregationist "Dixiecrats," was sworn in as chairman of the Senate Armed Services Committee—a grim irony, inasmuch as the integration of the armed forces was one of the reforms that inspired segregationists like Thurmond to bolt from Harry Truman's Democratic party.[7]

Savoring its victory, the Republican right has its own triumphalist version of history. According to the consensus among conservatives, the long march toward the Republican revolution of November 1994 began in 1955, when William F. Buckley, Jr., founded *National Review* as the vehicle for conservative ideas at odds with the then-dominant liberal orthodoxy. Crystallizing around *National Review* and organizations like Young Americans for Freedom (YAF), the conservative movement soon mustered enough strength within the Republican party to nominate Barry Goldwater for president in 1964. Though Goldwater was defeated by Lyndon Johnson in a landslide, the conservatives had strengthened their position within the GOP—and had found a new standard-bearer in Ronald Reagan, whose speech at the 1964 convention—"The Speech"—galvanized the partisans of the right. Denied the nomination by moderates in 1976, Reagan came to power in 1980; the Reagan revolution was completed in November 1994 by the Gingrich revolution. In retrospect, Goldwater's defeat marked the beginning, not the end, of the realignment of the American political order from liberal Democratic orthodoxy to conservative Republican hegemony.

This sanitized version of history grossly overemphasizes the importance of intellectuals in politics, and underestimates the effects of crude propaganda exploiting prejudice and fear. The success of Republican politicians owes little to the persuasiveness of conservative intellectuals like William F. Buckley, Jr. and Irving Kristol—and almost everything to Republican mastery of techniques of right-wing Southern demagogues like George Wallace.

Indeed, today's southern Republican right traces its lineage not to

Buckley's *National Review* circle or to the neoconservatives of the 1970s, but to the southern and western far right of 1932–1965 that opposed both the New Deal and the civil rights revolution. The present-day national conservative media network was anticipated, in many of its details, by the far-right media empire of the late Dallas oilman H. L. Hunt that flourished between the 1950s and the 1970s. Hunt's Facts Forum, founded in 1951, sponsored nationwide radio broadcasts played by hundreds of radio stations as well as TV shows, one filmed in Washington, that were carried by dozens of stations across the country. The Rush Limbaugh show and the conservative National Empowerment Television (NET) have more in common with Hunt's Facts Forum than with Buckley's *Firing Line.* Many of the themes of today's Republican conservatism—the alleged surrender of U.S. sovereignty to the United Nations, the supposed totalitarian tendencies of mainline Protestantism and Judaism—can be found in the titles of free books mailed by the Facts Forum library, a predecessor of the Conservative Book Club: *We Must Abolish the United Nations, Hitler Was a Liberal,* and *Traitors in the Pulpit.* Even gay-baiting, which played a minor role in the older mainstream conservatism, is an old theme of the southwestern far right; witness another Facts Forum title, *Behind the Lace Curtains of the Y.M.C.A.* Long before there was a Christian Coalition, Hunt (a notorious bigamist) was subsidizing the Campus Crusade for Christ; and before Pat Robertson established the Christian Broadcasting Network, Hunt had founded LIFE LINE, a nominally religious broadcasting and newspaper empire. The complicity of contemporary conservatives like Rush Limbaugh, Jerry Falwell, the editors of the *American Spectator* and conservative donor Richard Scaife in spreading crackpot conspiracy theories about Bill Clinton had a precedent, as well, in the scurrilous attacks on Kennedy and Johnson subsidized by Hunt. In some cases the links between Hunt's southwestern far right and the national right of today are direct. A young football player named Jack Kemp, along with Pat Boone, sat on the executive committee of Hunt's "District Speakers, Inc." Though Hunt's empire declined after his death in 1974, his son Nelson Bunker Hunt, an ardent admirer of the John Birch Society and a contributor to the Wallace campaign, helped preside at the marriage of the far right and the Republican party. In 1982, he and his allies raised $350,000 for the National Conservative Political Action Committee. In 1984, during the Republican National Convention, the younger Hunt hosted a barbecue for Republicans at his ranch outside Dallas. Jerry Falwell gave the invocation, and Pat Boone and Bob Hope entertained an audience that included Jesse Helms, Orrin Hatch, and Howard Phillips of the Conservative Caucus.[8] The center of gravity of the Republican party, in drifting to the far right, had moved south and west.

The new Southern elite in the Republican party brings with it obsessions and attitudes that have long been part of the political culture of Jefferson-Jackson conservatism. Conservative journalists may pretend all they want that the determination by today's southernized Republicans to slash taxes and abolish welfare represents some sort of rational response to modern social problems. The fact remains that southern and western conservatives are simply reenacting the ritualized approach to politics they inherited from their parents and grandparents and great-grandparents.

Consider the recurrent insistence by southern and western conservatives on massive tax cuts, at the expense, if necessary, of a balanced budget. This obsession may be rationalized in terms of "supply-side economics," a theory of the 1970s, but it really has its origins in a centuries-old regional political culture that has encouraged Southerners to take a slapdash approach to government finances since the days of Andrew Jackson and his "war" with the Bank of the United States. For two decades, regardless of the actual condition of the budget or the deficit, Republicans elected from the South and West have favored tax cuts. Budget-busting tax cuts are as southern and western as fiscal conservatism is midwestern and northeastern. In the Senate version of the 1978 Kemp-Roth tax-cut bill, which inaugurated the present era of massive deficits, not a single Republican senator from the Great Lakes and border states, and only 20 percent of the Republican senators from the Atlantic and New England states, co-signed the bill. In contrast, 40 percent of the Pacific Coast Republicans, 33 percent of the southeasterners, 60 percent of the southwesterners, and 100 percent of the Republican senators from the Mountain States co-sponsored Kemp-Roth.[9]

Some may argue that I am exaggerating the influence of white southerners on the conservative movement. After all, it might be objected, there is the southern California right, based in Orange County, that gave critical support to Nixon and Reagan. On close inspection, the southern California right turns out to be a cultural, indeed, an ethnic, offshoot of the southern right. The original Anglo-American settlers of southern California came from New England and the Yankee-settled Midwest, bringing with them a characteristic "Yankee" political culture that made them a major constituency for Progressive reform. During the Great Depression, however, a stream of migrants from the western fringes of the South, "Okies" and "Arkies," settled in central and southern California, bringing with them the political culture of the Scots-Irish Highland South. According to political scientist Daniel J. Elazar, "By and large, the radical right of southern California consists of former Southerners in revolt against what were, to them, unacceptable patterns of political and social life created by the dominant non-Southerners."[10]

The southern (and southern California) Republican right, which has inherited its views of the minimal state and the untrammeled market from the old Jefferson-Jackson Democrats, has gained an important ally in the form of the national business class. The U.S. business elite has abandoned the old Whig-Republican tradition of economic nationalism, based on massive federal investments in infrastructure (the railroads, the interstate highways) and high wages (even before the United States industrialized, the wages of its free workers were the highest in the world). The nationalist strategy served U.S. industry and finance well, as long as American banks and businesses were rising to world-class status in a giant domestic market protected from foreign competition. Today, however, multinational businesses and banks based in the United States pin their hopes on export markets abroad—and slaver at the thought of transferring industrial production and even routine service jobs to low-wage workers without unions or civil rights in Third World countries. Industrialists who teamed up with industrial workers at the expense of southern agrarians, who paid the costs of protectionism for U.S. industry, have now switched sides. A new, free-trade coalition—visible in the vote on NAFTA and GATT—allies multinational industry and finance with export-oriented agriculture in the South and West against industrial workers in the midwestern industrial heartland. (The major manufacturing industry in the South and West, the defense industry, is subsidized by the one federal program that Republican conservatives want to increase spending on.) The repudiation by the American business class of the "northern" model of high-wage, high-public-investment development in favor of the "southern" model of a low-wage, low-tax, low-public-service economy is a shift of historic proportions that has the potential to destroy the twentieth-century achievement of middle-class living standards for a majority of Americans.

The transfer of not only constituencies but worldviews between the Republican and Democratic parties, with the result that yesterday's Southern Democrats have become today's conservative Republicans, raises the question of which American party, which American tradition, can best be called "conservative." The answer depends on what "conservatism" is held to mean.

In a remarkable essay entitled "Conservatism as an Ideology" (1957), Samuel P. Huntington, one of America's leading political scientists, described three different definitions of conservatism.[11] The "aristocratic theory" defined conservatism as the ideology of aristocrats displaced by modern capitalism and democracy and wishing for a restoration of the *ancien régime* or an older feudal social order. Since few contemporary conservatives fit this description, Huntington dismisses the aristocratic theory. He also dismisses what he calls "the autonomous definition of conservatism" which defines conservatism as "an autonomous system of ideas which are generally valid." In the United States, the late Russell Kirk, who argued that conservatism was a transcendent ideology based on natural law, was identified with this position. Huntington dismisses the autonomous theory because "the conservative ideology lacks the broad sweep and catholic appeal of an ideology of universal and permanent relevance" like liberalism and Marxism, in their different varieties.

If conservatism is neither the worldview of aristocratic malcontents nor a political philosophy that is relevant in all times and all societies, then what is it? Huntington argues for the "situation definition" of conservatism, according to which conservatism is "the ideology arising out of a distinct but recurring type of historical situation in which a fundamental challenge is directed at established institutions. . . ." The patron saint of Anglo-American conservatism, Edmund Burke, for example, did not articulate a consistent theory of political and social order, but merely defended the (quite different) "establishments" of Britain, the American colonies, Ireland, India, and France against what he considered harmful innovation. "The plain fact of the matter," Huntington writes, "is that insofar as he had views on the desirable organization of society, in politics Burke was a liberal and a Whig, the defender of the Lockean constitution; in economics, he was a liberal free trader, his ideas at one with those of Adam Smith."

For Huntington, the opposite of conservatism is not liberalism but radicalism: "Conservatism and radicalism derive from orientations toward the process of change rather than toward the purpose and direction of change." It follows that, depending upon whether they are insurgents trying to seize power or part of an establishment trying to retain power, adherents of genuine (nonsituational) ideologies, like liberals, communists, fascists, or Muslim fundamentalists, may use "radical" or "conservative" arguments. In every case, the "establishments" defended by situationally conservative elites were the result of some revolution in the past. (Burke himself, in the late eighteenth century, was defending a British political order that dated back only to the Glorious Revolution of 1689.) Today's conservatism is invariably yesterday's radicalism, and today's radicals, if they are successful, will become tomorrow's conservatives.

If the situational definition of conservatism is the best, then the complaint by the American right about the use of the term "conservatives" to describe Soviet and Eastern European communist elites and "liberals" or "radicals" to describe their pro-market, democratic opponents, is without justification. Conservative communism—like that which existed in the last decades of the Soviet Union—is not a contradiction in terms, in the sense that "radical conservatism" *is* a contradiction.

In recent years, more and more so-called conservatives in the United States have been willing to describe themselves as "radicals" or "revolutionaries." The Republican right spoke of "the Reagan Revolution." Newt Gingrich sounds more like Robespierre than Burke. Irving Kristol's wife the historian Gertrude Himmelfarb has argued that the American right must not be conservative, in the situational sense, but counterrevolutionary, and her son William Kristol, editor of Australian media tycoon Rupert Murdoch's American conservative magazine the *Standard,* has attacked the defenders of the New Deal tradition as the real reactionaries.

I, for one, am willing to take the radicals of the Republican right at their word. They are not conservatives at all, in the situational sense. With all of the passion of left-wing anarchists, the radicals of the right vilify every major domestic institution of the American republic—the civil service, the universities, the public schools, and, increasingly, the police and the FBI—reserving kind words only for business, right-wing churches, and the military. Their goal, according to Newt Gingrich and Dick Armey, is not to slightly modify the Progressive–New Deal–vital center state, but to abolish it in order to establish a futuristic new "civilization" (Newt Gingrich's argument) or to restore the conditions of the nineteenth-century Gilded Age (Dick Armey's argument). The genuine conservatives today are indeed the liberals (including neoconservative Democrats), who seek to preserve the institutional and intellectual legacy of FDR, Truman, Johnson, and King.

Today's Republican right, then, is not conservative. Is it radical or counterrevolutionary? Does it seek to establish a new, utopian order, or to restore an idealized past? The question is misleading, because counterrevolution tends to blur into revolution. According to Huntington, "As time passes, the ideal of the reactionary becomes less and less related to any actual society of the past. The past is romanticized, and, in the end, the reactionary comes to support a return to an idealized Golden Age which never in fact existed. He becomes indistinguishable from other radicals, and he normally displays all the distinctive characteristics of the radical psychology." (Newt Gingrich, perhaps?)

Today's right, then, is a movement that is radical and revolutionary in its strategy. Its content, as we have seen, is Jefferson-Jackson populist liberalism—not in its eighteenth-century form, nor in its Old South form, but in its New South form. When they were the ruling class of a region, threatened from without by the federal government, elite white southerners were "conservatives," defending the post-Reconstruction status quo. Today, having hijacked the Republican party, they are "radicals," seeking, in alliance with the multinational corporate elite, to dismantle the New Deal and to impose their peculiar "New South" vision of the United States as a low-wage, low-tax, low-regulation economy in which economic segregation replaces formal legal segregation not merely in their native region but in the country as a whole. If they are defeated in national politics, the members of the southern right will no doubt fall back into a "conservative" mode and attempt to maximize their power at the state and local level in parts of the United States that they control with a minimum of federal interference.

The economic agenda of the southernized right can be enacted, of course, only if the right holds onto political power. Though Republican domination is by no means assured, trends are running strongly in favor of the GOP. The crack-up of the Democrats shows no signs of being reversed, and the emergence of a viable third party, in the form of Perot's Independents or some other group, that could replace the Democrats as the opposition to the Republican party is years or decades away.

The Republicans have a problem. The economic program of American conservatives, if enacted in its entirety, would devastate the middle class while helping the American overclass. Income would be redistributed upward, while taxes would be redistributed downward. The combination of a flat tax with the repeal of capital gains taxes would permit many millionaires and billionaires to pay a far lower proportion of their overall income in taxes than most middle-class and working-class Americans. The repeal of the minimum wage would permit employers to drive the wages of vast numbers of Americans toward Third World levels.

How can conservatives expect to win votes for an economic program so inimical to the middle class? The answer is they cannot—and they know it. Therefore, most conservative ideologues (including Patrick Buchanan, before his recent adoption of economic populism) have done their best to change the subject from the economy to what they like to call "the culture." In the next chapter, I will describe the "culture war" campaign of the Republican right. Both race-baiting and the politics of family values are part of the same Republican culture-war strategy of diverting the anger of the white working class from the owners and operators of the Republican party—the corporate elite and the hereditary rich—and focusing wrath on unpopular minorities: blacks, Jews, secular Americans, homosexuals, immigrants.

Chapter 6

The Culture War and the Myth of the New Class

Every now and then there really is a smoking gun. During the 1984 Reagan reelection campaign, Republican strategist Lee Atwater set forth the culture-war strategy of today's Republican right:

> Populists have always been liberal on economics. So long as the crucial issues were generally confined to economics—as during the New Deal—the liberal candidate would expect to get most of the populist vote. But populists are conservatives on most social issues. . . . When social and cultural issues died down, the populists were left with no compelling reason to vote Republican. . . .

Atwater's recommendation to the Republican party: change the subject from economics to "culture."[1]

The culture war was not original with Atwater. The goal of Republican strategists from the Nixon administration onward has been to replace the New Deal alignment based on economic class and region with a new alignment based on subcultures. Spiro Agnew called an early version of the conservative culture war "positive polarization," saying, "It is time to rip away the rhetoric and to divide on authentic lines." Patrick J. Buchanan, when he was working as an aide in the Nixon White House, outlined the strategy in a memo about the benefits of nominating a southern segregationist to the Supreme Court: "[I]t is a bitterly divisive issue for Democratic candidates. . . . Either they kick their black friends in the teeth, or they kick the South in the teeth. De facto . . . divisive."

Buchanan, who has since used the culture war to his own benefit in two runs for the Republican presidential nomination that have made him the leading conservative spokesman along with Pat Robertson, urged Nixon to adopt a political strategy that would "cut the Democratic Party and country in half. My view is that we would have far the larger half."[2] For some time, the Nixon–Agnew–Buchanan strategy of "positive polarization" has been succeeding in tearing the country in half and giving the GOP the larger half.

A Republican majority based on the exploitation of racial and cultural rather than economic divisions in the population would not be unprecedented. Culture-war politics in the United States is nothing new—one need only recall how the debate over prohibition between European immigrant "wets" and southern and western Protestant "drys" divided the Democratic party for generations between the Civil War and the New Deal, to the benefit of the dominant Republicans. The most important model for the culture-war politics of the American right, as I observed earlier, is found in the one-party politics of the segregated Democratic South.

The details of conservative culture-war rhetoric show the influence of the two traditions that have the greatest influence on modern conservative ideology: the Jacksonian populism purveyed by the likes of Pat Robertson and Patrick Buchanan, and the inverted Marxism of ex-leftist neoconservatives. Populism has its roots in seventeenth-century English Puritan radicalism: neoconservative ideology, in nineteenth- and early twentieth-century Marxism, especially Leon Trotsky's Marxist faction. It would be difficult, one might think, to synthesize two such unlike traditions. In fact, however, populism and inverted Marxism are similar, in their apocalyptic vision of the present and future, and their claim to represent the masses against sinister elites. It is much easier, in fact, to synthesize populist radicalism and ex-Marxist radicalism in a portmanteau radicalism of the right, than it is to reconcile either populist radicalism or ex-Marxist radicalism with traditional conservatism or moderate liberalism. Both populist conspiracy theory and inverted-Marxist class analysis come together in the conservative culture war.

Most societies have some version of the Golden Age myth. (The term itself comes from the ancient Greek poet and moral philosopher Hesiod, who traced the degeneration of mankind from an age of gold through ages of silver, bronze, and iron.) Once, it is said, there was a time when disorder and sin were nonexistent or far less prevalent than today. Children respected their elders; husbands and wives were faithful to one another; young men and women were virgins until marriage; people drank in moderation, and knew only dignified entertainments. Popular literature was highly intellectual, and tended to promote good character. Incorruptible statesmen served the public interest, not special interests. Everyone was learned, and a great number were wise. There were no commercials.

The myth of the Golden Age tends to be accompanied, in most human communities, by the Devil Theory—the American historian Charles Beard's term for the idea that adverse trends in society or economics can always be blamed, not on economic changes or the unintended consequences of institutional designs, but on the machinations of sinister (and often hidden) conspirators. If sickness sweeps the village, the cause must be sorcerors and witches. If the divorce rate goes up, then Hollywood producers and university professors must be to blame.

In recent years the intellectuals and publicists of the American right, drawing on both Jefferson-Jackson populism and Marxism, have developed a unique synthesis of the Golden Age and devil myths. The Golden Age in the United States, the right has decided, ended in the 1960s, when long-haired campus radicals took over the culture, or, at the earliest, in the 1930s, when FDR's New Deal liberals took over the country. (Some reactionary conservatives think the decline began with the Union victory in the Civil War, or the Reformation, or the Renaissance, or the thirteenth century, but they tend not to have much influence.) The agent of the fall from grace, the serpent in the American garden, was "the new class," a tiny group of professors, journalists, social workers, and Hollywood producers, of the sort once lumped together by the McCarthyite founders of modern conservatism as "parlor pinks." Despite their small numbers, these "new class" intellectuals and professionals, by virtue of their control of the mass media, have been able to brainwash substantial portions of the American population into going against their own sounder instincts and embracing a relativistic and hedonist anti-morality.

If this sounds like a caricature of the conservative position, consider a recent authoritative statement of the new orthodoxy in the Republican magazine *Rising Tide* by the eminent neoconservative scholar Michael

Novak.[3] "From this country's founding until well into the 1940s, the three words 'moral,' 'character,' and 'virtue' were like newly polished silver—as shown in the expression, 'a sterling character,'" Novak writes. "And then, as in a three-act play, such terms were devalued." We should be suspicious of any melodramatic interpretation of history that compares it to a three-act play—but let us read on.

"The novels and detective stories of the 1920s and thirties," Novak writes, "were a warning. Good guys began to be cynical. Ladies began to smoke, drink and swear" (he is talking about fictional ladies, without whose example, it seems, real-life ladies would not have thought of smoking, drinking, and swearing). At least Humphrey Bogart and John Wayne's rugged romantics only "tried to seem hardboiled." Bogie and the Duke were pusillanimous altar boys, compared to the anti-heroes who followed in the 1950s, the dreadful Beats. Sounding rather like *Dragnet's* Sergeant Joe Friday, Novak writes: "Deviance was the song of the Beats. Gunning their motorcycles and taking 'trips' on drugs, they abandoned words like 'virtue.' When they encountered men of character, they called them square, stiff, unbending and hopelessly out of date."

In some way—Novak never explains how—the Beats, who were anti-rational, anti-scientific, and anti-bureaucratic (and of whom there were at most five in the entire United States) were comrades in arms with Franklin Delano Roosevelt and his welfare-state mandarins: "millions of scientifically trained personnel." With the help of "the national media," this sinister nomenclatura shoved aside local elites: "The old ways lost luster. The new ways that drove them out shown as brightly as chrome." The Silver Age of the hardboiled but good-hearted 1920s and 1930s, which had followed a previous American Golden Age of soft-boiled virtue, was being succeeded in the fifties and sixties by an Age of Chrome.

"In these three acts"—Act One being the pre-WWI era, Act Two being the interwar period, and Act Three being the 1940s to the present—"a healthy ecology of liberty—the moral atmosphere, the inner world of images and guiding narratives that had shaped this nation since the Mayflower Compact—blew apart. . . . In its place arose a mutant, a new morality filled with noise and pride and the excitement of rotating strobe lights." Disco had arrived.

Novak's contrast between the old morality of virtuous Christian Rotarians and the new morality of bongo drum-pounding Beat poets and paper-pushing government technocrats deserves to be quoted at length:

> From about 1830 onwards, until well into the 20th century, about two-thirds of young people in America had attended Sunday school. There they learned such stories as that of the Good Samaritan: On the road to Jericho a man was set upon by highway robbers, beaten, robbed and left for dead. A man of a different tribe came along, found him, bound up his wounds, put him in a local inn to recuperate and paid for his lodging. . . .
>
> In the new moral ecology . . . under the guidance of experts in social science, the story of the Good Samaritan needed to be told in a new way: Two social workers covering their assigned territory come upon a poor fellow, beaten and robbed, on the road to Jericho. They look at his wounds and feel sorry. "These men who beat and robbed you," they ask, "how can we help them?"

"Until the mid-1960s," Newt Gingrich claims, in accordance with Novak, "there was an explicit long-term commitment to creating character." But then came the "counterculture" of the 1960s, which "is extraordinarily tolerant of violence, with a situation-ethics morality, in which your immediate concern about your personal needs outweighs any obligation to others."[4] If Gingrich's and Novak's accounts of the degeneration of America were even halfway accurate, then any thoughtful American today would be doing his best to emigrate. Fortunately, Novak's "three-act drama" of American history is historical fiction.

If you believe conservatives, public school teachers since the 1960s, or even since World War II, have been the shock troops of the "new class," endowing vulnerable American children with what Novak calls "a morality for amoral robots." In what school district have teachers been doing this? Certainly not in mine. I attended public schools throughout, from the first grade to the twelfth. If there had been courses in amorality, cultural relativism, and godless humanism, I think I would have noticed. The moral propaganda that I and my fellow students received from our unionized public school teachers was entirely conventional—Be on Time, Finish Your Homework, Count to Ten When You Are Angry. I suppose that some hardshell conservatives might see a dangerous instance of "relativism" in the occasional lecture, in my lily-white and almost exclusively gentile suburban elementary school, about the need to be nice to people of other races and religions—but the banalities routinely expressed by conservative politicians trying to sound ecumenical can hardly be corrupting of youth when enunciated by teachers. What is the alternative, anyway—teaching racial pride and intolerance for heresy?

The picture Novak and other conservatives paint of an America that turned into an orgiastic Sybaris after the 1960s, then, seems utterly unreal to those of us who grew up in mainstream America between the 1960s and the present. How could conservative intellectuals be so wrong? How could they exaggerate the liberalism, and underestimate the social conservatism, of American society so absurdly? Demagogy plays a role, but many of the elite conservatives I know appear to be sincerely confused. They think that their fellow Americans are much wilder than they really are.

There are two answers, I think. The first, and most important, is that many of the intellectuals of the right have spent much of their lives either on elite college campuses or in big cities. Academics and journalists living in Cambridge, Massachusetts or Manhattan tend to grossly overestimate the strength of radicalism in the country. (Conservatives seldom note that this illusion tends to hurt the left, whose intellectuals are recurrently stunned by the lack of popular support for their positions in the continent outside of their coastal, metropolitan bohemias.)

Another reason for the often hysterical exaggeration of the influence of cultural radicalism in the United States has to do with the relaxation of censorship in books, movies, television, and music since the 1960s. The most thorough studies of American sexual behavior reveal a population in which the overwhelming majority have few partners in their lifetimes and quite conservative tastes. There is far more sex in mass entertainment, it appears, than there is among the masses themselves.

The moralistic conservatives think this is a problem. Perhaps it is. But it is a problem to which leading conservatives themselves have contributed. In his successful spy novels, William F. Buckley, Jr. has his hero, Blackford Oakes, fornicating repeatedly outside of marriage. In the first novel of the series, *Saving the Queen,* the intrepid spy has sex with the Queen of England. In his first book, *God and Man at Yale* (1951), Buckley alerted the regents of Yale to a professor who had suggested at a conference of the American Social Hygiene association that taboos against premarital sex were "unrealistic." "As a professor," the young Buckley warned, "Mr. Murdock has wide influence, and it cannot be expected that his remarks and attitudes will have no influence on his students."[5] If the mere mention of premarital sex by Professor Murdock, away from campus, was enough to turn Yale undergrads into crazed sex fiends, imagine the effect of the smoldering pages in Buckley's spy novels in which his hero and his hero's girlfriend—both Yale students, both unmarried—do what Buckley wanted Professor Murdock to be fired for mentioning. Nor is Buckley's fiction alone in posing a potential threat to today's impressionable youth. Newt Gingrich has written a novel, *1945,* in which a "Nazi sex kitten" does various things to his protagonist that cannot be mentioned in a family book like this. Then there is Texas Senator and Republican presidential candidate Phil Gramm, who back in the 1970s sought to invest in a series of soft-core porn movies, with titles like *Beauty Queens.*[6]

Let us call the problem of sexual explicitness in literature and film the Buckley-Gingrich-Gramm problem. Let us assume that writers and investors like the editor of *National Review,* the Speaker of the House, and the co-author of the Gramm-Rudman Act, by writing or subsidizing soft porn, really are contributing to the delinquency of minors. What is to be done? Irving Kristol, in the past several years, has repeatedly called for government censorship of sexually explicit material, even "soft" pornography. As a practical matter, this would mean a great expansion of government bureaucracy, at the state and local level, if not at the federal level. Thousands, perhaps tens or hundreds of thousands, of civil servants would have to be employed to pore over books, magazines, and movies scanning carefully for naughty bits.

Most western democracies abandoned regimes of strict censorship in the past several generations, precisely because of the high cost compared to the dubious results. Before 1989, however, the communist governments of the Soviet Union and its Eastern European satellites maintained a regime in the cultural realm that should have made any American conservative proud. On point after point in their critique of the western media and western literature, indeed, the communist apparatchiks agreed with the would-be cultural commissars of the American right like Irving Kristol and William Bennett. They hated the same things, like modern art ("bourgeois formalism" to the Soviet-bloc left, the "avant-garde" to the American right). They preferred classical music and ballet (the older, the better) to jazz, rock and roll, and modern dance, which struck them as entirely too suggestive. In fashion, as in matters of sexual behavior, the Soviet left, like the American right, tended toward the puritanical. By calling for censorship of the sort that has only recently been dismantled in communist Europe, Kristol and his allies are simply completing the parallel between their views of culture and those of such prim defenders of public and private decency as Stalin and Fidel Castro.

The best answer to conservative advocates of heavy-handed censorship (as opposed to the limited censorship that even a liberal community will engage in) comes from the great eighteenth-century English conservative man of letters, Doctor Samuel Johnson, in a conversation with his biographer James Boswell about the poet Matthew Prior:

> I asked whether Prior's poems were to be printed entire; Johnson said they were. I mentioned Lord Hailes's censure of Prior, in his preface to a collection of "Sacred Poems," by various hands . . . where he mentions "those impure tales which will be the eternal opprobrium of their ingenious author." JOHNSON. "Sir, Lord Hailes has forgot. There is nothing in Prior that will excite to lewdness. If Lord Hailes thinks there is, he must be more combustible than other people."[7]

Even when I considered myself a conservative, I was skeptical about the nostalgic picture of a wholesome, virtuous small-town past. (I refer here only to the state of personal morals and mores within the white majority; the institutionalized immorality of slavery and segregation is an entirely different question.) Today we have the Hell's Angels; back then, they had Hell's Kitchen. The inner-city black and Hispanic gangs of today are better armed, but no more vicious, than the brutal Irish-American urban gangs of late nineteenth-century New York, like the Dead Rabbits and the Five Pointers. Al Capone owned much of the Chicago political class and police, during the very era that many contemporary conservatives look back on as a Golden Age. Somehow today's moralistic conservatives manage to overlook the fact that the Golden Age of political corruption in the United States was inaugurated by the single greatest effort at conservative moral reform by law in American history: Prohibition.

The conservative theory of morality, as I observed above, combines the myth of the Golden Age with the devil theory of history. The older southern Democratic right that taught today's Republicans how to wage culture-war politics was not afraid to name particular groups of devils: blacks, Catholics, Yankees, Jews, communists. Today's Republican right prefers to describe the enemies of God-fearing white Christian folk in vague terms: "the cultural elite," or "the media elite," or—the favorite demon in right-wing demonology—"the new class."

The idea of "the new class" has two sources—dissident communists in the early twentieth century, like the Pole Max Nomad and the American James Burnham, who explained Stalinism by saying that "a new class" of intellectuals and party operatives had taken over in post-capitalist Russia instead of proletarians, and the Austrian-American economist Joseph Schumpeter, a conservative who worried that the liberal business civilization of the West was breeding anti-capitalist intellectuals in its midst who would ultimately destroy capitalism. Neither the socialist nor the Schumpeterian versions of the new-class thesis appears convincing today. Stalin's dictatorship, far from representing the triumph of the intellectuals, rested on the traditional agencies of tyrannical regimes: the military and the secret police. Intellectuals in the Soviet Union who questioned the government line were systematically harassed, imprisoned, or executed. Schumpeter's prophecy that intellectuals would seize power in the West and impose socialism seems equally absurd today. Throughout the western world, socialist parties are in a state of disarray. What is more, there is no western democracy, apart from France, in which intellectuals have any significant influence or prestige in politics, compared to conventional party politicians. If the new class really exists and has planned to lead the industrial democracies into socialism, it has been remarkably ineffective.

None of this necessarily discredits the contemporary conservative version of the "new class" theory, in which the term, severed from its origins in the writings of Nomad, Burnham, and Schumpeter, has become simply a catchphrase that lumps together moderate conservatives, liberals, and socialists into a single category, and implies that they belong not simply to one of several opinion factions, but to a distinct social stratum or class. In his recent book *The Freedom Revolution,* House Majority Leader Dick Armey of Texas divides the country into virtuous "doers" and sinister "talkers." The latter constitute the new class—a group subdivided into six subspecies: "politicians, educators, journalists, lawyers, theologians, and entertainers." (Armey, an educator before he became a politician, must be the exception to the rule that people like him should be doubly distrusted.) The "doers" know what the "talkers" deny: "The market is rational and the government is dumb."[8]

What is the source of the irrational enthusiasm for tyrannical state power on the part of deluded new-class "talkers"? Jeane Kirkpatrick explains: "Rationalism, optimism, and activism have been and still are the source of liberal and radical political action. They also are characteristics of the politics of the new class."[9] They are also—it should be pointed out—characteristics of the Republican political class; remember Ronald Reagan's "Morning in America"? What is supply-side economics, if not the archetypal example of a utopian political-economic program as rationalistic as it is optimistic? What is Jack Kemp, if not the embodiment of an optimistic, utopian "talker"? Kirkpatrick herself, when she spoke at the 1984 Republican convention, did not see fit to promote virtues that were the opposite of new-class vices like "rationalism, optimism, and activism"—say, virtues like irrationalism, pessimism, and sloth.

Another equally dubious version of the new-class theory posits a quasi-Marxist class struggle between professionals (who are collectivist and therefore bad) and the business class (whose members are for free enterprise and therefore good). According to Irving Kristol, "The simple truth is that the professional classes are engaged in a class struggle with the business community for status and power." Are dentists and lawyers really engaged in a power struggle with corporate vice presidents? According to the most thorough study of the American professional class, Kristol's "simple truth" is simply false. A study of attitudes among American professionals conducted by Steven Brint, a sociologist at the University of California at Riverside, has demonstrated that professionals do not have the left-wing, anti-business attitudes imputed to them by conservatives. True, highly educated professionals tend to be secular and relatively liberal on subjects like civil liberties, sexual rights, and tolerance of political dissent. On economic matters like labor and welfare rights, however, Brint discovered that affluent professionals tend to be far more conservative than average Americans—and far to the right on the issues of crime and the military. Brint concludes, "Even the most liberal segment of professionals—the people who would be counted as members of the 'new class' in any version of the theory—were, by and large, far from unconventional in their tastes or decidedly left-of-center in their political views, and they certainly show little opposition to the basic organizing principles of a business civilization."[10] Brint's findings should come as no surprise. For decades, even as neoconservatives were fantasizing about a leftist crusade by members of the new class, Americans with advanced educations and high incomes have been far more likely than average Americans to vote Republican.

The "new class," then, is a figment of the neoconservative imagination. Professionals and business executives alike tend to belong to a single class, the dominant elite in the contemporary United States—the managerial-professional overclass, which tends to be liberal on social issues and conservative in its economic views. If neoconservatives sought to be genuine populists, they would attack the overclass, in the name of the socially conservative and economically liberal working-class majority in the United States. But such genuine populism would mean attacking the overclass media, including the *Wall Street Journal,* and overclass institutions, like the conservative foundations that funnel money to writers supporting lower regulation on business and lower taxes on the rich.

If the idea of the new class confuses the adversary culture with the professions, the neoconservative notion of "the bourgeoisie" hopelessly confuses *patriciates* and *business classes.* This mistake is easier to make in English and French, where "bourgeois" since the nineteenth century has come to mean "mercantile," than in German, where *bürgerlich* retains the older political and social connotations of the burgher, the citizen. For an equivalent in English, one must imagine that the term "burgesses" had survived—and described eminent citizens from old families, not just the rich or corporate executives.

The bourgeoisies of early modern Europe were not mere business classes; they were urban patriciates, groups that were political and social elites as much as they were economic elites. The term "genteel," in its origins, has nothing whatsoever to do with capitalism; its root is *gens,* or family; it refers to aristocratic or patrician lineage, not to money. The great bourgeois dynasties, like Thomas Mann's family in Lübeck, Germany, were more like aristocratic families than like the lower-middle-class shopkeepers idealized by Thatcherites in Britain and neoconservatives in the United States. The ethos of the great bourgeois families stressed public service in city-state or national politics; the idea of a strict separation between government and business, to say nothing of the idea that government is inherently wicked and corrupt and the market good and constructive, would have struck members of the old European bourgeoisie as absurd. Though this kind of bourgeoisie made its living, at least in part, from commerce, modern industrial capitalism, by shifting the locus of economic power away from merchant-princes to national and multinational corporations with salaried managers, destroyed the social conditions that made an old-fashioned bourgeois elite possible. The real enemies of the old-time bourgeoisie are the sponsors of the conservative movement on Wall Street.

It is questionable whether many of the virtues that the neoconservatives ascribe to the bourgeoisie are "bourgeois" virtues at all. Many so-called bourgeois virtues (as the late Christopher Lasch, a populist of the left, pointed out) are characteristic more of lower-middle-class and working-class and rural folk than of the metropolitan rich and the corporate elite. The "Confucian" work ethic of many Asian-American immigrants, in its Chinese origins, has nothing to do with a bourgeois or commercial society at all. Although many first-generation immigrants from Asia, like European immigrants before them, are compelled to take minor jobs in the private-sector economy, the Confucian value system of East Asia is the product of a society in which government office, based on academic merit, was the highest goal of the ambitious. Confucian values are not the virtues of the bourgeois, but of the mandarin, of the state bureaucrat. In this, they resemble the work ethic that Anglo-Americans noted among immigrants from German-speaking Central Europe in the nineteenth and twentieth centuries. The old-fashioned "Prussian" or "German" virtues of discipline, obedience, and erudition were those of a thoroughly statist and collectivist cultural region, in which the middle class, the *Mittelstand,* literally, the class in the middle, tended to consist not of shopkeepers but of minor government functionaries. Since the virtues prized by statist, communitarian societies tend to produce individuals who function well in modern, bureaucratized, industrial capitalist enterprises, the fact that the two leading capitalist countries in the world, apart from the United States, are the former authoritarian states of Japan and Germany should come as no surprise. However, it casts doubt on the American conservative dogma that "statism" and "capitalism" are somehow incompatible. In reality, modern government and modern industrial capitalism are both highly bureaucratic—and the modern societies that flourish tend to be secular Confucian and Teutonic nations in which the "bureaucratic virtues," rather than the "bourgeois virtues" or laissez-faire "individualism" shape communal norms.

The neoconservatives, then, are as mistaken about the bourgeoisie as they are about the new class. The only postwar American conservative who got matters right was James Burnham, the former Trotskyist intellectual who became an editor of *National Review.* In his 1940 book *The Managerial Revolution,* Burnham argued that the old bourgeois-capitalist order was giving way to a new system of managerial capitalism. Nostalgia for the old days of small-scale proprietary capitalism was useless; the task confronting western civilization was to find institutional means to preserve individual liberty and national independence in a world of military and trade blocs and bureaucratic elites (in both the public and private sectors). Had later conservatives built upon Burnham's insights, the conservative intellectual movement would not have wasted half a century on preposterous conspiracy theories about leftist journalists and pinko professors. But then, the conservative intellectual movement would not have been useful in promoting the narrow interests of members of the rapacious private-sector managerial overclass seeking to pass themselves off as members of a benevolent and virtuous "bourgeoisie."

Although it was never plausible and has been convincingly discredited, the neoconservative version of the new-class theory has become one of the cliches of the Republican right. The reason is that it gives the appearance of social-scientific validation to the apocalyptic conspiracy theories of the mostly southern and western Protestant fundamentalists upon whom conservatives now depend for votes. By talking about a new-class conspiracy of "amoral elites" trying to brainwash "our children," Ivy League intellectuals on the right like Kristol and Novak and Bennett and Kirkpatrick appear to be giving credibility to the deepest nightmares of deluded working-class white evangelical Protestants.

In 1994, conservative evangelical circles across the United States were swept by rumors that the Disney corporation was beaming subliminal sexual messages into the minds of young viewers of its popular animated films. *Communique,* a biweekly newsletter of an anti-abortion group called the American Life League, warned its readers of a scene in *The Lion King* in which clouds in the background supposedly spell out S-E-X. In its March 1994 issue, *Movie Guide,* a "Christian" movie review magazine in Atlanta, published an article entitled "Aladdin Exposed." According to *Movie Guide,* during a scene on a balcony between Aladdin and the Princess, Aladdin murmurs "All good teenagers, take off your clothes." (In reality, the line is "Scat, good tiger, take off and go.") A third rumor claimed that a minister in *The Little Mermaid* had been portrayed in a state of sexual arousal.

Movie Guide eventually retracted its claim—but not until after hordes of alarmed evangelical Christians across the country (to say nothing of their titillated children) anxiously scanned the three Disney movies for the alleged pro-sex propaganda. "I felt I had entrusted my kids to pedophiles," one conservative evangelical Protestant homemaker in upstate New York told the *Wall Street Journal.* "It's like a toddler introduction to porn." She dumped the Disney videos in the trash.[11]

The rumors on the Christian right about pedophilia in the Magic Kingdom constitute what social scientists call "moral panics." Moral panics—witch-hunts, rumors of Jews poisoning wells, claims that day-care center operators are inducting children into satanic rites—are destructive enough to society when they are spontaneous. The calculated manipulation of popular fears of secretive, all-powerful elites like "the new class" or "the liberal media elite" or "the cultural elite" by cynical conservative politicians and propagandists can only be described by one of those moral terms that conservatives want to reintroduce into public discourse: evil.

The myth of the new class is not the only weapon in the right's culture-war arsenal. One of the methods by which conservatives promote their goal of stimulating an artificial "moral panic" among Americans is the systematic distortion of language. Consider, for example, the term "the Judeo-Christian tradition." This term was invented in the nineteenth century by anti-Semites, who sought to discredit Christianity by stressing its Jewish origins. After World War II, ecumenical liberals gave the term a new meaning. Since the 1970s, conservatives have claimed, with ever-increasing shrillness, that their package of pro-business measures and Protestant sectarian legislation is the natural outgrowth of the Judeo-Christian tradition.

A few decades ago it was liberals like Reinhold Niebuhr and Will Herberg who pointed to Social Security and the National Labor Relations Board as examples of the manifestation of the "Judeo-Christian tradition" in politics. Today's conservatives claim that the same "Judeo-Christian tradition" requires capital gains tax cuts and the elimination of a federal guarantee of welfare for the destitute.

As these examples suggest, the "Judeo-Christian tradition" can be used to justify any public policy by any group: liberals, conservatives, environmentalists, survivalists, supporters of legal abortion and its opponents. Christian Coalition leader Pat Robertson, reasoning from the "Year of Jubilee" in the Old Testament, has even suggested that the Judeo-Christian tradition may require the redistribution of property every fifty years. The debates are unlikely to be resolved, as the Christian and Jewish Scriptures for the most part are silent on the subject of the details of public policy in a modern industrial democracy.[12]

Only in the United States, among the English-speaking democracies, is conservative rhetoric soaked by pharisaical public religiosity. In Britain, the homeland of the Anglo-American conservative tradition, one rarely encounters the kind of cant about "the Judeo-Christian tradition" that competes with calls for a capital gains tax cut for first place in frequency of repetition in American right-wing rhetoric. "It is wholly anachronistic," the British conservative philosopher John Gray has written, "to expect that Christianity . . . will ever have the political significance in England that it possessed throughout the seventeenth, eighteenth and nineteenth centuries."[13] "Eschewing an agenda of political morality," one student of British conservative thought has written, "British conservatives maintain that society will dissolve if the central state is not endowed with the authority to maintain public interaction and coordinated activity. . . . From this perspective, the Church and Christianity in general are ignored by British conservatives, as they can neither enhance nor inhibit the state's authority."[14] I vividly recall a speech former British Prime Minister Margaret Thatcher gave to an audience of worshipful cadets at the Virginia Military Academy a few years back. One awe-struck cadet asked Mrs. Thatcher, "How did you manage to keep going, through all of the difficulties and criticism you encountered?" Any American conservative politician would have answered, "My loving spouse, my darling children, and the Good Lord above." The Iron Lady replied, with supreme and unsentimental egoism, "I kept going because I knew *I was right and they were wrong.*" If there is an Almighty, I suspect that He prefers English conservatives like Mrs. Thatcher, who are less likely than their American cousins to invoke His name in vain.

Not that the American right, in its upper echelons, is all that much more religious than the British right. Though a few elite conservatives are genuinely religious, for many others, religion appears to be less valuable for its supernatural aspects than for its contribution to a social climate in which Wall Street and the *Fortune* 500 can flourish. In the words of Irving Kristol, "It is not too much to say that the Judeo-Christian tradition, in its Protestantized form, is the Old Testament for liberal capitalism."[15] Another Jewish conservative, the scholar Jacob Neusner, has been less willing to endorse the instrumental use of religion. According to Neusner, "[t]heologically and historically, there is no such thing as the Judeo-Christian tradition. It's a secular myth favored by people who are not really believers themselves."[16] Neusner is one of the few conservative intellectuals to point out that the religious right's efforts to reintroduce prayer into public schools violate basic tenets of genuine religion. "State-sponsored, nonsectarian prayer," Neusner writes, violates "theological norms":

> When it comes to prayer, pretending that we all can and should address God in one and the same way teaches two bad lessons. First, it denigrates important particularities: our way to God, known in a particular church or synagogue or mosque, now gives way to another path to God, in which we must walk. Second, it fabricates a common faith where there is none, and so places our common Americanness into conflict with our significant points of difference.[17]

The conservative war on plain language does not end with the attempt to blur the distinction between short-term Republican policies and the eternal truths, however defined, of the "Judeo-Christian tradition." Conservatives also seek to stack political debate in their favor by means of tendentious phrases like "Christian conservatives," "pro-family voters," and "people of faith." The purpose of the term "Christian conservative" is to pass off the narrow, and often bizarre, political-moral agenda of the tiny minority of Americans who are far-right Protestant evangelicals as the agenda of the substantial number of Americans who are both Christian (in one or another tradition) and conservative (usually in a rather vague and moderate way). The phrase "Christian conservative" inflates a moral minority into an electoral plurality, even a majority. Consider the difference between these two sentences: "Christian conservatives seek to make their voices heard on Capitol Hill" and "Southern Baptists, Pentecostalists, and other Protestant sectarians seek to make their voices heard on Capitol Hill." The former lulls, the latter alarms, center-right Methodists, Episcopalians, Lutherans, and Catholics.

Christian Coalition executive director Ralph Reed has introduced a new cant phrase into American public discourse: "people of faith." The same conservatives who have spent the past decade making fun of the politically correct phrase "people of color" now solemnly intone about the mistreatment of "people of faith." The cant of victimology is borrowed from the left, almost unchanged, by Protestant fundamentalists and their conservative allies. Another phrase, "pro-family voters," is an even greater masterpiece of rhetorical sleight-of-hand and psychological manipulation. The phrase collapses the distinction between ordinary voters who prefer intact families to broken homes—and who doesn't?—

and weird sectarians who follow television evangelists and want to outlaw abortion and persecute homosexuals. In addition to passing off the views of the radical minority as those of the moderate majority, the phrase "pro-family voters" implicitly creates an enemy: anti-family voters. The syllogism follows: Republican conservatives are pro-family, therefore Democratic liberals must be anti-family! Few conservative propagandists, of course, are so crude as to explicitly call those who disagree with them "anti-family." But their audiences can be expected to connect the dots.

The cynicism of the culture-war strategy can be illustrated by the case of House Majority Leader Newt Gingrich. In one of the videotapes circulated by the foundation that Newt Gingrich formerly headed, GOPAC, the Speaker of the House gives a lesson in Orwellian Newspeak that would have made Big Brother proud. "Notice the power of the word 'gay' versus the word 'homosexual,' and notice how it changes the whole dynamic of the discussion." At Gingrich's direction, GOPAC passed out a list of phrases that would help Republican candidates "speak like Newt." The aspirants to public office were advised to smear Democrats by linking them with phrases like "sick," "traitors," "corrupt," "bizarre," "cheat," "steal," "devour," "self-serving," and "criminal rights."[18]

Not too long ago, Gingrich gave the most perfect performance in this mode to date. After Susan Smith drowned her two children, Gingrich announced that this illustrated the moral decline caused by liberalism and the Democratic party. It turned out, however, that this disturbed woman had been molested in her youth by a male relative who later became one of the local leaders of Pat Robertson's Christian Coalition.[19]

The purpose of the culture war, as I have argued, is to divert the wrath of wage-earning populist voters from Wall Street and corporate America to other targets: the universities, the media, racial minorities, homosexuals, immigrants. Patrick Buchanan was one of the architects of this strategy as an advisor to Richard Nixon, Ronald Reagan, and George Bush. In his 1996 campaign for the Republican presidential nomination, however, Buchanan united culture-war politics with the class-war politics of a populist demagogue in the tradition of William Jennings Bryan, Huey Long, and Father Charles Coughlin. The outrage of the conservative establishment at Buchanan's new, consistent populism—at once anti-intellectual and anti-business—is understandable. In place of the conventional Republican strategy—culture war instead of class war—Buchanan offered a new synthesis of culture war and class war, a synthesis powerful enough to make him the winner of the first 1996 Republican primary, in New Hampshire.

It seems doubtful that Buchanan's genuine cultural and economic populism will replace the purely cultural populism of the New York–Washington conservative establishment. It is worth noting, however, that confronted with genuine populism, in the form of the Buchanan insurgency, many of the same conservatives who recently have been ridiculing "elites" in the name of "the people" suddenly discovered the conservative virtues of hierarchy and elitism. The reaction of Rush Limbaugh to Buchanan's attacks on corporate America showed that at least some prominent conservatives were having second thoughts about the identification of conservatism and a fraudulent version of populism: "Pat Buchanan is not a conservative," Limbaugh declared. "He's a populist." After years of attacking the establishment in the name of the culture war, conservatives like Limbaugh found themselves defending the monied establishment against one of their own. The culture war of the right, devised to divert attention from the class war of the overclass against the middle class, now shows signs of giving way to a class war on the right, between middle-class conservatives and the Wall Street–Washington conservative elite. The progression from culture war against the center to civil war within the right is enough to make one believe in poetic justice.[20]

Chapter 7

Three Conservative Hoaxes

How the Right Has Fooled the American People
About Taxes, Education, and Illegitimacy

Since the 1960s, conservative politicians, journalists, and intellectuals have succeeded in shifting the national consensus to the right on many issues. Chief among these are the disputed subjects of taxation, education, and welfare. On these three matters, conservatives have managed to convince many centrists and neoliberals to agree, if not with the details, then with the general drift of their arguments. Thanks to the success of conservatives in altering the terms of political debate in the United States, many Americans now take it for granted that excessive taxation has burdened the American economy; that America's system of public education is among the worst in the world; and that excessively generous welfare is a contributing factor to, if not the primary cause of, a dramatic increase in illegitimacy among poor blacks in the inner cities.

All three of these conservative dogmas have become part of the conventional wisdom. More important, they provide the legitimacy for the major domestic policy initiatives of the present-day American right. The claim that low productivity growth in the United States is the result of the discouraging effect that high taxes produce on investors and corporations is the theory that justifies the tax-cut program of Newt Gingrich's congressional Republicans, as it justified the upper-bracket tax cuts of the Reagan era. The claim that America's public schools are in critical condition appears to support the radical cure proposed by the right: "school choice" or public financing of private schools, including private religious schools. Finally, the assertion that the federal government has inadvertently encouraged illegitimacy by means of welfare is the primary argument invoked by the coalition of economic and social conservatives that has sought to dismantle the federal commitment to welfare dating back to FDR's New Deal.

Conservative arguments about supply-side economics, the failure of public education, and the epidemic of illegitimacy are familiar, widely believed, and respected even by adversaries of conservatism. There is only one problem: they are demonstrably wrong. The facts, when objectively examined, do not support conservative views about taxation, public education, and illegitimacy. On these three subjects, the right is not merely wrong, but dead wrong. This has ramifications outside of the world of scholarship, inasmuch as misguided policies based on fallacies promulgated by the conservative movement—beginning with supply-side economics—have already done enormous damage to the prosperity and social fabric of the United States.

It would be tragedy enough if conservatives had been innocently mistaken in promoting fallacies about taxation, education, and welfare. The tale of conservative thought about these issues is not a tragedy, though; it is a scandal. Repeatedly, since the late 1970s, conservative politicians, public policy experts, and journalists have ignored, dismissed, or (as in the case of the Sandia report about American public education, discussed below) attempted to suppress evidence that contradicts conservative dogma about social policy. What is more, the same small group of conservative Republican intellectual impresarios including Robert Bartley, editorial page editor of the *Wall Street Journal,* and Irving Kristol, editor of the *Public Interest,* has played a key role in popularizing ill-founded misconceptions in the areas of public finance, public education, and welfare. Their sacrifice of objectivity to political expediency has gone far beyond the normal tendency of partisans of all persuasions to stack evidence in favor of policies they prefer.

It is an irony of the first order that the neoconservative network centered on the *Public Interest* should have played such a large role in popularizing the dubious theories on which conservative policy reforms like deficit-expanding tax cuts, school voucher proposals, and the proposed abolition of welfare are based. After all, it was in the pages of the *Public Interest,* in the 1960s and 1970s, that neoconservative intellectuals like Daniel Patrick Moynihan articulated what remains a compelling critique of the tendency of left-liberals to base radical and ill-considered

policy reforms on poorly understood or ambiguous social-science data
(an example would be the way that school busing for racial "balance"
was justified by questionable studies that purported to show that black
students were psychologically harmed by learning in mostly black envi-
ronments). Although the initial neoconservative critique was formulated in response to the abuse of social science by the left, the greatest
examples of the unholy union of dubious data and radicalism in policy
since the 1970s have been found on the right.

In this chapter, I will demonstrate the making of not one but three
political hoaxes—supply-side economics, the education crisis, and the
alleged illegitimacy epidemic. I will show how the well-funded conservative propaganda machine disseminated these fallacies until they became part of a new political consensus, and I will describe the special
interests that benefit from the acceptance of these falsehoods as fact by
the political class and the public in general. The story of the promulga-
tion of any one of these public-policy myths would reflect poorly upon
the intellectual and ethical integrity of the leaders of American conservatism; taken together, the three great conservative hoaxes constitute
one of the most shameful episodes in the history of the intersection of
scholarship and politics in the United States.

The earliest and by far the most damaging of the three great conservative hoaxes of late-twentieth-century America has been supply-
side economics. Supply-side economics was based on the "Laffer
curve," named after economist Arthur Laffer, who claimed that tax rates
in the United States in the 1970s were so high that they were discouraging investors and businesses from engaging in productive investment.
The vast majority of economists, liberals and conservatives alike, dismissed Laffer's theory as nonsense. Rejected by the economics profes-
sion, supply-side economics was picked up by a small group of
conservative journalists, of whom the chief were Jude Wanniski, a pop-
ularizer of economic ideas, Robert Bartley, Jr., the editor of the *Wall
Street Journal*'s influential editorial page, and Irving Kristol, editor of the
flagship journal of neoconservative public policy science, the *Public Interest*. Kristol introduced Wanniski to Congressman Jack Kemp, who
became the most ardent promoter of supply-side economics in Congress. Wanniski and Kemp, in turn, helped to convert presidential
candidate Ronald Reagan. Although George Bush, reflecting old-
fashioned Republican fiscal conservatism, mocked supply-side eco-

nomics during the 1980 race for the Republican nomination as "voodoo economics," the supply-side mantra became the central dogma of "Reaganomics."

The victory of supply-side economics over fiscal conservatism owed nothing to its intellectual credibility and everything to its political utility. The fiscal-conservative approach to reducing the $79 billion deficit that Ronald Reagan inherited from Jimmy Carter was as painful as it was sound—cut spending and raise taxes. Reagan and his political advisors, however, did not want to incur the wrath of the voters by cutting spending on the popular middle-class entitlements like Social Security and Medicare that accounted for a substantial proportion of the deficit (as for defense, Reagan proposed the most massive peacetime military buildup in U.S. history, to counter a genuine but grossly exaggerated Soviet threat). The other option, raising taxes on the major constituents of the Republican party, the rich and the corporations, was out of the question for the Reagan administration. Arthur Laffer's theory provided a way out of this political dilemma. According to supply-siders, massive tax cuts would produce a correspondingly massive economic boom. Higher economic growth, stimulated by lower rates, would result in higher revenues for the federal government than it had been collecting at higher rates. Thanks to the miracle promised by supply-side economics—a miracle for which the only precedent seems to have been Jesus Christ's reported multiplication of fish and loaves—the federal government could slash taxes, finance growing entitlements, pay for a huge military buildup—and balance the budget within a few years. Reagan promised a balanced budget at the end of his second year in office, and a $100 billion surplus in his third.

Once in office, Reagan pushed through a 25 percent tax spread over a three-year period. The result is the central fact of American politics today—the deficit, which peaked in 1992 at $290 billion (by 1995, thanks to deficit-cutting measures passed in 1990 and 1993, the deficit shrank to $164 billion).[1] Most of the deficit, it is important to note, was run up under Reagan and Bush. Here are the numbers: under Ford and Carter $450 billion was added to the federal debt. By contrast, the federal government under Reagan and Bush added an additional $3.5 *trillion*.[2] During Reagan's two terms, the deficit hovered at $200 billion, almost three times as much as it had been in the Carter years. Between 1950 and 1980, the federal deficit had grown at a rate of only $50 billion a year; in the first six years of the Reagan administration, thanks in large part to the successful promotion of Arthur Laffer's theories by Irving Kristol, Robert Bartley, and Jude Wanniski, the deficit grew at an annual rate of $161 billion. (Clinton and the Democratic Congress of 1992–94, it should be noted, cut the deficit in half—by slowing spending *and* by raising taxes on the richest Americans.)

No matter what supply-siders may claim today, the U.S. deficit would have been far smaller (though no doubt still significant) if the 1980 presidential race had been won by Jimmy Carter, or by George Bush or any of the more conventional Republican candidates who lost the nomination to Reagan, the standard-bearer of the right. The blame for today's crippling deficit rests with Ronald Reagan, Jack Kemp, and the circle around the *Wall Street Journal* and the *Public Interest*. In his memoir, *The Triumph of Politics,* former Reagan budget director David Stockman has described the efforts of conservative leaders to persuade the Reagan administration to ignore doubts about the supply-side project. "On the conservative side," Peter G. Peterson, the former commerce secretary, has observed, "writers like Irving Kristol were adamant in their message to Republicans" to ignore or downplay the deficit in the interest of making the Republican party popular.[3]

In the aftermath of the supply-side deficit disaster, some Reaganites have sought to defend their folly. Perhaps supply-side economics did not produce the wonders that were promised, they reason, but Reagan's capital gains tax cuts did have *some* effect in promoting prosperity. A pleasant thought—but one that the historical record does not support. The conservatives and their allies have been slashing capital gains taxes for years, and the promised effects have never materialized.

In 1978, after the maximum capital gains tax rate was cut from 39 percent to 28 percent, the GDP dropped by 1 percent in the next year and a half. In the two years following the tax cut, the annual growth rate of the economy was a miserable 0.3 percent—a huge drop from the 5.8 percent growth rate that preceded the downward revision of capital gains taxes. Unemployment also rose after the capital gains tax cut.

Perhaps this simply reflects the business cycle, or the effect of other factors like high interest rates. Perhaps the same excuse can be made for the failure of the second major capital gains tax cut, in 1981, which cut the maximum rate to 20 percent, to stimulate the economy. (Once again, though, the growth rate of the economy after the tax cut was lower than it was before—falling from 3.5 percent in the twelve months preceding the change to 2.8 percent in the two years that followed.)

Perhaps all of this can be explained away. Still, the conservative support-ers of capital gains tax cuts have a lot of explaining to do. They must ex-plain not only why massive cuts in capital gains taxes failed to stimulate the economy, but also why economic growth increased following in-creases in the capital gains tax in the 1976 Tax Reform Act (from 3.9 percent in the prior twelve months to 5.2 percent in the next two years) and in the 1986 Tax Reform Act (from 2.2 percent in the preceding year to a two-year average of 3.8 percent following the tax hike).[4]

Nor did the tax cuts of the 1980s produce higher productivity growth; the U.S. economy grew at 2.3 percent per year from 1979 to 90, compared to 2.4 percent between 1973 and 1979, and 2.8 percent from 1968 to 73. In other words, the U.S. economy grew more impres-sively before the Reagan-era tax cuts than after them. So much for Pro-fessor Laffer and his curve.

After supply-side economics, the second great public-policy hoax to be concocted by conservative strategists and experts and dissemi-nated by the conservative press has been the alleged crisis of American public education. Thanks to a decade and a half of well-coordinated conservative propaganda, many Americans have been persuaded that America's public schools are miserable failures and that American stu-dents are among the worst in the industrialized world. Those who be-lieve these assertions, it turns out, have been misled.

In their 1995 book *The Manufactured Crisis: Myths, Fraud, and the At-tack on America's Public Schools,* two leading educational researchers, David C. Berliner and Bruce J. Biddle, document how the American right has manipulated, and in some cases tried to suppress, data in order to create a misleading image of public-school failure. The story begins in 1983, when the Reagan White House released a highly publicized report entitled *A Nation at Risk* that claimed that America's public schools were disastrous failures compared to those of countries like Japan. Although the report claimed to be based on empirical research, Berliner and Biddle note that "none of the supposedly supportive 'evi-dence' actually appeared in *A Nation at Risk,* nor did this work provide citations to tell Americans where that 'evidence' might be found."[5] Since the appearance of *A Nation at Risk,* conservative authorities on education like William Bennett, Chester Finn, and Lynne Cheney have accused American public schools of everything from failing to teach basic skills to promoting left-wing social values and demeaning patriotism and morality. Not coincidentally, this grim portrait of an American public educational system in crisis has provided the most important rationale for the adoption of "school choice"—the Republican proposal to funnel taxpayer dollars to private church academies, prep schools, and other private schools.

The constant repetition of conservative claims about the inadequacy of American public schools leads many to assume that there must be something to their critique. Close examination of the evidence, however, reveals patterns very different from the ones that the conservative opponents of public education claim to perceive. Here are just a few examples of the conservative truisms that turn out, on closer inspection, to be untrue.

The right's critique of public schools has gained credibility from the claim that American public education is grossly inferior to that of other industrial democracies. This is a fallacy, based on a failure to interpret data correctly. For example, in aggregate comparisons of the mathematical abilities of American and Japanese students, Japanese students do better. However, this reflects differences in curricula between the United States and Japan. When American and Japanese students who have taken comparable courses are compared, American students sometimes do better than Japanese.[6] The same pattern emerges in other cross-national comparisons. One would think it would be commonsensical to note that students at elite German *Gymnasiums* should be compared to students at American prep schools, or to students in advanced classes in public high schools, not to a statistically concocted "average" American high school student—and yet this is neglected by the conservatives who invoke misleading aggregate data as evidence for an educational "crisis" they are determined in advance to find.

Conservatives have also claimed that falling SAT scores prove that American public education is failing. Between 1963 and 1975, aggregate SAT scores declined slightly, before leveling out. As Berliner and Biddle point out, this decline reflects the fact that more students from unimpressive educational backgrounds have chosen to take the SAT, a pre-college test. Far from being proof that American public education is failing, the slight decline in SAT scores merely proves that more students who would not have gone to college in the past are now planning to attend college.

What is more, according to Berliner and Biddle, once SAT data are disaggregated, the following pattern emerges: "(1) scores for verbal achievement have been holding steady; (2) scores for mathematics achievement have shown modest increases; (3) white students have been holding their own; (4) students from minority homes are now earning higher average scores." Berliner and Biddle conclude: "How on earth can America's teachers and schools be failing the nation when SAT scores for white students have recently been stable, the average SAT score for Native Americans has increased thirty-nine points, and average scores for blacks has [*sic*] gone up a whopping fifty-five points? Citizens should rejoice at this marvellous news."[7]

Data from tests other than the SAT also refute the conservative myth of a catastrophic decline in American education. All-time highs have been reached recently for scores on seven of nine areas in math, science, and reading evaluated by the National Assessment of Educational Progress. The increase in the number of students taking difficult Advanced Placement Tests, from 98,000 in 1978 to 448,000 in 1994, has greatly outstripped the increase in the student population.[8] Indeed, American children are smarter on average than their parents and grandparents. The average IQ score for white Americans (for whom the data is most easily available) has risen by 0.3 points per year. Berliner and Biddle point out that "the number of students expected to have IQs of 130 or higher—a typical cut-off point for defining giftedness in many school districts throughout the nation—is now about seven times greater than it was for the generation now retiring from leadership positions in the country and often complaining about the poor performance of today's youth."[9]

Contrary to popular belief and conservative propaganda, the American public school system does not waste vast amounts of money on idle educational bureaucrats. In fact, bureaucrats in central public educational offices account for only 1.6 percent of the staff of the public school system, and principals and other supervisors in schools themselves for another 2.9 percent, so that the bureaucrats make up only 4.5 percent of the total staff of public schools. What is more, most of the increased funding that has gone to public education in recent years has gone, not to lazy bureaucrats, but to the mentally retarded and emotionally disturbed students who are the subjects of special ed programs and the teachers who serve them. A recent study by Richard Rothstein and Karen Hawley Miles of the Economic Policy Institute showed that on average special education and other special programs like bilingual and vocational classes received 60 percent of all new school funding. New York City spends $23,600 per special-education student, compared to a mere $5,200 per student in conventional education.[10] A case might be made against spending so much money on the disabled, but it is not one that conservatives have sought to make. No doubt actual legions of handicapped children with expensive needs make less promising targets of conservative rhetoric than mythical legions of overpaid, underworked bureaucrats.[11]

In their eagerness to vilify the public schools, conservatives themselves have sometimes fallen for hoaxes. In 1994, the press in the United States was suddenly full of references to two lists of behavior banned in public schools, one from the 1940s and the other from the 1980s. In the 1940s, it was said, "the [top] problems were: (1) talking; (2) chewing gum; (3) making noise; (4) running in the halls; (5) getting out of turn in line; (6) wearing improper clothing; (7) not putting paper in wastebaskets." In the 1980s, however, the major problems were: "(1) drug abuse; (2) alcohol abuse; (3) pregnancy; (4) suicide; (5) rape; (6) robbery; (7) assault." Conservative pundits like William Bennett, George Will, and Rush Limbaugh triumphantly pointed to the contrast between the two lists as proof of the right's claim that society has dramatically deteriorated since the 1940s—and that the decline is liberalism's fault.

The two lists, it turns out, were a complete fraud. Journalist Barry O'Neill discovered that the lists originated with "T. Cullen Davis of Fort Worth, a born-again Christian who devised the lists as a fundamentalist attack on public schools." From Davis the bogus lists were disseminated among the true believers of the far right by activists like Phyllis Schlafly and Tim LeHay, from whom they passed into respectability via gullible conservative pundits like Will and Bennett.[12] It should come as no surprise that another often-repeated conservative horror story about education, about the failure of American students to recognize historical figures and facts that were familiar to students fifty years ago, is equally dubious. The report, it turns out, unfairly compared average present-day American high school students to elite college freshmen at Columbia University in 1943.[13] When educational researcher Dale Whittington compared the answers to similar questions on history tests administered today and in 1915, she discovered that today's students scored roughly the same as did their grandparents' generation.[14]

The facts about public education, then, do not bear out the conservative claim that the country faces a meltdown of educational standards unless it adopts radical reforms like school choice. Why, then, have conservatives gone to such lengths to try to discredit public education? As in the case of supply-side economics, politics has triumphed over scholarship.

Today it is often said that the initiative for school choice, as a major policy initiative of the right, originated in the late 1970s with religious schools protesting the Carter administration's effort to deny tax exemptions to racially segregated Southern religious schools. Race actually played a larger part in the Republican party's support for school choice than even this would suggest. Richard Nixon, not Ronald Reagan, was the first Republican president to make school choice part of his agenda. School choice was a key element in the southern strategy crafted by Richard Nixon to win the votes of the followers of George Wallace. Its primary appeal was not to religious-right voters but to former southern segregationists who did not want their children to attend racially integrated schools, and to northern white ethnics who sought an alternative to court-ordered busing for their children. Originating in the Republican scheme to exploit the white backlash against integration, the school-choice project of the right has since found favor with Protestant fundamentalists and Catholic parents of children in parochial schools (who seek to be reimbursed for the religious instruction of their children by taxpayers who do not share their beliefs). No doubt the idea also appeals to members of the Republican economic elite, who might use school vouchers toward the cost of educating their children at expensive private academies like Groton or St. Mark's. Though school choice has been a Republican scheme since Nixon, not until the Reagan administration, with *A Nation at Risk,* did conservatives find a way of packaging this special-interest program as something necessary not just to reward the constituents but to save American education, perhaps even American society, from catastrophic decline.

The accusation I am making deserves to be stated in its boldest form: *Conservative educational proposals are not a rational response to genuine problems of American public education. They are an after-the-fact rationalization for Republican school-choice policies adopted by the Nixon administration and its successors to win the votes of northern white "ethnics" and southern Protestant fundamentalists.* The historical record is quite clear. We do not see a catastrophic decline in the quality of most public schools, followed by an agonizing reconsideration of public education by conservative scholars who reluctantly conclude that no choice remains but the privatization of education. Instead, we see cynical Republican operatives seizing upon school choice as a wedge issue to split the Democratic coalition along racial and religious lines, an attempt followed—almost a decade later—by the discovery, by the Reagan and Bush administrations and a small number of foundation-subsidized conservative intellectuals, of a nationwide educational crisis so severe as to make the abolition of public education thinkable. Having announced, in the early 1970s, that school choice was the cure, conservatives began trying to find a malady grim enough to justify it.

That the conservative educational strategy is being driven less by concerns about quality education than by the need to lure far-right voters into the Republican camp is evident in the hostility of the right to federal funding and national standards. If the conservatives who bemoan the supposed inferiority of American schools to Japanese and German schools were sincere, one would expect them to favor Japanese and German remedies—national funding of local schools, national standards imposed by an education ministry, little if any role for parents in the choice of curricula. In other words, if conservatives were sincere in their admiration of Japanese and German education, they should favor, not the privatization of education, but a system of public education far more centralized, bureaucratic, and uniform than the one that we have. Instead, they complain that our decentralized school system is worse than the centralized systems of Europe and East Asia—and call for further decentralization. The conservative remedy for the ills of fragmentation is more fragmentation. This is not what one would expect, from a dispassionate analysis of the problem. But it is exactly what one would expect if the entire exercise, from the very beginning, has been an attempt to justify government subsidies for Baptist and Pentecostalist church schools teaching children that the dinosaurs drowned in Noah's Flood.

Ironically, what began as a wedge issue for the right may be on the verge of becoming a wedge issue for liberals seeking to separate one part of the conservative coalition—fundamentalist Christians—from their business-class allies. The Republican business elite does not share the enthusiasm for decentralization and school choice of Republican politicians courting the fundamentalist right. At the National Education Summit of governors and CEOs held in April 1996, Alcoa executive Paul O'Neill wondered "why on earth we can't insist on universal standards at least for 9-year-olds. Can't a 9-year-old multiply 9 by 9 and get the same answer in all 50 states?" The host of the meeting, IBM chairman Louis Gerstner, explained, "This is a political issue, Paul—not a rational issue."[15] Sooner or later, the need of American business for highly educated workers trained in math and natural science is likely to collide with the desire of the fundamentalist minority to abolish the public schools in order to protect their children from secular humanism and Darwinism.

T he third of the great conservative hoaxes of our time is the idea of the illegitimacy epidemic. The conservative account of illegitimacy begins with a demonstrable fact: the number of births out of wedlock, as a percentage of all births, has risen dramatically in western democracies in recent decades. Within the black community, the increase in the proportion of births to single mothers has been particularly dramatic: from 23 percent in 1960 to 28 percent in 1969, to 45 percent in 1980, to 62 percent at the beginning of the 1990s.[16] To this indisputable statistic, conservative policy experts join another conclusion which is contested by left-liberals, but which moderate liberals and centrists have every reason to accept—namely, that children in female-headed households tend to be worse off in economic terms, and perhaps in psychological terms as well, than the children of intact families.

These two facts alone—the rising population of illegitimate births, and the difficulties associated with single parenthood—do not, in themselves, support the conservative social agenda. The conservative theory of illegitimacy links these facts with an explanation of illegitimacy (it is caused, or encouraged, by liberal welfare policies and/or a permissive media culture), and a proposed solution for the problem that follows from the explanation (the cure is to restrict or abolish welfare, to censor television and movies, or both). The contemporary conservative consensus on illegitimacy has emerged almost entirely from two great media coups.

The most important was a *Wall Street Journal* op-ed of October 29, 1993, entitled "The Coming White Underclass" by Charles Murray, in which the right's favorite social expert drew attention to the rising proportion of illegitimate births among whites as well as blacks.[17] For years, Murray had been arguing that welfare policies promoted illegitimacy, but none of his earlier work, not even his influential book *Losing Ground,* had the impact of his *Wall Street Journal* op-ed. "Every once in a while the sky really is falling, and this seems to be the case with the latest national figures on illegitimacy." Murray pointed out that in 1991 almost 30 percent of births in the United States were out of wedlock—a proportion "higher than the black illegitimacy rate in the early 1960s that motivated Daniel Patrick Moynihan to write his famous memorandum on the breakdown of the black family." Murray went on to observe that "the 1991 story for blacks is that illegitimacy has now reached 68% of births to black women. In inner cities, the figure is typically in excess of 80%." The reader was left with the impression that poor black women were having babies out of wedlock at a rate three or four times the rate [during] John Kennedy's presidency. Murray furthered this impression by writing of the "long, steep climb in black illegitimacy" and of the post-1960s era in which "illegitimacy became epidemic within [the black] minority."

The other event that crystallized the new conservative consensus about the illegitimacy epidemic was Vice President Dan Quayle's speech denouncing the CBS-TV series *Murphy Brown* for encouraging illegitimacy by portraying an upper-middle-class professional woman choosing to have a baby out of wedlock. When the *Atlantic Monthly* ran an article with the provocative title "Dan Quayle Was Right," many Americans who do not follow policy debates closely concluded that Dan Quayle must have been right about the illegitimacy question—after all, even the "liberal" *Atlantic Monthly* agreed.[18] The Murray op-ed and the Quayle speech gave conservative extremists the needed cover to attempt to do what they had wanted to do all along anyway—abolish welfare for the poor altogether, and, as an added benefit, restore a pre-1970s regime of censorship to television and cinema. Even more significant was the demoralizing effect the new conservative consensus had on centrists and liberals. Liberals, it was thought, could no longer deny that there was an illegitimacy explosion; they had to come up with their own solution for this escalating crisis. (I myself held this view, until I began to research the question.)

The liberals who reached this conclusion, it turns out, were conceding too much to the conservatives. *For there is no illegitimacy epidemic in the United States, of the sort that conservatives describe.*

Let us return, for a moment, to the growing percentage of illegitimate births among black Americans: 23 percent (1960), 28 percent (1969), 45 percent (1980), 62 percent (1990). What conservatives want you to believe is that these numbers reflect a tendency for unwed moth-

ers to have more children on average in response to rising welfare benefits and more permissive attitudes toward premarital and extramarital
sex. According to the common conservative interpretation of these
data, a poor black woman in 1990, in order to take advantage of greater
welfare benefits, and encouraged by today's permissive culture, might
have three children out of wedlock, whereas a comparable woman in
1950, when benefits were lower and the culture was stricter, would
have chosen to have only one. On the face of it, this is not an unreasonable explanation. Unfortunately for the conservative opponents of the
welfare state, it is an explanation that is based on a complete, indeed a
ludicrous, misreading of the relevant data.

The increase in the proportion of illegitimate births in the black
community is a result, not of a strikingly greater tendency in recent
decades on the part of poor blacks to have more children out of wedlock, but of the striking tendency of middle-class and affluent blacks to
have fewer children in wedlock. Poor black women have had illegitimate children at a rate during the age of post-1960s "liberalism" only
slightly above the rate that prevailed for poor black women during the
supposed Golden Age of pre-1960s social conservatism. According to a
1995 Census Bureau Report on Characteristics of the Black Population, "the rate of babies being born to unwed black teenagers—about
80 per 1,000 unmarried teenagers—remained virtually the same from
1920 through 1990."[19] The rise in the number of illegitimate births
from 23 percent in 1960 to 62 percent in 1990 reflects, not greater fertility by poor blacks, but a significant decline in the number of legitimate births among the non-poor black majority. Harvard scholar
Christopher Jencks has estimated that if married black women had
borne as many children in 1987 as they did in 1960, "the proportion of
black babies born out of wedlock would have risen only from 23 percent in 1960 to 29 percent by 1987."[20] It may be that any number of
out-of-wedlock births is a problem. Still, it is hard to imagine conservatives riding into power by promising to combat a "crisis" consisting of
the rise of illegitimacy among the black poor from 23 to 29 percent.

Jared Bernstein of the Economic Policy Institute has devised a useful
graph that makes the relationship between rising illegitimacy rates and
declining fertility among married couples clear (Figure 3). As the graph
indicates, the proportional rise of illegitimacy, far from reflecting a
breakdown of social norms across the entire society, is an ironic testi-
mony to the growth in affluence among most white and black families

FIGURE 3

Expected Lifetime Births by Marital Status and Race, 1960–1989

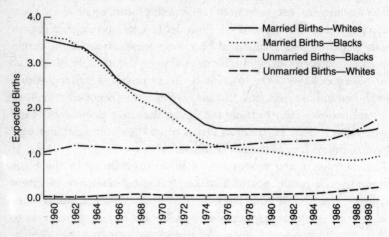

Source: Lawrence Mishel and Jared Bernstein, *The State of Working America, 1994–95* (Washington, D.C.: Economic Policy Institute, 1994). Used with permission of the Economic Policy Institute.

in the twentieth century—a growth in affluence that took place, for the most part, on the watch of liberal Democrats between the 1930s and the 1970s. Between 1890 and 1990, the reproductive behavior of the white and black poor had hardly changed at all. It is the behavior of the rest of the population that has changed, as a result of rising incomes. In the United States, as in other industrial democracies, middle-class and over-class families tend to have fewer children than their poor fellow citizens—or their parents and grandparents.

There is no illegitimacy epidemic. Poor black people are having babies out of wedlock at only slightly more than the rate they did in the early twentieth century, when there were no federal welfare programs, when the media were heavily censored, and when, in addition, black Americans were persecuted in a police-state regime of racial segregation. The rise in the proportion of illegitimate births among black Americans (and white Americans, too) is almost exclusively a result of the decision of the majority of intact American families who are not poor to have a higher living standard with fewer children rather than to have more children with fewer resources for each.

One can read most of the literature of conservatives on the family without ever finding an acknowledgment that the main influence on family formation is not the media or public policy but rather the economy. From 1800 until the present, according to anthropologist Marvin Harris, the birthrate in the United States steadily declined (the sole exception being the "baby boom" of 1945–57). Large families, in particular, have become relatively rare; in 1850, there were seven times as many families with four or more children as there are today. The steady decline in the birthrate, and the growth in the number of families without children, cannot be attributed to post-1960s liberalism. The decline went on during the very era, from the American Revolution through the 1950s, that modern conservatives look back on as the Golden Age of "traditional family values."[21]

What is more, the decline of the traditional family is a worldwide phenomenon. In many developed countries, divorce rates doubled between the 1970s and 1990s; even in developing countries, one-fourth of first marriages tend to end by the time women reach their fifth decade. The number of children born out of wedlock is rising around the world; as many as a third of the children in Northern Europe are born to unwed mothers. (Japan, where there are very few out-of-wedlock births, is the striking exception.) While the United States leads the industrialized world in the number of divorces—almost half of all marriages—the divorce rate has risen in most other industrial countries. The fact that family structure is changing in a similar way in quite different societies renders nonsensical the facile conservative explanation that people are being hypnotized into changing their mores by sex education in public schools or by watching reruns of *Murphy Brown*.[22]

If an excessively generous welfare state and a sinister liberal media elite in the United States are not responsible for family shrinkage and breakup, what is? The answer, it seems, is the political and social emancipation of women, and their entry into the work force in modern or modernizing economies. Douglas Besharov, a resident scholar at the American Enterprise Institute, is one of the few conservative intellectuals honest enough to acknowledge that economics, not "the cultural elite," is the driving force behind changes in family structure: "We are dealing here with the liberation of women. In the post-industrial age, when the earning power of men and women becomes quite equal, that creates a very different relationship between men and women and makes it easier for women to leave unhappy relationships."[23]

What, then, can be done to encourage the large, strong families of the nineteenth and eighteenth centuries? To start with, all the factories can be destroyed and the cities blown up. Most Americans can be herded back to farms. In a neo-agrarian society, large numbers of children who can help out with farm chores would once again be considered an indispensable investment by most women and men. If pro-family conservatives are too squeamish to contemplate such Khmer Rouge tactics, there are other, slightly less draconian options available. The liberalization of divorce laws in the United States and other countries might be reversed, to make it difficult if not impossible for people to obtain legal divorces, no matter how miserable their marriages. This legal reform might be accompanied by an informal policy of ostracism toward those who divorce. In particular, men who have divorced their first wives—such as Ronald Reagan, Bob Dole, Newt Gingrich, and Rush Limbaugh—might be shunned by the community as living, breathing symbols of immorality, while couples who have stayed together through rough times—say, Bill and Hillary Clinton—might be honored and praised.

If even this seems too harsh, then there is really little that can be done by government to strengthen the family. Tinkering with the tax code won't reverse the decline in family formation and family size; few individuals are so calculating as to marry in order to receive a few hundred or thousand dollars in tax benefits. What about censoring pornography? In Japan, pornography, particularly of a violent kind, is far more accessible than in the United States, and yet Japan has a much lower rate of out-of-wedlock births and divorces. In other words, there appears to be no relationship between pornography and family solidarity.

How about another proposal of the "pro-family" right—defending the right of government agencies, landlords, and employers to discriminate against homosexuals? One of the favorite themes of the religious right is that the legal recognition of homosexual couples will undermine the traditional heterosexual family. Exactly why legalizing gay marriages would have this effect is not clear. Are heterosexuals going to refuse to get married, out of childish spite, if homosexuals are allowed to? Is the denial of marriage to gay and lesbian citizens one of the things that makes marriage appealing to the straight majority? Somehow, one doubts it. Just for the sake of argument, let us suppose that the religious right succeeds, not only in continuing to prevent gay marriage, but in restoring the pre-1960s pattern of persecution of homosexuals in the United States. Let us suppose that gay and lesbian Americans are driven into hiding, on fear of being arrested and rounded up in concentration camps, as far-right conservatives now and then propose (the Nazis, it is worth recalling, tried to exterminate Europe's homosexuals as well as Europe's Jews and gypsies). Let us suppose that homosexual citizens are persecuted as viciously here as in Castro's Cuba and Communist China. In this anti-homosexual America, will the divorce rate go down one percentage point? Will any fewer children be born out of wedlock, once all the homosexuals are arrested or forced into hiding? It seems unlikely.

What about a revival of Christianity in the United States (mass conversions to Judaism, Islam, or Buddhism being unlikely)? Both the opponents and the allies of the religious right take it for granted that orthodox Christianity has been "pro-family" throughout the ages. No American conservative has been as honest about this matter as Ferdinand Mount, the English conservative who edits the *Times Literary Supplement*. This former ally of Margaret Thatcher, in his 1992 book *The Subversive Family,* drew attention to the rather embarrassing fact that the Christian Church, for much of its history, has been the enemy of the strong family (conservatives in Britain are permitted to say such things). As Mount points out, any idea of "the spiritual importance of marriage . . . is wholly absent from the Gospels." For St. Paul, "Existing marriages are to be maintained, but only as a concession to human weakness and as a social expedient." It is preferable to be celibate than to have sex, even within marriage. The Catholic Church institutionalized this bias against married people by limiting its hierarchy to celibate priests. Catholic thinkers, moreover, counsel people from lusting after their own spouses. According to John Paul II, if a man "looks in this way at a woman who is his own wife, he would commit adultery in his heart." "The wise man," wrote St. Jerome, "should love his wife with judgment, not passion." Mount notes that this cannot be blamed on misinterpretation of the Gospels, for Jesus himself says, "If any man come to me, and hate not his father, and mother, and wife, and children, and brethren, and sisters, yea, and his own life also, he cannot be my disciple." A prophet who tells his followers to abandon their families and follow him can hardly be described as "pro-family." The British conservative concludes, "The Sermon on the Mount is a wonderful, intoxicating sermon. But it is a sermon for bachelors."[24]

It is worth recalling that John Bunyan's *Pilgrim's Progress,* that classic of evangelical Protestantism, begins with Pilgrim running away from his wife and his children, with his fingers in his ears so that he will not hear them calling to him. Bunyan is merely restating the point that Christ made: if excessive attachment to one's family gets in the way of one's individual salvation, then one has a duty to repudiate one's family. With reason, then, pagan Greeks and Romans in the ancient world, and Confucian East Asians in recent centuries, have seen the emphasis on individual salvation in Christianity as a subversive threat to strong family ties and national loyalties.

Luther, a former monk who got married, bequeathed a higher opinion of marriage to Protestants than that of Catholic tradition. The multiplication of Protestant sects, however, has rendered any generalization about Protestant attitudes toward marriage and divorce impossible. Conservative Protestants in the modern United States at least pretend to be opposed to divorce (while voting for divorced conservative politicians). John Milton, the greatest evangelical Protestant poet of all time, and no mean theologian, argued eloquently for the Scriptural foundations of divorce—and polygamy, too. The Mormons, who tend to be solid supporters of the Republican right, have a substantial minority who believe that the federal government was wrong to outlaw Mormon polygamy. How can pro-family conservatives disagree? After all, if marriage is such a good thing, surely plural marriage is best of all.

Even a religious revival in the United States, then, would not necessarily restore premodern family structures. At any rate, different religious traditions themselves give different answers to questions about the family. Indeed, if religious sentiment in the United States grew in intensity, the "culture war" would probably consist of bitter interreligious conflict, as Catholics, Protestants, and Mormons argued over whose version of Christianity was the True Faith.

To be sure, it is not inconceivable that some government measures might actually promote intact families. Criminalizing divorce, or making it more difficult, might do wonders to promote family cohesion. Curiously, however, the Christian Coalition, in its "Contract with the American Family," leaves out one word: D-I-V-O-R-C-E. Self-described "pro-family voters" have mobilized to pass initiatives in dozens of states across the country that would deny civil rights to homosexuals. They have put far less energy into initiatives that would revoke no-fault divorce. Why? Why is making it difficult for gay men and lesbians to rent or get decent jobs a greater threat than liberal legal reforms that have made it easy for parents to split up? For that matter, why does the Christian Coalition think that a $500 "child tax credit" for a parent making $200,000 a year—amounting to *one four-hundredth* of his or her annual income—is important enough to make a central part of its "pro-family" agenda, but not divorce-law reform? The answer has nothing to do either with the family or with God and everything to do with politics. Homosexuals, being an unpopular and politically weak minority, make useful scapegoats for demagogic Republican politicians trying to create or capitalize upon artificial moral panics (this explains the anti-gay initiatives), and the dominant elite within the Republican party consists of rich Americans (thus the insistence of "pro-family conservatives" that the rich should not be excluded from the "child-care tax credit").

What, then, should be "done" about the family? The genuine conservative answer would be: nothing should be "done" at all, least of all by the government. Genuine conservatives of the Burkean sort are suspicious of heavy-handed efforts by a remote and impersonal bureaucratic government to fine-tune individual behavior—particularly in areas as intimate as sex and marriage. Surely there is a deep contradiction between the American right's opposition to crude social engineering in the form of busing for racial balance and minority set-asides, and its belligerent support for even cruder social engineering in the form of tax credits or censorship policies that supposedly will "strengthen the family."

The facts about the (mythical) illegitimacy epidemic and the (genuine) demographic problem will undoubtedly come as a surprise to many readers, of all political persuasions, who have been convinced by incessantly repeated conservative propaganda that because of welfare and/or the media, poor black women are having more babies out of wedlock today, on average, than they did in the 1950s or 1920s. That this blatant falsehood has been turned into a widely accepted "fact" in public discussion is a tribute to the power of the corporate and foundation-subsidized conservative brain trust in disseminating disinformation.

In promulgating the myth of the illegitimacy epidemic, the conservative intelligentsia cannot be excused as being sincerely mistaken. Conservative intellectuals have known all along, or have had reason to know, that the conservative "line" on illegitimacy rates among the black and white poor was simply wrong. As proof, I refer the reader to a 1991 article by James P. Scanlan, "The Perils of Provocative Statistics."[25]

Scanlan takes as his subject the misuse of statistics in three cases: the "feminization of poverty," or the increase in the proportion of poor families headed by single mothers; the disproportionate disqualification of blacks from intercollegiate athletics by a rule promoting higher academic standards; and the rise in the ratio of the black infant mortality rate to the white infant mortality rate. In the latter two cases, left-liberals misunderstood or distorted statistics in order to find "racism" where none in fact existed. In the case of the feminization of poverty, it is conservatives who have rushed to base sweeping policy proposals on data they have not understood, or do not want to understand.

"Female-headed families comprise a larger proportion of the poor than they did the preceding year; the observer concludes that female-headed families are worse off," Scanlan writes. Although this might seem a rational conclusion, in fact it is "utterly wrong." Scanlan's analysis deserves to be quoted at length:

> To see how the conventional understanding is often in error, imagine a country with a population of eight families. Six families, or 75 percent, are poor. Two of those are female-headed families, so in this society 33 percent of poor families are female-headed. Ten years later poverty is down to 25 percent, or two families. But one female-headed family—one less than before—is still poor. Commentators point to the familiar fact that the female-headed families, who once composed 33 percent of the country's poor families, now make up a shocking 50 percent. Although this scenario might appear to be farfetched, the use of what seems bad news to hide what may really be good news has become common in discussions of social policy.[26]

In fact, Scanlan points out, "a major reason for the dramatic increase in the feminization of poverty . . . was an unprecedented reduction in poverty that included major reductions in the poverty of female-headed families. . . . Though far less poverty-prone than in 1959, members of female-headed families had almost doubled their representation among the white poor (from 15 percent to 27 percent). . . ."[27] Note that two years before Charles Murray warned of a "coming white underclass," Scanlan showed that the rise in the proportion of female-headed families among the white poor resulted from the *success* of public policy in reducing poverty among whites from the 1950s to the present.

Scanlan's subject is the rise in female-headed families as a proportion of poor families, not the rise in illegitimate births as a proportion of the whole in both black and white America. Nevertheless, his critique of "the use of what seems bad news to hide what may really be good news" applies to the use by conservatives of the scary but misleading statistic—the black illegitimacy rate rose by 39 percent between 1960 and 1990!—instead of the more relevant, but less alarming, statistic— the proportion of black babies born out of wedlock increased by *only 6 percent* between 1960 and 1987, from 23 to 29 percent, when the reduction of fertility on the part of married black women is factored out.

The Scanlan article demolishing the kind of statistical argument that conservatives have employed to support their claim of an illegitimacy epidemic did not appear in a liberal publication, or in some obscure scholarly journal. It was published in the leading public policy journal of the right, edited by the central figure in the conservative brain trust, Irving Kristol. While the *Public Interest* has a relatively small readership, it is a major source for ideas that are disseminated through more popular organs of the right such as newspapers, magazines, and radio and TV shows.

All of which raises an interesting question. Kristol and the other leaders of the conservative intellectual movement, if they had wanted to, could have turned the Scanlan article about the feminization of poverty into a major media event. Kristol might have urged the *Wall Street Journal,* for which he frequently writes op-eds, to display an adaptation of the Scanlan article prominently on its op-ed page. Kristol's friend and ally Robert Bartley, the editorial page editor, might have written one of his passionate and stinging editorials, pointing out the significance of Scanlan's conservative critique of conservative illusions about illegitimacy rates. From the headwaters of the *Public Interest* and the *Wall Street Journal,* the facts about the feminization of poverty—and, perhaps, the statistical truth about the slightness of the rise in the rate of out-of-wedlock births by unmarried black women—might have been spread downstream to the conservative rank and file, via *National Review, American Spectator, Commentary,* and the Rush Limbaugh program, as early as 1991. The entire debate about illegitimacy and welfare might have been radically different.

Needless to say, the intellectual and political readers of the right did not praise and publicize Scanlan's *Public Interest* article. Why didn't they? Why did the intellectual and political right, given a choice between the unsound use of statistics by Charles Murray and Dan Quayle, and the accurate analysis of James P. Scanlan, promote the former rather than the latter? The reason is obvious—the theory of a black illegitimacy "epidemic," misleading as it is, adds to the arsenal of conservative culture-war politics, whereas Scanlan's cold facts disarm the radical right. It is not surprising that the leaders of American conservatism distorted the facts about illegitimacy, in the interest of political gain. After all, they had simply ignored the facts about the feminization of poverty—even when those facts were presented in their own flagship social-science publication!—and hoped that nobody would notice.

Supply-side economics, the myth of public school failure, and the illegitimacy-epidemic hoax are only the tip of the iceberg. Other examples of the dissemination of half-truths and falsehoods by the foundation-subsidized conservative intelligentsia that writes for the *Wall Street Journal* and the *Public Interest* are not difficult to find. For example, we now know that the scientific basis of Reagan's Strategic Defense Initiative or "Star Wars" was far more dubious than conservative foreign policy experts admitted during the 1980s. Indeed, conservative journalists and intellectuals without scientific backgrounds were misled, along with Reagan and SDI supporters in Congress, by physicist Edward Teller's misrepresentations of the actual state of science and technology in the area of missile defense.[28] In 1994, the General Accounting Office revealed that the Pentagon had rigged key SDI tests in 1984, by heating target missiles and putting bombs on board to ensure that they would explode when approached by interceptor missiles. The Pentagon's evident purpose was to deceive Congress, which might not have voted to continue research on SDI had its leaders known the facts. Senator Sam Nunn, chairman of the Senate Armed Services Committee, did not learn about the deception until 1993. By that time, Congress, not realizing it had been hoaxed, had voted to spend almost $30 billion on SDI research.[29]

The conservative disinformation apparatus went to work again, to prevent President Clinton's plan to provide health care coverage for all Americans from ever reaching a vote. Clinton's plan would have been the most conservative, pro-business version of universal health insurance in any western democracy. Nevertheless conservatives were desperate to stop it, in order to deny the Democrats a political victory. The cynical reasoning of Republican strategists was spelled out by Irving Kristol's son William: "It will revive the reputation of the party that spends and regulates, the Democrats, as the generous protector of middle-class interests."[30]

The conservative campaign against health care reform found its greatest champion in Elizabeth McCaughey.[31] McCaughey was an archetypal member of the subsidized conservative intelligentsia—she was a John M. Olin Fellow at the Manhattan Institute. (Recall that the architect of the foundation-sponsored conservative intelligentsia, William E. Simon, had been president of the Olin Foundation, and that the Manhattan Institute, by lavish promotion, had turned Charles Murray from an obscure social scientist into a celebrity). In the pages of the *Wall Street Journal,* and then in the *New Republic,* McCaughey claimed that "the bill prohibits doctors from accepting payments directly from you for the basic kinds of medical care" covered by insurance. This was simply not true; as *New Republic* senior editor Mickey Kaus pointed out, the Clinton plan would have allowed any patient to pay any doctor from the patient's own funds (even without Clinton's reform, most health maintenance organizations—HMOs—do not pay doctors who are not on their lists). McCaughey also claimed that the Clinton plan outlawed "fee-for-service (choose-your-own-doctor) insurance" (it did not).[32]

Despite the fact that its central claims were demonstrably false, McCaughey's *New Republic* article, "No Exit," won the *New Republic* a National Magazine Award for "Excellence in Public Interest." McCaughey, for her part, won election as the Republican lieutenant governor of New York. Largely because of misleading claims by conservatives like McCaughey, support for health care reform crumbled and the Clinton plan was never even brought to a vote.

The foundation-subsidized right has disseminated other fallacies in the area of health care policy. The Washington Legal Foundation, a conservative think tank, has paid for advertisements reading: "If a murderer kills you, it's homicide. If a drunk driver kills you, it's manslaughter. If the FDA kills you, it's just being cautious." The claim that "red tape" and bureaucracy prevent great numbers of Americans from receiving lifesaving drugs fits in with the anti-government message of the right (even as it promotes the interests of the pharmaceutical industry that is a major funder of Republican candidates and conservative think tanks). However, the notion that the U.S. government is slower than other governments to approve drugs is false. An FDA study comparing the approval of new drugs by the United States, Japan, Germany, and Britain (which together account for 60 percent of global pharmaceutical sales) showed that the United States usually approved a drug first.[33] Thus another widely believed "fact" disseminated by the subsidized policy experts of the right turns out to be bogus.

The three major theories animating conservative domestic policy during the past decade and a half—supply-side economics, the illegitimacy epidemic, and the crisis of public education—on close inspection turn out to have been hoaxes, perpetrated by conservative propagandists to justify reforms that benefited Republican special interests: the business elite, the Protestant fundamentalist lobby, or both.[34]

Did the conservatives realize they were mistaken? If they did not know the facts, they at least had ample opportunity to find out. The conservative leaders who have not been guilty of consciously misleading the public can be accused of a cavalier disregard for truth. The term "cavalier" is not my term; it comes from Irving Kristol himself. In the recent thirtieth anniversary issue of the *Public Interest,* Kristol confessed that he and his allies never really understood economics; what they were after was merely a something-for-nothing gimmick that would help elect Republicans:

> Among the core social scientists around The Public Interest there were no economists. (They came later, as we "matured.") This explains my own rather cavalier attitude toward the budget deficit and other monetary or fiscal problems. The task, as I saw it, was to create a new majority, which evidently would mean a conservative majority, which came to mean, in turn, a Republican majority—so political effectiveness was the priority, not the accounting deficiencies of government.[35]

The "accounting deficiencies of government," that is, the deficit, now exceeds 164 billion dollars.

The cavalier promoters of supply-side economics have not been alone in sacrificing scholarly objectivity to the short-term interests of the Republican party and its special-interest constituencies. The educational experts of the American right have shown a remarkable talent for ignoring data that contradict their lurid picture of an American public educational system in collapse. For example, a 1992 study by the International Association for the Evaluation of Educational Achievement that reported that American nine-year-olds placed second in the world when it came to reading achievement was ignored by the very same conservatives who had routinely quoted other data from the same source that seemed to show that American public education was failing.[36] No op-eds by William Bennett; no cover stories in *National Review.* The Bush administration even refused to publish a report on

American student achievement that the administration itself had commissioned from Sandia National Laboratories—evidently because the report's skepticism about the supposed education crisis undermined conservative fear-mongering.[37] The Sandia analysts had discovered that, when contemporary test takers were matched with students with the same demographic attributes taking the test fifteen years earlier, the contemporary students did better; the contemporary 50th percentile was equivalent to the 60th percentile in 1975.[38] No wonder the Republican enemies of public education wanted to bury news as good as this. The report was finally published by R. M. Helskamp in 1993.[39]

The clearest example of the abuse of social science data by contemporary conservatives remains Charles Murray's contribution to the myth of the illegitimacy epidemic. In his inflammatory "The Coming White Underclass" op-ed in the *Wall Street Journal*, Murray barraged the reader with analyses of statistics, with one significant exception. He did not mention the reason that the proportion of illegitimate births in the black community has risen to 60 percent since the 1960s (the declining birth rates of middle-class and affluent blacks). The result, as I have noted, was to lead unsuspecting readers (including me at the time) to conclude, wrongly, that poor black women were having babies out of wedlock at approximately three times the rate as in the 1960s. If he did not intend to encourage such a misconception, Murray at least permitted it, by leaving out the critical data and writing instead about the supposed "long, steep climb in black illegitimacy," describing the last three decades as an era "when illegitimacy became epidemic within a comparatively small ethnic minority."

This was not the first time Murray's selective use of data or misinterpretations of statistics happened to support conclusions that his conservative constituency wanted to hear. In *Losing Ground*, perhaps the most influential book about welfare among conservatives, Murray purported to show that the American welfare state encouraged illegitimacy and discouraged work. His claims were quickly demolished by other researchers. The constant-dollar value of welfare benefits declined by 20 percent after 1972—even while out-of-wedlock births rose (among women who did not receive welfare as well as among welfare recipients). Between 1972 and 1980, in fact, the number of black children dependent on AFDC actually declined.[40]

Not only was Murray's welfare-causes-illegitimacy thesis wrong, but so were many of the most important details of his argument. Murray illustrated his theory by means of a "thought-experiment" involving a Pennsylvania couple, Harold and Phyllis, who choose not to marry when Phyllis becomes pregnant because Phyllis can make more money as a single mother on welfare. Robert Greenstein showed that Murray had done his math wrong: "In 1980—even in Pennsylvania—Harold and Phyllis would have one-third more income if Harold worked than if he remained unemployed and Phyllis collected welfare."[41] Equally damning was Christopher Jencks's discovery that Murray's figures purporting to show an increase in poverty in the past three decades (which would prove that the War on Poverty had been a failure) were based on disputed work by an economist named Timothy Smedding. Using sounder figures, Jencks calculated that the population below the poverty line in 1980 was half as large as the poor population of 1965—and only one-third as large as the group under the official poverty line in 1950.[42]

Murray's basic claims about the welfare state, to say nothing of many subsidiary arguments, had been discredited. Nevertheless, Murray's reputation as the leading public policy expert of the right was not affected in the least, and his influence continued to grow. The reason is that Murray is the leading member of the "counterintelligentsia" that the ex-leftist Kristol and Wall Street tycoon William Simon decided to create in the 1970s. Charles Lane has pointed out that in the 1980s Murray was raised from obscurity by William Hammett, the president of the Manhattan Institute, part of the right-wing intellectual front. On the basis of a pamphlet Murray had written, Hammett paid for Murray to spend two years researching *Losing Ground,* then sent seven hundred free copies, at an expense of $15,000, to key journalists, politicians, and academics. Hammett even hired a public relations expert, Joan Taylor Kennedy, to transform Murray into a celebrity intellectual. In addition to booking TV and radio appearances, the Manhattan Institute paid influential politicians and journalists honoraria of $500 to $1500 to participate in a seminar on Murray and his thought.[43] (Although the Manhattan Institute severed its connection with Murray when it discovered that the book on which he was collaborating with the late Richard Herrnstein would argue for genetic differences in intelligence between the conventionally defined races, another foundation-subsidized conservative think tank, the American Enterprise Institute, became Murray's new sponsor.)

From the time that he was handpicked by the Manhattan Institute's William Hammett, Murray's career as a foundation-subsidized conservative expert has resembled that of a political candidate, groomed by handlers and sponsors, more than that of a scholar. At every stage, most experts in the fields in which Murray has dabbled have rejected his reasoning and his use of data. His failure to convert the experts with his scholarship has not prevented him from becoming a superstar among public-policy writers. He has flourished, unlike better scholars who happen to share conservative views, because his work has given the appearances of scholarly cover to the banal prejudices of the rank-and-file right (poor women have babies to make money from the government, white people are genetically superior to blacks and Hispanics).

The promotion of Arthur Laffer, an economist with views rejected by most in his field, and Charles Murray, a social scientist whose arguments persuade few other social scientists, as the leading public policy experts of the American right does more than testify to the cynicism of the tiny network of foundation presidents, program officers, editors, and publishers who run the intellectual conservative network from behind the scenes. It also offers additional proof, if any be needed, that the tradition with the greatest influence on American conservatism is American populism. Laffer and Murray—each with his radical, cure-all reform (supply-side tax cuts, the abolition of welfare)—fit the populist model of the great thinker.[44] For two centuries, the typical American populist intellectual or political leader has been the crank, often the monetary crank, peddling this or that simple and sweeping economic or institutional policy reform as a panacea for a whole range of social and even diplomatic problems. Jefferson was convinced that his embargo on exports from the United States would end the Napoleonic wars by making the European nations realize their dependence on America. Andrew Jackson's panacea was the abolition of the Second Bank of the United States. For the followers of William Jennings Bryan, the use of silver as currency would restore rural prosperity, end American dependence on the Old World, and further the causes of Christianity and progress. The core group in the Republican electorate today, as I have noted, consists of the descendants of southern and western Democrats in the Jefferson-Jackson-Bryan tradition. We should not be surprised that the grandchildren of free-silverites should become enamored of supply-side economics in the 1980s and the flat tax in the 1990s, nor that they should be easily persuaded that American life would be much better if only public education and federal welfare were utterly annihilated, just as the "Monster Bank" (the Second Bank of the United States) was destroyed by Andrew Jackson.

To reject conservative myth-making about federal taxation, education, and welfare is not to deny that there are genuine problems in all three areas. Though the deficit would have been much smaller than it is, had it not been for Ronald Reagan and the supply-siders, the growing costs of Medicare and Medicaid alone would sooner or later have forced budgetary reforms on the federal government. The budget ought to be balanced the old-fashioned, fiscal conservative way—by cutting a defense establishment that is larger than necessary in present conditions, by cutting entitlements (starting with entitlements that go to the well-off), and by raising taxes (beginning with higher progressive taxation on the affluent). Despite the promise of the neo-Reaganite right in the Contract with America to slash taxes further, there should be no further tax cuts for the well-off until the federal budget is in the black.

American public education faces serious problems, though these hardly add up to the kind of apocalyptic crisis spoken of by the right. The chief of those problems arise from the difficulties public schools in metropolitan areas face in educating poor urban black and immigrant children (similar challenges do not exist in ethnically homogeneous Japan, with its policy of zero legal immigration). The troubles of public schools in urban areas are compounded by the irrational American system of organizing primary and secondary education into a patchwork of often small independent school districts—and by the equally irrational method of financing public schools out of local property taxes, instead of general state or federal revenues. The solution to the organizational incoherence of public education is for the states and the federal government to impose uniform—and higher—standards for teacher competency and student achievement. And the solution to the problems caused by the underfunding of schools as a result of taxpayer revolts aimed at lowering property taxes is to finance schools primarily out of state and federal revenues. Having the state and federal governments assume the responsibility for funding schools, on an equal per-student basis, can reduce, though not eliminate, the grotesque discrepancies between the crumbling schools of many inner cities and the well-funded, clean, attractive schools of the suburbs.[45] The adoption of these centrist liberal reforms ought to be accompanied by the rejection of left-liberal mistakes like busing for racial balance and Afrocentric education.[46]

It is even possible to imagine a system of vouchers for primary and secondary education that would be compatible with the goals of ensuring equal access to quality education by all American children. An acceptable school choice plan would have two features that would distinguish it from conservative schemes. First, only schools that met rigorous standards in objective fields like mathematics and natural science would be permitted to participate in the program (bible academies teaching the story of Noah's ark as history would not qualify). Second, the children of the wealthy would not be eligible for the vouchers, on the grounds that the middle and working classes should not subsidize the rich. Needless to say, both of these features of a thoughtful school choice plan would make it unacceptable to the major constituencies of educational reform on the right: Protestant fundamentalists and wealthy families who enroll their children in expensive private academies.

The question of welfare reform is one that defeats any simple solutions, liberal or conservative. As I have demonstrated, Charles Murray's suggestion that there is something that can be described as an "epidemic" of illegitimacy among the poor is a myth, based on a statistical illusion. Does this mean that we should not be concerned about illegitimacy rates in general, and about black illegitimacy rates in particular? Not at all. There are two genuine problems associated with illegitimacy. The first has already been pointed out—children growing up in female-headed households tend to have fewer life chances than those growing up in intact families, not least because there is much less money around. The fact that a minority of American children are born out of wedlock would be a problem for public policy, even a tragedy—but hardly one of the major crises confronting the United States at the end of the twentieth century. To this problem, Daniel Patrick Moynihan, not Charles Murray, remains the soundest guide—and Moynihan, as a senator and a scholar, has passionately rejected the dumb idea that the way to reduce illegitimacy is simply to throw single mothers and their children off welfare into destitution.

The other problem caused by the rise in the proportion of illegitimate births arguably does constitute a crisis, a crisis at once demographic and political. In the very long run, it does not so much matter whether poor women are having babies at a greater rate, or middle-class and affluent women are having babies at a reduced rate. The ultimate result will be the same: the country will be repopulated by the descendants of today's poor. Because of the justifiable decision of well-off black women to have fewer children, most black Americans in the twenty-first century will be the children and grandchildren of today's inner-city black poor.

"The poor are outbreeding the rich"—this has been the great nightmare of upper classes throughout history. Caesar Augustus was so concerned about the political and social implications of the differential in fertility levels between the Roman elite and the Roman masses that he advocated his own version of "pro-family" legislation, including tax penalties for upper-class bachelors. The fear of being outbred not only by blacks but by Irish, Poles, Czechs, Greeks, Italians, and Jews, and by the supposedly inferior among the Anglo-American population, animated the craze for eugenic sterilization and birth control in late nineteenth and early twentieth century America. (It is worth recalling that Planned Parenthood was promoted by upper-class WASPs as a means of keeping down the numbers of non-WASPs.)

Faced with demographic decline among its own ranks and the growth, as a percentage of the population, of other groups, an elite is faced with three choices: it can pursue a divide-and-rule strategy, preventing a hostile majority coalition from forming by pitting one nonelite group against another; it can try to reduce the relative growth of the nonelite population (by means ranging from birth control to sterilization, ethnic cleansing and outright genocide) or it can attempt to replenish its own ranks from the ranks of the growing majority. A racial strategy of divide and rule, pitting whites against blacks, has been the core of Republican electoral strategy since Nixon; in a nonwhite-majority America, elite white conservatives might pursue a different divide-and-rule strategy, pitting Hispanics against blacks, and blacks against Asians. In *The Bell Curve,* Charles Murray and Richard Herrnstein in effect propose that the government take the second strategy, reducing the relative growth in nonwhite numbers by reducing nonwhite immigration and discouraging reproduction by poor blacks, whites, and Hispanics by cutting off welfare and making contraceptives easily available to the poor. Though Murray and Herrnstein do not advocate more radical measures, making abortion easily available to the poor, and sterilizing the poor, as was done in many states in the early twentieth century, would have the same effect. The proposal that poor black women be sterilized by Norplant implants as a condition of receiving welfare is found today only on the lunatic fringe. This offers small comfort, inasmuch as in less than a decade, the ideas of Murray and Herrnstein have migrated from the fringe to the respectable center of conservative thinking.

The liberal approach to alarming demographic trends rejects both divide-and-rule politics and kinder, gentler genocide in favor of integration. Liberals want to reduce the ranks of the poor, not by encouraging or coercing the poor to have fewer children, but by enabling the children of the poor to join the ranks of the middle and upper classes. Not only can this be done, it has already been done in the United States—by the great midcentury liberals from FDR to LBJ. Thanks to liberal programs promoting social mobility, from public education and the G.I. Bill to home-ownership subsidies, Social Security, and Medicare, most of the children and grandchildren of the ignorant, teeming immigrants and poor whites who horrified upper-class Americans in the 1890s managed to join the middle class and the overclass by the 1990s. Black social progress has been less complete, but just as real—only a minority of black Americans today are poor. Thanks largely to the reforms undertaken by FDR, Truman, and Johnson and their allies, the relative decline of Anglo-Americans as a proportion of the U.S. population has not meant the relative decline of either the broad middle class or the elite. The American middle class and the American overclass at the end of the twentieth century are full of people with names like Reagan and Kristol.

Surely it is no coincidence that the great era of social mobility in the United States also happened to be the great era of Democratic liberalism, from the beginning of the New Deal to the last years of the Great Society. Nor can it be mere coincidence that the era of conservative Democrats and conservative Republicans, from Carter to Clinton, has seen the historic rise of the American middle class checked and in many cases reversed. We cannot be sure that an updated version of the FDR-Truman-LBJ project will do as much for today's poor blacks, whites, and Hispanic and Asian immigrants as midcentury liberalism did for poor blacks, native-born whites, and European immigrants in the early twentieth century. We can be sure, however, that Carter-Reagan-Bush-Clinton conservatism will fail to turn the poor of today into the middle class of tomorrow. We will be lucky indeed if conservative policies do not turn the middle class of today into tomorrow's poor.

Chapter 8

The New Social Darwinism

The Revival of Racism on the Right

The Republican party today—despite the presence of a few token figures like Supreme Court Justice Clarence Thomas—is a white person's party. Increasingly, it is a party of white southerners. The success of the Goldwater-Nixon southern strategy in luring white southern conservatives into the GOP has come at a price—the abandonment, by the party, of its proud tradition as the party of Abraham Lincoln and Frederick Douglass. As I have shown in previous chapters, the Republican party of today owes less to the Republican party of Dwight Eisenhower than to the States' Rights party of Strom Thurmond, the segregationist candidate for president in 1948 who became one of the earliest white southern politicians to abandon the Democrats for the Republicans.

Appealing to the racial anxieties of white voters has become a central element of the strategy of the Republican elite for gaining and maintaining political power, as it was for the conservative Bourbon Democrats who lorded it over the South in the first half of the twentieth century. In most cases, the racist appeals are coded, like Nixon's support for "school choice" (intended to give white southerners a way to escape the integration of public schools), Ronald Reagan's attack on "welfare queens," and Phil Gramm's sneering, pseudo-folksy references to those who want to ride in the wagon and not pull. In the 1990s, even the circumlocutions began to be abandoned, in favor of unapologetic racialist theorizing—not by elected politicians, but by highly esteemed members of the conservative intelligentsia like Charles Murray, Dinesh D'Souza, and Peter Brimelow.

The new racial politics of the Republican right has been helped, if only inadvertently, by the disastrous racial politics of left-liberal Democrats. When the left-liberals annihilated the New Deal–vital center national liberals in the Democratic party in the 1960s and 1970s, they also killed the genuine liberal alternative to segregation—race-neutral or color-blind antidiscrimination law. Racial preference, and multiculturalism, the theory that justifies it, have been the central elements of the left-liberal approach to race in the post-apartheid United States. Racial preference, together with busing to achieve "racial balance," has done more to send white voters in the direction of the Republican right than any number of "Willie Horton" commercials could have done. The worst effect of left-liberal racial politics have been a subtle one: by constantly emphasizing that blacks, Hispanics, and Asian-Americans are cohesive groups whose identity must be preserved, left-liberals, without intending to, have given credibility to white racists who argue that "Euro-Americans" constitute a similarly cohesive group whose identity and traditions equally deserve government recognition and support.

In addition to benefiting from the idiocies of left-liberalism, the Republican right has been able to take advantage of the slowly growing unease among the white population inspired by figures purporting to prove that whites will be reduced to minority status in the twenty-first century. The figures may be disputed; they are based on the assumption, which may not be realistic, that the United States will indefinitely continue to allow high levels of immigration from Latin America and Asia. Nor do the calculations take into account the high intermarriage rate among whites, Asians, and Hispanics, a phenomenon that is slowly but surely blurring the white-nonwhite distinction. Even so, the reduction of nonwhites to minority status in cities like Los Angeles and New York has already occurred, and whites may soon be a minority in the most populous states like California, Texas, and New York. A demagogic race-baiting strategy originally aimed at white southerners afraid of being overwhelmed by blacks may prove equally useful in obtaining the votes of whites in the sunbelt alarmed about the rise in numbers of Hispanics and Asians.

The right's record on race is the subject of this chapter. It is a tale mostly of evil and expediency, lit only occasionally by flashes of enlightenment, compassion, or patriotism that extend to the whole of the American nation and not merely to a privileged part.

Modern American conservatism was warped and contaminated by racism from the beginning. The members of the conservative movement led by William F. Buckley, Jr. and centered on *National Review* spent the 1950s and the early 1960s denouncing federal efforts to dismantle America's version of apartheid and voicing support for continued European rule of nonwhite populations in Africa and Asia. The *National Review* conservatives were too genteel, of course, to indulge in blatant racism. Their official opposition was based on their concern for "states' rights." That this was a mere pretext is proven by the fact that not a single prominent conservative in those days proposed state (as opposed to federal) civil rights legislation. Conservatives like Buckley also justified their anti-anti-segregationism by vague references to the superior "civilization" of white southerners. That civilization, it appears, was under threat by the prospect of black suffrage even outside of the South; on one occasion in the 1950s, William Rehnquist—now Chief Justice of the Supreme Court, and then a Young Republican—had to be ordered away from a polling place in Arizona because he was demanding that black voters be forced to prove they could read by reading the Constitution before being allowed to mark their ballots.[1]

If Buckley, Goldwater, and their allies had prevailed, I would have grown up, like my ancestors, in a segregated Texas, with black and white drinking fountains, white-only businesses and restaurants, and so on. Fortunately, the southern segregationists and their conservative allies elsewhere were defeated by Martin Luther King, Jr., and Lyndon Johnson, whose 1964 Civil Rights Act is the single most important piece of legislation in the twentieth century United States—more important even than the historic legislation of FDR's New Deal. As he signed the Civil Rights Act, Johnson predicted to an aide that he had lost the South for the Democratic party. His words proved all too prophetic. Having done everything they could to prevent black Americans from voting, the conservatives regrouped in the 1970s and 1980s to form a new nationwide Republican coalition of whites voting *against* black Americans, using issues like welfare, busing, and racial preferences to inflame passions.

The historic commitment of "the party of Lincoln" to equal rights for nonwhite Americans is easily exaggerated, of course. Lincoln himself hoped almost to the end of the Civil War that black Americans could be shipped out of the country; his tentative plans for Reconstruction would have excluded all but a small percentage of "intelligent" blacks from the suffrage. His Republican successors abandoned the effort to use federal power to protect civil rights in the South, making an informal deal with the southern oligarchy that permitted segregation and one-party Democratic rule in the South for almost a century. Between Reconstruction and the civil rights revolution, the Republican commitment to civil rights was minimal, consisting of unenthusiastic support for a few black Republican political bosses and token gestures like Theodore Roosevelt's dinner at the White House with Booker T. Washington, which Roosevelt later regretted. Even Progressive Republicans like TR shared the racism of their age, which envisioned whites in general, and Anglo-Saxons in particular, at the top of a hierarchy with Asians in the middle and Africans at the bottom.

During the Little Rock crisis of 1954, Dwight Eisenhower used federal troops for the first time since the end of Reconstruction to enforce civil rights for black Americans in the South, and in 1957 he signed the first federal civil rights legislation in almost a century, the Civil Rights Act of 1957. He did so only reluctantly, however. Eisenhower, who enjoyed telling racist jokes, complained: "No single event has so disturbed the domestic scene in many years as did the Supreme Court's decision of 1954." His vice president, Richard Nixon, lost the black vote to Kennedy when Nixon hesitated to express support for Martin Luther King, Jr., jailed in Reidsville, Georgia (a call from Robert Kennedy to the judge who had denied King bail led to King's release). Nixon was a racist of the crudest sort; when he learned that there were federal scholarship programs for blacks, he said: "Well, it's a good thing. They're just down out of the trees."[2] According to H. R. Haldeman, Nixon said "that there has never in history been an adequate black nation, and they are the only race of which this is true. Says Africa is hopeless."[3] Nixon instructed Kissinger to include something about Africa in a foreign policy address by telling him to "make sure there's something in it for the jigs."[4] Anticipating the thesis of Charles Murray and Richard Herrnstein in *The Bell Curve*, Nixon told Ehrlichman that social programs directed at black Americans were a waste of money: "America's blacks could only marginally benefit . . . because blacks were *genetically inferior* to whites."[5]

Hoping to win the "blacklash vote" of formerly Democratic white southerners and northern white ethnics who had voted for George

Wallace in 1968, Nixon subordinated civil rights policy to a divide-and-rule strategy. On the one hand, Nixon denounced busing and racial quotas, and unsuccessfully nominated two southern segregationists, Clement F. Haynesworth, Jr. of South Carolina and G. Harrold Carswell of Florida, to the Supreme Court. At the same time, Nixon inaugurated the present era of affirmative action by pushing through the Philadelphia Plan, a scheme for imposing racial quotas in unions that the Johnson administration had killed. Some liberals, like Nixon's biographer Stephen Ambrose and historian Herbert Parmet, have thus claimed that Nixon was actually a great friend of black Americans; according to Parmet, "It would do a great injustice to deny [Nixon's] intellectual and spiritual commitment to racial equality." In fact, Nixon's purpose in reviving and implementing the Philadelphia Plan was to split the Democratic coalition by pitting white labor against the black civil rights movement. Ehrlichman later explained: "Nixon thought that Secretary of Labor George Shultz had shown great style in constructing a political dilemma for the labor union leaders and the civil rights groups. Before long, the AFL-CIO and the NAACP were locked in combat over one of the passionate issues of the day and the Nixon administration was located in the sweet and reasonable middle. . . . After that, Shultz was just naturally invited in to help out with school desegregation."[6] Having served as Nixon's compliant tool in divisive racial politics, George Shultz rose within the GOP until he became Secretary of State under Reagan.

Another divide-and-rule policy that dates from the Nixon administration is the use of the Voting Rights Act by Republican administrations to replace biracial liberal congressional districts with ghettoized black-majority districts and "whiter" conservative districts. Although this strategy only began to pay off after it was employed by Reagan and Bush, it was suggested by Nixon campaign advisor Kevin Phillips, who argued that "abandonment of civil rights enforcement would be self-defeating" for the reason that "maintenance of Negro voting rights in Dixie, far from being contrary to GOP interests, is essential if southern conservatives are to be pressured into switching to the Republican party."[7]

Though Ronald Reagan angrily denied that he was a racist, he became the right's favorite politician largely on the basis of a dramatic lie he told repeatedly, to voters, members of Congress, and even foreign leaders, about a black "welfare queen" in Chicago. The woman in question, Linda Taylor, was convicted in 1977 for fraud and perjury involving only $8,000 in welfare checks. As Reagan told the story, however, Taylor had used "eighty names, thirty addresses, twelve Social Security cards" to acquire "veterans' benefits on four non-existing deceased husbands" which, joined with other welfare benefits, gave her a tax-free income of more than $150,000.[8] Neither William F. Buckley, Jr. nor Irving Kristol nor William Bennett nor any other conservative intellectual or journalist ever pointed out that Reagan was spreading a preposterous lie. Even if Linda Taylor had defrauded the government of $150,000, rather than $8,000, she hardly would have been representative of the minority of poor black women on welfare. Reagan, a good politician, was telling conservative voters what they wanted to hear— that the typical poor black on welfare is a cunning con artist, and rich, to boot.[9]

Despite Reagan's coded appeals to white racism, it looked for a while in the 1980s as though the right might have been freed from its segregationist origins. Throughout the 1970s and 1980s, liberals routinely accused all conservatives who criticized liberal positions on civil rights of being racists. This was neither fair nor accurate. While the right undoubtedly contained a number of unreconstructed racists who had never accepted the legitimacy of integration, the conservative movement was enlarged after the 1960s by an influx of former liberals, the neoconservatives, most of whom had supported integration but opposed race-conscious government policies like busing and affirmative action. These views were shared by a small but prominent group of black conservatives, including Clarence Thomas, Thomas Sowell, and Walter Williams. White conservatives like Jack Kemp and William Bennett stressed their admiration for Martin Luther King, Jr., in order to distance their conception of the right from the segregationist conservatism of the recent past. Jack Kemp said that the Republican party had "missed the opportunity" to fight racism: "I wasn't there with Rosa Parks or Dr. King or John Lewis, but I am here now and I am going to yell from the rooftops about what we need to do."[10] In the 1980s Republican operatives could argue, with some justification, that the disproportionate number of crimes committed by the black poor did not make "law and order" an innately "racist" issue.

The liberal left was sometimes crying wolf, then, when it saw resurgent racism in conservative critiques of affirmative action and multiculturalism—critiques which a growing number of liberals and leftists have come to endorse. The point of the story about the boy who cried wolf, though, was that eventually a wolf *did* show up. The resurgence of old-fashioned racism that liberals had mistakenly thought they perceived on the mainstream right in the 1980s finally arrived in the 1990s, shaggy and drooling.

The debate about race on the right has been transformed by three books, all published within a few years of one another in the mid-1990s: *The Bell Curve* by Charles Murray and the late Richard Herrnstein, *The End of Racism* by Dinesh D'Souza, and *Alien Nation* by Peter Brimelow.[11] The thesis of *The Bell Curve* is that the position of blacks and Hispanics in American society, and of lower-income whites as well, is best explained by their genetic inferiority compared to upper-income white Americans, not by any historical or economic factors. The American class and caste system, in other words, is the more or less inevitable result of the underlying genetic distribution of potential as well as actual intellectual ability in the population. Devoting resources to educating poor blacks, Hispanics, or whites is a waste of time, since they are doomed by nature to lives of drudgery in low-skill occupations. Welfare ought to be abolished, because it is encouraging "dysgenesis," that is, the outbreeding of smart whites by dumb whites, blacks, and Hispanics. Immigration by blacks and Hispanics, who tend to score less well on IQ tests than white Americans, also ought to be restricted in the interests of upgrading the quality of the American gene pool. (Presumably immigration by genetically superior Nordic Aryans from Europe ought to be encouraged, although Herrnstein and Murray leave this conclusion to be drawn by the reader.)

In *The End of Racism*, Dinesh D'Souza is careful to insist that he is not making claims about genes, but about "civilization." Still, there is little in his book that an American white supremacist could disagree with. D'Souza's rambling book combines undisputed facts and figures about inner-city pathology with extenuating arguments with respect to segregation (it protected blacks, he says, and not many blacks were lynched, anyway). The greatest threat to black Americans, D'Souza writes, is not white racism but "liberal antiracism" (by unlucky coincidence, the book was published about the time that the Mark Fuhrman tapes shocked Americans with their revelations about how deeply ingrained white-supremacist attitudes remain in police forces like that of Los Angeles). By a somewhat different method, D'Souza arrives at the same conclusion as Murray: white Americans have no responsibility toward the black poor, and efforts to help them are probably counterproductive. The black poor are the problem of the black middle and upper classes, not of affluent and influential Americans of all races. Whites should not only not be forced to pay for programs to help the black poor; they should be allowed to engage in "rational discrimination." D'Souza calls for repealing the Civil Rights Act of 1964, insofar as it applies to businesses and individuals. According to D'Souza, it should be legal for restaurants once again to deny service to nonwhite customers.

The third book in the triptych of the new conservative racial thought is Peter Brimelow's *Alien Nation*. Like the other two books, this polemic interpolates legitimate arguments for reducing the number of immigrants (such as their likely contribution to lower wages for low-skilled native-born workers) with page after page of lurid rhetoric appealing to white prejudice and white panic. The centerpiece of Brimelow's book is his answer to the Murray-Herrnstein bell curve of IQ distribution—a chart showing a Census Bureau projection of the relative growth of nonwhite populations at the expense of white Americans in the future: "I call this 'The Pincer Chart.' For obvious reasons." The nonwhite "pincers"—one black and Asian, the other Hispanic—are squeezing the white majority in America into a minority. Brimelow treats the projected reduction of white Americans to minority status as an apocalyptic event. The shrinking proportion of whites (still well over 80 percent today) means that the American nation "is now in the grip of an ethnic revolution"; it "is being dissolved by public policy."

Brimelow compares the United States to multinational empires, where a single ethnic group—the "umpire"—maintained social peace by either overwhelming numbers or a policy of divide and rule. The United States "faces the direct equivalent of being abandoned by an imperial umpire." The result, he predicts, will be the polarization of American society into ethnic voting blocs. "The uneven distribution of immigration will tend to force the country's regions even further apart." Brimelow reaches absurdity when he writes: "The experience of an Anglo-Cuban society like Greater Miami is going to have little in common with an Anglo-black society like Atlanta or even with an Anglo-Mexican society like San Antonio. These will be communities as different from one another as any in the civilized world. They will verge on being separate nations." Brimelow concludes: "The contradictions of a society as deeply divided as the United States must now inexorably become, as a result of the post-1965 influx, will lead to conflict, repression, and, perhaps, ultimately, to a threat thought extinct in American politics for more than a hundred years: secession." Note the confident verbs of the prophet: "must now inexorably;" "will." Brimelow repeatedly invokes a delphic formula, a variant on the phrase "race is destiny": "Race and ethnicity are destiny in American politics." "Once again: ethnicity, and demography, is destiny in American politics."

In the book's most preposterous section, Brimelow compares today's immigrants from Latin America and Asia to ancient Germanic barbarians: "In some ways, the nearest thing to a precedent for today's world in motion appears to be the famous Volkwanderung [*sic*—he means *Völkerwanderung*]—the great 'movement of peoples' in the Fifth century that saw Germanic tribes overrun the Western Roman Empire." Brimelow hastens to add, in defense of the Goths, that the "German war bands" were actually less of a threat to Roman cultural unity than Mexican-American and Korean-American immigrants are to the integrity of American society, because "the Germans were Western Europeans." It seems that Theodoric the Goth had more in common with Boethius than, say, Lee Trevino has with Arnold Palmer.

Brimelow does not join Herrnstein and Murray in opposing non-white immigration because of supposed "dysgenic" effects on the American gene pool. Still, Brimelow's Spenglerian argument about the decline and fall of white America bears no small resemblance to that found in *The Bell Curve*. In both the pincer chart and the bell curve, crude white prejudices find striking, pseudoscientific symbols.

The chief significance of these three books is not scientific, but social and political: their appearance and reception shows how extreme the conservative movement has become in the 1990s. Herrnstein and Murray, in particular, have engaged in a sort of intellectual laundering operation, repackaging the arguments of marginal scholars in a respectable form. Their entire argument about racial differences in IQ therefore stands or falls on the credibility of their sources—which, as it happens, tend to be far outside the mainstream of modern social science, liberal or conservative.

In *The Bell Curve,* Herrnstein and Murray rely heavily on the dubious data of a small and eccentric band of scholars who have argued the case for white superiority and innate black inferiority for decades. According to Charles Lane, writing in the *New York Review of Books,* Herrnstein and Murray "cite in their book no fewer than thirteen scholars who have benefited from Pioneer Fund grants in the last two decades—

the grants total more than $4 million."[12] The Pioneer Fund, founded by Wyckliffe Draper, a textile tycoon who admired the eugenics policies of Nazi Germany, was established in 1937 with the purpose of "race betterment, with special reference to the people of the United States." (The fund got its name from the desire of Draper and his allies to promote the reproduction of descendants of the "white pioneers," presumably threatened by the fecundity of recent European immigrants and nonwhite Americans.) One of the first projects consisted of cash grants to encourage pilots of the Army Air Corps to have children and pass on their "superior stock"—an American counterpart to the SS *Lebensborn* program of Nazi elite "stud farms."

Since World War II, the Pioneer Fund has lavished grants on scholars like the psychologist Arthur J. Jensen and the physicist William Shockley willing to argue for an innate genetic basis for black poverty and poor educational performance. (Shockley proposed a "Sterilization Bonus Plan" which would pay the intellectually inferior not to reproduce). In recent years, the most important spokesmen for this school of thought have included two Pioneer Fund grantees, J. Philippe Rushton and University of Ulster (Northern Ireland) psychologist Richard Lynn, editor of *Mankind Quarterly,* a journal in which many of the scholars on whom Herrnstein and Murray rely have published their findings, despite the fact that mainstream anthropologists reject the magazine as racist. (One of Josef Mengele's mentors, Ottmar von Verschuer, a leading light of Nazi racial pseudoscience, served on the editorial board of *Mankind Quarterly* in the 1950s.)

Herrnstein and Murray devote two pages of the appendix of *The Bell Curve* to defending J. Philippe Rushton against charges that his work is pseudoscientific racism. The authors of *The Bell Curve* are not the only conservatives who have recently sought to convince the conservative reading public that Rushton is an eminent thinker whose views deserve respect. A few months before *The Bell Curve* was published, *National Review*—which in matters of race as well as immigration has moved far to the right in recent years—published a rave review of Rushton's book *Race, Evolution, and Behavior: A Life History Perspective.* The reviewer damns scientists skeptical of genetic origins for social differences among races, and praises Rushton because he "is willing to accept the results of his science." Here are the results of Rushton's "science," according to the puff piece in *National Review:* "On the average, according to the data Mr. Rushton reports, Orientals are more intelligent, have larger brains for their body size, have smaller genitalia, have less sex drive, are less fecund, work harder, and are more readily socialized than Caucasians; and Caucasians on average bear the same relationship to blacks." This is nothing but an updated version of nineteenth century white supremacy theory, with Caucasians representing the perfect balance between cunning, unemotional, and undersexed "Orientals" and dumb, emotional, and oversexed "Negroids." To these old stereotypes, Rushton adds the rhetoric of modern population biology, which distinguishes between animal species with "k-strategies" (few offspring and sustained parental involvement) and those with "r-strategies" (many offspring which receive little or no parental care). "Based on the data he reports," *National Review* readers learned, "Mr. Rushton observes that Orientals are the most k-strategizing of the human races, and blacks are the most r-strategizing." Translation: blacks have a *genetic imperative* to have more children than everyone else—and to neglect them. The source of this genetic imperative, according to Rushton, is the fact that blacks "evolved in Africa in an abundant but unpredictable environment that favored reproduction over nurturance. . . . The harsh environment of northeast Asia in which Orientals evolved favored more nurturing, socialization, and greater intellectual capacity. Caucasian evolution in Eurasia imposed intermediate pressures."[13] The work ethic of Korean immigrants, it appears, has less to do with Confucian culture or the economic opportunities for immigrant middlemen in modern cities than with a genetic predisposition to work long hours that evolved in reaction to the Ice Age. This kind of crackpot theorizing—at once ludicrous and despicable—is what Herrnstein and Murray felt compelled to defend at length, and which *National Review*'s editors have chosen to treat respectfully.

The connection of the Pioneer Fund with the conservative movement did not end with Murray and Herrnstein. From 1973 to 1977, a lawyer named Thomas Ellis served as a director of the Pioneer Fund. Ellis had opposed the 1954 Supreme Court school desegregation decision, writing that the goal of integration "is racial intermarriage and the disappearance of the Negro race by fusing into the white." In 1976, Ellis admitted distributing leaflets to Republican primary voters in North Carolina which claimed that President Gerald Ford was considering choosing a black as his running mate. In 1983, the Reagan administration was forced to withdraw Ellis's nomination to a position on the Board of International Broadcasting because of his connection with the

Pioneer Fund. Undaunted, Ellis drew attention again in 1990, when he helped to craft Senator Jesse Helms's successful campaign for the U.S. Senate against his black rival, Harvey Gantt. Ellis and other Helms advisors came up with the infamous ad showing the hands of a white person crumpling a rejection letter; the voice-over explained that a "minority" had gotten the job.

In the winter of 1995–96, Ellis surfaced once more—this time as a friend of Malcolm Forbes, Jr., and an "informal advisor" to the Forbes campaign.[14] Within weeks of the scandal surrounding Ellis's participation in the Forbes bid for the Republican presidential nomination, Larry Pratt of Gun Owners of America was forced to step down as a co-chairman of the Buchanan campaign following public revelations of his repeated association with leaders of white-supremacist organizations like Aryan Nations and the Christian Identity Movement. The prominence of extremists like Ellis and Pratt in the candidacies of Republican presidential contenders as different as Forbes and Buchanan showed that individuals with ties to the white racist fringe are somehow managing to acquire influential positions at the highest levels of Republican national politics.

All of this raises a question—why now? After all, the conservative foundation/think-tank/publishing network in which Murray and D'Souza work, and which has promoted their new works on race, has been around since the 1970s. During most of that period, the mainstream intellectual right was indifferent or hostile to arguments that conservative editors, think-tank presidents, and foundation officers now endorse or at least take seriously. It is not as though theories of black genetic inferiority or enthusiasm for eugenics were unknown in the 1970s and 1980s. Richard Herrnstein himself ignited a controversy in 1971 with an *Atlantic Monthly* article entitled "IQ" in which he introduced the claims that he later set forth with Murray in *The Bell Curve*. He and other eugenics theorists, including William Shockley and Arthur Jensen, were relegated to the far right—not just by liberals, but by mainstream conservatives.

In 1990, former Ku Klux Klan leader David Duke ran for the Republican nomination for the office of U.S. senator from Louisiana on a platform of eugenics. He argued for abolishing affirmative action and ending welfare. In addition, Duke proposed rewarding people with high IQs—a group that is disproportionately white—in order to encourage them to breed more. Anticipating Murray and Herrnstein, Duke argued, "Right now the government is doing the reverse. The low income, low IQ people [who] are least able to function in our society have the highest birthrates in our society. And so government is encouraging the least capable and least talented people that have the highest birthrate. I think that's disastrous. . . . That's against evolution."[15] These sentiments led the Republican party to denounce Duke in 1990. Four years later, most of the conservative intelligentsia, though not Republican politicians, embraced Murray and Herrnstein for making an almost identical argument (though their proposals differed—while Duke wanted to reward high-IQ whites for reproducing, Murray and Herrnstein proposed discouraging low-IQ blacks from having children, by cutting off welfare and making birth control more accessible to the poor).

The revival of eugenics theory by Murray and Herrnstein would not have been treated so respectfully had the Kemp wing of the conservative policy elite not been defeated in the early 1990s by the far right. In the late 1980s, Jack Kemp, joined by conservative political scientist James Q. Wilson, was a proponent of a conservative war on poverty. As housing secretary in the Bush administration, Kemp waged a campaign to increase spending on the poor, to the dismay of most of his former admirers on the right. In the early 1990s, I remember hearing conservatives muttering that Jack Kemp had gone soft on the blacks. The hero of the Kemp-Roth tax cuts had now become the advocate of government action to help the black poor. Jack Kemp had become too liberal. Kemp's solicitude toward the black poor, as much as anything else, doomed him as a possible Republican presidential contender in the social Darwinist 1990s.

When one considers the hardening of attitudes toward welfare and the black poor in the past few years, and the growing importance of right-wing white southerners in the Republican voting base and the Republican leadership alike, it is impossible to avoid concluding there is a connection. My argument is not that the southernization of the right influenced Murray and Herrnstein, or D'Souza or Brimelow, in writing their books, but rather that the transformation of ex-Democratic white southerners into the major constituency of conservative Republicans ensured a more fertile reception for their ideas than there would have been if the American right, in 1995, were primarily a movement of the North, the Midwest, and the Pacific coast. Race, sex, breeding, class—these are the classic themes, not of Taftian conservatism or the sunbelt right, but of Tidewater conservatism.

Whatever the cause, there can be no doubt that in the past several years, conservatives by their own statements have eroded the taboo against overt racism in public. Politicians and media personalities, along with right-wing intellectuals and journalists, have encouraged this trend. During the House debate over the Republican welfare bill in early 1995, Representative John L. Mica (R-Florida) held up a sign that read, "Do Not Feed the Alligators." He said, "We post these warnings because unnatural feeding and artificial care creates dependency." Representative Barbara Cubin (R-Wyoming) similarly compared welfare recipients (who in the public mind are all black) with wolves.[16] Rush Limbaugh's racist rhetoric is even more blatant. Limbaugh told a black caller, "Take that bone out of your nose and call me back." "The NAACP should have riot rehearsals," he announced on another occasion. "They should get a liquor store and practice robberies." Whenever Senator Carol Moseley-Braun's name is mentioned on his program, Limbaugh plays the theme song "Movin' On Up" from the all-black situation comedy "The Jeffersons." "Have you ever noticed how all newspaper composite pictures of wanted criminals resemble Jesse Jackson?" he asked listeners. (William Bennett, who has decried the loss of standards of decency and civility, calls Limbaugh "possibly our greatest living American" and "extremely sophisticated, extremely smart. . . . He's very serious intellectually".)

Not all conservative thinkers approve the adoption by the Republican party of Dixiecrat-style black-baiting and Murray-style eugenic theory. Tony Snow, a conservative columnist and former speechwriter for George Bush, recently criticized the anti-black attitudes of his fellow conservatives. Republicans, Snow writes, "have a tendency to treat black Americans as if they belonged to a separate species." By doing so, they are missing an opportunity to win black voters who are disillusioned with the Democratic party and conservative on many social issues.

In the tradition of Jack Kemp, Snow proposes an agenda of economic empowerment for inner-city blacks. According to Snow, "Congress should slash taxes and business regulations, especially on the mom-and-pop operations that create many of our jobs and can revitalize inner cities." In addition, Republicans "should take aim at employment barriers, such as the Davis-Bacon Act, which originally was drafted as a way of preventing black construction workers from competing for federal contracts, against white firms in the Northeast." Finally, a Republican Congress should offer "poor citizens educational choice. Public schools in most major cities stink. Low-income Americans must accept whatever education the system gives them. In the days of Jim Crow, conscientious black parents could create and insist upon good schools—and against all odds, they often succeeded in building halls of learning. Poor parents have no such recourse today. As a result, we have educational apartheid. . . ."[17]

As promising as they sound, Snow's Kempite proposals offer the promise of black advancement at the price of the certainty of lower wages. Consider his suggestion that the black poor will be helped by the same agenda of slashing taxes and business regulations that helps the white rich. Is this true? Precisely what regulations does Snow propose to slash? The "mom-and-pop operations" that Snow idealizes are far less likely than large firms to provide health coverage and pay decent wages to their workers. Does Snow believe that Congress should make it easier for small employers to refuse to provide health coverage for disproportionately black poor workers? What about the minimum wage? Already full-time employment at the minimum wage is insufficient to keep a worker out of poverty. Most conservatives, however, want the minimum wage to be maintained at the present level (while losing value as a result of inflation), or even abolished. How would permitting employers to pay entry-level workers three dollars an hour or fifty cents an hour help poor blacks to work their way out of poverty? Such a reform would actually reduce the benefits of effort, by plunging more full-time workers into poverty. With Republican friends like these, black Americans do not need enemies.

At least Snow does not mention another discredited idea of Jack Kemp's—"enterprise zones" in urban areas in which federal and state wage minimums and regulations are waived, in order to attract investors. The idea of enterprise zones was never convincing; mere economic incentives were unlikely to lure businesses to inner cities, as long as other costs—for example, those imposed by high crime rates— remained substantial. Perhaps it is just as well. If enterprise zones had taken root, then workers everywhere would have been hurt. Workers outside of the inner city would have seen their jobs relocated in ghettos where employers were allowed to pay substandard wage rates and forego health coverage for their employees. Some inner-city blacks might have gained employment—but at the cost of sacrificing the wages and benefits that all Americans have a right to expect. All of the optimistic rhetoric about enterprise zones could never disguise the fact that they were simply updated versions of an old institution where black workers labored and where legal standards were waived—the plantation.

The rest of Snow's recommendations are equally dubious. Indeed, when he discusses the Davis-Bacon Act and education, Snow rewrites history in a manner worthy of George Orwell's Big Brother. According to Snow, "the Davis-Bacon Act . . . was drafted as a way of preventing black construction workers from competing for federal contracts against white firms in the Northeast." Really? Perhaps Snow can name one or two black-owned construction firms in the segregated South that competed nationwide for construction contracts in the 1930s. In reality, the Davis-Bacon Act was passed during the New Deal era to prevent corporations from hiring nonunionized blacks as strikebreakers to bust unions. Inasmuch as most unions were segregated, the act can be criticized as racist, and it undoubtedly reduced employment for blacks who did not belong to unions. But since most blacks then worked in the nonunionized service sector and agriculture, the idea that black workers would have been better off in general if it had never been passed is ludicrous. At most, black workers would have been allowed to compete with white workers for low-paying jobs with firms that had defeated efforts at unionization. What is more, the fact that unionized labor today is disproportionately black means that efforts to reduce union power, like repealing Davis-Bacon, will hurt more black workers than they help.

In his discussion of education, Snow tortures history until it confesses what conservatives want to hear. If Snow is to be believed, the era of segregation was a veritable Golden Age of black education: "In the days of Jim Crow, conscientious black parents could create and insist upon good schools. . . ." Today, however, we "have educational apartheid." What, if not "educational apartheid," does Snow call the old Jim Crow system of "separate-but-equal" white and black schools? That the separate schools were not equal is attested by the memory of living individuals, to say nothing of documentation of different rates of spending on white and black schools by segregated states and the segregated District of Columbia. As for school choice, Snow implies that the segregated educational system of Jim Crow granted black parents more choice than they have in today's integrated public school system. Under Jim Crow, however, blacks were not permitted to choose between schools; they were assigned by state governments to all-black neighborhood or city schools.

Snow is not entirely incorrect to link the school-choice movement with Jim Crow. As I have noted earlier, the enthusiasm of conservatives for school choice began in the 1950s, as a response to court-ordered de-segregation. Conservatives supported school choice as a way of empow-ering white parents to send their children to all-white schools. In Alabama, for example, the response of conservatives in the legislature to *Brown v. Board of Education* was to promote a "school placement bill," an ancestor of today's conservative tuition voucher schemes. Alabama Governor "Big Jim" Folsom, a populist who was not a racist—"I just never did get all excited about our colored brothers . . . I have found them to be good citizens"—was quick to point out that tuition voucher schemes would not only permit whites to avoid contact with blacks, but would also subsidize rich parents who wanted to insulate their children from middle-class and poor children. Folsom turned the school-voucher debate from a conservative wedge issue into a populist class-war issue: "I wouldn't want to sign a bill that would let rich folks send their kids all to one school and the poor folks to another school."[18]

Folsom was more honest about the consequences of school choice than Snow or the other contemporary conservatives who support them. If school vouchers were not accompanied by government-imposed tu-ition cost controls, then expensive private schools would simply raise their tuitions by the amount of the voucher. If the voucher were worth $6000, then a prep school that today charges $10,000 would be tempted to raise its tuition to $16,000, maintaining the same exclusive, upper-middle-class and wealthy student body as before, at no greater cost to affluent parents—but at a much greater cost to taxpayers in general. Elite private schools, of course, would accept the occasional token poor student. Under a voucher system, though, most poor black parents would only have a choice between schools for poor children—in prac-tice, perhaps a choice between two or three schools, if there were any choice at all. Most of the new private schools that would spring up would compete for middle-class and wealthy youngsters. At the same time, black parents, if they paid taxes, would be forced to subsidize school vouchers for affluent children attending schools segregated by income.

The "pro-black" conservatism suggested by Tony Snow would be al-most as harmful to black Americans as the harshest anti-black conser-vatism. The truth is that no conservatives, white or black, have the best interests of the black poor and working classes at heart. If they did, then conservatives would support measures to raise entry-level wages, instead of to lower them; to expand health coverage, instead of to allow it to be cut back; and to strengthen disproportionately black unions, instead of to weaken them. Inner-city public schools, as I noted in a previous chapter, are a disaster—but their problems are largely a result of subcultural pathologies which teachers and principals have little power to remedy, and tax revolts by white suburbanites that have led to inadequate financing of majority-nonwhite schools. In most industrial democracies, public schools are financed out of general tax revenues by the central government. Only in the United States is the education of the next generation financed primarily by local property taxes—the very taxes that are most likely to inspire tax revolts. Equalization of school funding by the states or the federal government would not solve all of the problems of inner-city schools, but it would do more for the inner-city poor than vouchers permitting them to trade third-rate public schools in the ghetto for third-rate private schools in the ghetto. (It says a lot about the southernization of the right that the chief conservative proposal for black education is school choice, a reform invented by southern white racists to replace formal legal segregation with informal economic segregation.)

The southern-style racial politics of the right are being given a boost by the nationalization of "southern" racial patterns resulting from the immigration of blacks to large urban areas in every region of the country and the massive immigration from Latin America and Asia that followed reforms in immigration policy in the 1960s. In the past, the white Protestant majority in each region faced different "others": European Catholic immigrants in the North and Midwest, blacks in the South, Mexican-Americans along the border, East Asians in California. Today in metropolitan areas nationwide one tends to find the same pattern—blacks, Hispanics, and Asian-Americans in the inner city and virtually all-white suburbs beyond.

The parallel with the South can be extended. In the New South of 1875–1965, as in the antebellum Old South, the most significant geographic division was between the heavily black, but white-elite-dominated tidewater and the middling-to-poor white upcountry or Piedmont. A similar division seems to be emerging on a nationwide scale in the United States, with a division between the "brown belt" metropolitan areas of the coasts and lowlands, where both minorities and rich whites are concentrated, and the states of the Rocky Mountains and the northern interior, where there are few nonwhites and fewer extremes of wealth and poverty (all of the most "typical" American cities—with Tulsa, Oklahoma, in the lead—are found in the American upcountry). The lowland brown belt itself is divided between minority-dominated inner cities and homogenous white suburban and exurban rings.

While most of the new nonwhite immigration is concentrated in a few coastal states like California, Texas, and New York, there is an ongoing white exodus from those same states. This raises the disturbing possibility that the old southern Bourbon strategy of uniting affluent, outnumbered whites in the lowland black belt with poor and middling whites in the lily-white southern upcountry in a coalition against lowland black majorities might be emulated, in the twenty-first century, by a national Bourbon strategy. Outnumbered members of the wealthy white overclass in the suburbs of coastal states like California, Texas, and Florida might find allies against local nonwhite majorities in middle-income whites in the Rocky Mountain and Plains states whose political power is grossly exaggerated by the malapportionment of the U.S. Senate. Instead of the nationalization of the South, we may be witnessing the southernization of the nation.

I began this chapter by suggesting that southern-style black-baiting, in both its crude forms and in the genteel form of pseudoscientific racist scholarship, serves the interests of the white corporate-professional overclass by exploiting the hostility of white voters toward the black poor and nonwhite immigrants. For many years, during my association with the conservative movement, I resisted this explanation; it seemed too trite, too reductionist. That was before two of the leading members of the foundation-funded "counterintelligentsia" organized in the 1970s by William Simon and Irving Kristol sought to revive eugenic theory and long-forgotten apologies for Jim Crow, and before a lurid and deeply misleading attack on nonwhite immigration was published by a senior editor at *Forbes,* a magazine that advertises itself proudly as a "capitalist tool." It was also before the editors of *National Review* and *Commentary,* rallying to the defense of Murray and Herrnstein, gave the appearance of credibility to claims that opponents of pseudoscientific racism are nothing more than liberals frightened of daring scholarship.

Perhaps I and other former conservatives who have been astonished at the revival of undisguised pseudoscientific racism on the right in the past several years should not have been surprised. At a time when the conservative economic elite and populist conservatives disagree over economic issues like free trade, the symbolic denigration of black Americans (and sometimes other nonwhites) can unite the conservative coalition. The new racism appeals to populist conservative politicians and activists because it can win white working-class and middle-class votes. At the same time, it appeals to business-class conservatives because it provides what appears to be a scholarly rationale for slashing funding for entitlements and education directed at the black poor (and the white and Hispanic poor as well)—namely, the rationale that welfare merely encourages genetically inferior people to breed, and that the poor are too stupid to benefit much from schooling. In a somewhat similar fashion, the formula of white supremacy, ritually repeated at elections, bound together the white Bourbon ruling class and the exploited white masses in the South.

It is a grim prospect. If the conservatives manage to consolidate a white majority or plurality based on race-baiting, pseudoscientific race theory and eugenics (expressed, perhaps, in coded terms), then George Wallace will turn out to have been prescient when he declared, "Alabama has not joined the nation. The nation has joined Alabama!"

Chapter 9

The Confederate Theory
of the Constitution

For generations, American conservatives have presented themselves as the valiant defenders of the U.S. Constitution, the faithful guardians of the sacred charter of American liberty against liberal misinterpretation and subversion. At the same time, they have shown an increasing willingness to tinker with the document in the pursuit of short-term partisan goals. Almost all of the proposals for constitutional amendments that have gained attention and support in recent years have come from the right. Conservatives have sought to amend the constitution to ban abortion and impose term limits. They have even sought to write a prohibition of flag-burning into the federal charter of government.

Much of this is nothing more than opportunistic grandstanding, designed to appeal to single-issue groups for short-term political gain. Indeed, it is difficult to talk about a single conservative theory of the Constitution, because the theory changes, from decade to decade and even from year to year, depending on the electoral fortunes and short-term plans of the Republican party. During the 1950s, conservative thinkers like James Burnham and Willmoore Kendall defended the prerogatives of Congress and denounced the power-grabbing presidency. Since the 1970s, however, conservatives have tended to complain that an "imperial Congress" (to use the term of a Heritage Foundation book) is endangering liberty in America by sapping the power of an enfeebled executive. The reason for this complete reversal of conservative attitudes toward the executive and legislative branches is obvious. During the New Deal era from FDR to LBJ, Congresses controlled by the "conservative coalition" of right-wing southern Democrats and northern Republicans tended to be much further to the right than liberal or moderate presidents. Since the era of Republican presidential hegemony began with Richard Nixon's election in 1968, however, the White House has been more hospitable to conservatism than Congress. If Republicans hold on to their new majority in Congress for any length of time, we can expect a revival of long-forgotten conservative defenses of a strong legislative branch. This is likely to be the case, even during the tenure of Republican presidents, who will be tempted to move toward the center in order to ensure their reelection. In a united Republican government, the most diehard conservatives are likely to be found in Congress, not in the White House—and, within Congress, in the House, rather than the Senate (senators, like presidents, have to be more moderate to appeal to diverse groups in their large constituencies).

For all the opportunism and inconsistency that characterizes conservative constitutional thought, present-day conservatives do tend to share a distinct and identifiable theory of the Constitution. The constitutional theory of the Republican right is not Republican in its origins; it is inherited, like so much else in today's Republican party, from the conservative Democrats of the South. The tradition that informs modern conservative thinking is the Jeffersonian-Jacksonian tradition of the southern and western states. The basic themes in this tradition are animus against government at all levels, states' rights, a cult of firearms linked to a supposed right of armed insurrection, and support for a variety of political gimmicks like term limits that give the illusion, though not the reality, of popular democracy.

The Republican right, then, does have a venerable and consistent theory of the constitution. It just happens to be the Confederate theory.

In this chapter, I examine the implications of the southern states' rights theory that has become the constitutional orthodoxy of the conservative movement. Conservative proposals for decentralization range from the moderate (the combination of state and local discretion with federal funding) to the seditious (the alleged right of anti-government radicals to form private storm trooper units and to amass weapons to use against law enforcement officers). Whether in its mild or extreme form, the Confederate theory of the Constitution promises to do as much harm to the twenty-first century United States as a whole as it has done to the South for two centuries.

Throughout American history, there have been two rival schools of constitutional thought—the Federalist or Hamiltonian theory, and the Anti-Federalist or Jeffersonian theory. The Federalist theory was passed on by the Federalists to early nineteenth-century National Republicans like John Quincy Adams, Whigs like Daniel Webster and Henry Clay, and Republicans like Abraham Lincoln. By way of early twentieth century Republican Progressives like Theodore Roosevelt and Herbert Croly, the Federalist theory, in modified form, was bequeathed to contemporary liberalism and what Dwight Eisenhower called "modern Republicanism." The Anti-Federalist theory—originally the philosophy of opponents of the U.S. Constitution who preferred the weaker Articles of Confederation—was handed down from Thomas Jefferson to Andrew Jackson. As Jackson's strong stand against the possibility of South Carolina's secession demonstrated, the Anti-Federalist tradition can be compatible with Unionism, of a minimal sort; the Confederates, though, drew the conclusion that secession was among the rights specified by the doctrine of states' rights, and on the basis of Anti-Federalist theory alone it is hard to disagree. In the twentieth century states' rights again became the center of Anti-Federalist thinking, as white southern segregationists tried to invoke the doctrine to resist federal efforts to defend the civil rights of black southerners.

Both the Federalist and the Anti-Federalist traditions have equal claim to being "conservative." The claim of the Federalist tradition is somewhat stronger; from the eighteenth to the twentieth century, the Hamiltonian tradition was identified with the socially conservative, propertied, nationally minded financial and industrial elite, while the more extreme forms of Jeffersonianism and Jacksonianism were espoused by agrarian and urban radicals. The term "conservative" in connection with a national political tendency was first used by Daniel Webster, who described the philosophy of the Whig party as "national conservatism" and opposed it to the radicalism of southwestern followers of Andrew Jackson. Only in the twentieth century, when Progressives like Herbert Croly called for wedding national programs of social-democratic reform to the older pro-business nationalism of the Federalists, Whigs, and Republicans, did the elitist Hamiltonian tradition become popular (even as it remained hostile to populism of the Jefferson-Jackson sort).

The Anti-Federalist theory of the Constitution has a much weaker claim to representing "conservatism" in an American context. This tradition has tended to attract Americans who think of themselves as radicals or populists rather than conservatives, in the sense in which Daniel Webster or Edmund Burke used the term. From the very beginning, members of this school have seen themselves as the champions of a doctrine of radical liberty that emerged during the American Revolution. No sooner had the tyranny of the British government been thrown off than new, comparable threats to American liberty appeared at home—or so Anti-Federalists have consistently claimed. At times the new tyranny, the successor to King George, has been identified with the federal Constitution (which most Anti-Federalists accused of creating an overly centralized, repressive state); the administration of George Washington; the First and Second Banks of the United States; the Republican party under Abraham Lincoln; the Federal Reserve; the New Deal; and the federal judiciary in its role of vindicator of civil rights. From the eighteenth century to the present, the Anti-Federalist fear of imminent tyranny (always mistaken, so far) has been the same, and so has the Anti-Federalist solution—immediate and radical reduction of government functions, decentralization of power to the states and local communities, the rotation of officeholders by term limits (for elected officials) and the spoils system (for appointees), and the adoption of versions of direct democracy including initiative and referendum and provisions for the "recall" of politicians between elections.

The Federalist theory, as I noted above, has its roots in northern and eastern soil, whereas the Anti-Federalist theory has tended to flourish in the swamps and prairies of the South and the West. The two traditions have left their distinctive mark on state constitutions in the two regions. The constitutions of the northern states tend to provide for strong executives, and to be difficult to amend. Southern and western state constitutions, by contrast, tend to provide for weak, figurehead governors (whose powers of appointment are limited by direct election of dozens of state executive and judicial officers). State constitutions in the South and West, in addition, are often easy to amend, with the result that most are loaded down by dozens or even hundreds of amendments. In California, where populist reformers in the early twentieth century took the logic of Anti-Federalist direct democracy to an extreme, voters must decide the fate of numerous ballot initiatives in every election, many of them dealing with complex and controversial issues that would better be handled by a deliberative legislature. (The tax-revolt initiative Proposition 13 of 1978 or the 1994 Proposition 187 on immigration reform fall into this category.)

For a brief time after World War II, it appeared that the Anti-Federalist theory of the constitution was dead, at least in national politics. Under Eisenhower, the Republican party had appeared to reconcile itself with the basic reforms of the New Deal Democrats. Eisenhower, firmly if reluctantly, sent federal troops into the South to protect the civil rights of black southerners for the first time since Reconstruction. In accepting the need for a strong national government and exercising federal power on behalf of individual liberty as well as interstate commerce, Eisenhower and other modern Republicans were simply returning to the older tradition of the party of Lincoln.

An observer in 1965, witnessing the collapse of the southern segregationist Democrats, might have concluded that the northern theory of the Constitution had prevailed over the southern theory at last. Sadly, this was not to be. The children and grandchildren of the southern segregationists—in some cases, segregationists like Strom Thurmond—themselves moved into the post-Eisenhower Republican party and took it over. The new white southern Republicans in Washington have brought with them in their carpetbags the constitutional theories of Thomas Jefferson and Andrew Jackson, of John C. Calhoun and Jefferson Davis. Now that the southern-dominated Republicans control Congress—and may soon control the presidency and the judiciary—the Confederate theory of the United States Constitution is enjoying a renaissance that no one could have predicted only a few decades ago.

The most striking example of the revival of southern constitutional ideas comes not from the political arena but from the Supreme Court, which as a result of appointments by Republican presidents since Nixon has a center-right, though not extremely conservative, majority. The radical right was disappointed by the Supreme Court's striking down of state-imposed term limits on U.S. representatives in *U.S. Term Limits v. Thornton* (1995). Although conservatives were disappointed by the majority's opinion that states could not add to the qualifications for members of the U.S. Congress enumerated by the federal Constitution, the Republican right found some consolation in the fact that four justices—Rehnquist, Thomas, O'Connor, and Scalia—dissented. The dissenting opinion by Justice Thomas offered even more hope to the extreme right, by showing a rehabilitation of the states' rights theory of the Confederates and the segregationist Dixiecrats.

The majority was clearly right, and the dissent clearly wrong, in holding that the qualifications prescribed by the Constitution for U.S.

representatives—they must be over twenty-five, citizens of the United States for at least seven years, and inhabitants of the states in which their districts are found—and for U.S. senators—they must be over thirty, citizens of the United States for at least nine years, and citizens of the states they represent—are the *only* legal qualifications. One of the oldest rules of legal construction is *inclusio unis, exclusio alterius*—if the drafters of a law or constitution include some requirements, they must be assumed to have considered and rejected others. To argue, as Thomas does, that "the Constitution is simply silent on this question" of eligibility requirements for representatives and senators is simply not to read the Constitution.

In attempting to argue that the states can add to the eligibility requirements imposed by the federal Constitution, Thomas goes so far as to resurrect the old southern theory of the Constitution as a "compact" of "sovereign states." Thomas writes: "The ultimate source of the Constitution's authority is the consent of the people of each individual state, not the consent of the undifferentiated people as a whole." This throws out the theory of *The Federalist Papers,* which holds that there is an undifferentiated American "people," which, in matters like ratifying the federal Constitution, is divided along state lines merely as a matter of convenience. Thomas also rejects the constitutional theory of Abraham Lincoln, who, with others in the Federalist-Whig tradition, argued that the authorization of inhabitants of the former British colonies to form states by the Continental Congress proved that the national government actually preceded the state governments in time. The gravest weakness of Thomas's attempt to revive the compact theory is the Fourteenth Amendment, which established federal citizenship for the first time, putting Americans in a direct relationship to the national government. Even if the Constitution before the Civil War was not based on the theory of a single American people, rather than as many "peoples" as there are states, the Civil War amendments should have finished off the compact theory for good.

The southernization of the right has opened the debate once again, by making support for "states' rights" a litmus test for conservative Republican appointees to the highest court in the land. Though they belong to the party of Lincoln, Rehnquist, Thomas, Scalia, and O'Connor are promoting the constitutional theory of Jefferson Davis and John C. Calhoun.

The states' rights theory leads conservatives to support the malapportionment of the United States Senate as a necessary evil—perhaps even a positive good. Today a majority of the American people reside in a minority of states. Half of the American people live in the eight most populous states—California, Texas, New York, Florida, Pennsylvania, Illinois, Ohio, and Michigan (in order of diminishing population). Added together, the citizens of the Big Eight make up roughly 137 million people—slightly over one-half of the U.S. total (again, for 1994) of 260,340,900. The twelve largest states have roughly 166 million inhabitants—about sixty-five percent of the people in the United States as a whole. The populations of the states vary enormously, from the largest, California (31,430,697 in 1994, the latest date for which figures are available) to the smallest, Wyoming (475,981).

The disparities in population between the states were far from this extreme when the framers of the Constitution assigned each state two senators. In 1790, two years after the Constitution went into effect, the difference in population between the largest state, Virginia (748,000) and the smallest, Delaware (59,000) was of the ratio 12:1; today the difference in population between California and Wyoming is 66:1. What is more, in the early years of the republic the populations of the smallest three-quarters of the states would have added up to more than half of the nationwide total. Even today, if the United States were limited to the original thirteen states—Connecticut, Delaware, Georgia, Maryland, Massachusetts, New Hampshire, New Jersey, New York, North Carolina, Pennsylvania, Rhode Island, South Carolina, and Virginia—the population of the ten smallest states would add up to well more than half of the national population.

The requirement that amendments be ratified by three-quarters of the states initially guaranteed that a numerical majority of American voters, through their representatives, would approve them. This is no longer the case. Patrick Buchanan has proposed to change the Constitution to allow any single state, rather than Congress, to initiate constitutional amendments. This reform, combined with the existing constitutional provision allowing two-thirds of the state legislatures to ratify an amendment, would permit a numerical minority, resident in a majority of thinly populated states, to amend the Constitution against the wishes of an overwhelming majority of Americans. This is not what the Founders had in mind. The Founders were not prophets—they did not foresee the addition of thinly populated prairie and Rocky Mountain states, or the growth in metropolitan population density in a few states—but neither were they proponents of minority rule. They were framing a government to protect legitimate minority rights, but they had no intention of establishing a government permitting overrepresented minorities to lord it over majorities.*

Conservative arguments for states' rights are not limited to constitutional theory. There are practical arguments as well. One is that individual liberty is best protected in a system of strong states and a weak central government. The other is that states with a lot of leeway to experiment in public policy can be centers of innovation—"laboratories of democracy."

The first argument—states' rights and freedom go together—is not supported by either American history or the history of other countries. In the United States, of course, the state governments, particularly those in the South, have tended to be the greatest enemies of personal freedom, in matters like civil rights and sexual privacy. The federal government and individual liberty, in the United States, have usually been synonymous. Even the grossest violations of civil and human rights by the federal government—the removal of the Cherokees, the internment of Japanese-Americans and Japanese citizens during World War II—were collaborative efforts between states (Georgia, California) and the federal government, in which the initiative for the atrocities came from the state governments.

It might be argued that states' rights has been too tangled up with white oppression of blacks, Indians, and Asians for there to be a fair test of the idea of federalism. In a post-racist United States, perhaps the states might defend individual liberty against federal oppression, rather than serve as fences within which local majorities can tyrannize local minorities. Obviously it would require another two centuries to test this

---

* Republican presidential candidate and *Forbes* publisher Malcolm Forbes, Jr. has proposed that Canada adopt a senate as malapportioned as our own. In contrast to Canada, Forbes has written, "the U.S. does have an upper chamber where Wyoming, our least populous state, has the same number of votes as does California, our most populous state. Our federalism better protects minority interests. . . . The answer for Canada is simple. Create a senate that has equal powers in its House of Commons, that has equal representatives from each province and that is directly elected." The reason for Forbes's interest in Canadian affairs is his belief that Canada's western provinces, if overrepresented in a new U.S.-style senate, might force the adoption of "a vigorous regime of massive tax cuts and a Gingrich-Kasich approach to reining in spending." Malcolm S. Forbes, Jr., "Whither Canada?" *Forbes,* November 20, 1995, p. 23.

notion (assuming what seems doubtful, which is that racism and other forms of bigotry are insignificant in the United States). A test of a sort, though, is provided by a comparison of other modern liberal democracies, in the past century—some unitary states, others federal states. There appears to be no correlation at all between federalism, personal freedom, and stable democracy. After World War I, Britain and France—both unitary states—remained democratic, while the federal democracy of the Weimar Republic succumbed to National Socialism. Within the English-speaking world itself, there is little or no difference, with respect to liberty and democracy, between centralized Britain and federal Canada and Australia. Freedom and democracy, it seems, have more to do with a deeply rooted and vigorous liberal democratic culture than with any particular distribution of power between central and subordinate governments.

The practical argument for strong federalism that sees the states as "laboratories of democracy" is just as dubious. In the United States, for two centuries, the state governments have been anything but innovative. Consider the design of democratic institutions. Democracies around the world today come in a variety of forms. Most modern democracies are parliamentary regimes; a minority (most of them in Latin America) are based, like the United States, on the separation of powers between a legislature and an independently elected executive. Electoral systems are equally diverse. While the United States and a few other English-speaking countries, including Britain, retain the plurality or winner-take-all electoral system, most contemporary democracies elect their legislators by means of some version of proportional representation. Among countries with bicameral legislatures, there is great diversity with regard to the powers of upper houses and the criteria by which their members are selected. Judicial systems, too, vary dramatically among today's democratic countries. Finally, there is great variation in the powers of central governments—some democracies, like Britain and France, are unitary states, while others, like the United States, Germany, Canada, and Switzerland, are federal.

If the individual American states really were laboratories of democracy, then one would expect the diversity of political structures within the United States to equal the diversity found around the democratic world. Instead, in two hundred years scarcely any of the states has significantly modified the forms inherited from the colonial and founding eras. Not one American state has rewritten its constitution to adopt a parliamentary form of government, like those of the Canadian and Australian states. Why? Why must every state government, with its executive, house and senate, be a miniature facsimile of the federal government (itself a slightly altered version of the late-eighteenth-century New York state constitution)? Only one state in the Union, Nebraska, has a unicameral legislature—and this slight departure from the cookie-cutter pattern of the state constitutions is considered rather exotic. There is somewhat greater variation when it comes to state judicial systems—many states, for example, have separate courts of criminal and civil appeals—and some states, but not others, permit initiatives and referenda—but these interstate differences are still extremely minor. Not one state has even attempted to replace the eighteenth-century English plurality system of voting with proportional representation, though the latter has been the norm in western democracies for generations. Two hundred years of constitutional experiment in fifty democratic laboratories—and the result is dreary redundancy.

When all other arguments fail, conservative states' rights theorists resort to a populist argument: the state governments are "closer to the people." It is difficult to understand the argument that state officials are "closer" to the people, in anything other than a geographic sense. After all, the same electorate votes for state legislators and members of the U.S. Congress. What is more, there tends to be higher turnout for federal elections, particularly presidential elections, than for state and local elections. That being the case, federal elected politicians would seem to have *more* democratic legitimacy than governors and statehouse legislators.

The idea that the states are "laboratories of democracy," then, finds little support in history. On the other hand, there is abundant data to support the most compelling argument against a high degree of decentralization in public policy, which holds that national and multinational corporations will play one state against another, forcing all of the states in a "race to the bottom" in the areas of taxation, regulation, and spending for public education and public amenities.

One of the purposes of the federal Constitution was to prevent states from engaging in economic warfare with each other. Today, though, one of the chief goals of governors and state legislatures is devising ways to lure business from other states in the Union. One method, adopted by many states, has been offering "tax abatements" to businesses that build new plants or offices in the state. In some cases, this has resulted in the creation of new jobs. But in many cases, the economic bonanza has not occurred, and the only lasting result of attempts to bribe corporations to relocate has been to shift the burden of taxes from corporations to ordinary citizens. Nationwide, the corporate share of local property taxes has plunged from about 45 percent in 1957 to about 16 percent in 1990.[1] In Louisiana, thanks to a 1974 constitutional change that exempted corporations investing in manufacturing from property taxes for ten years, companies have paid $2.5 billion less than they would have— a sum that amounts to an annual loss of $1.5 million to each public school in Louisiana. Thanks to state favoritism to corporations, Louisiana also lost around $1.5 billion that might have gone to public services in the 1980s.[2] During the same period the city of New Orleans, lacking the funds to repair the streets, began an "Adopt-a-Pothole" program, in which the city would rent municipal crews to residents who raised the money themselves to pay for holes in the road.

The perverse incentives of economic federalism led neighboring states to try to undermine one another, rather than cooperate in regional projects to rebuild the infrastructure, create jobs, and reduce pollution. According to one estimate, New York, New Jersey, and Connecticut lose $1 billion a year in the form of tax incentives seeking to lure businesses away from their neighbors or to keep them at home.[3] The only beneficiaries of federalism run amok are large corporations that can use a threat to relocate as leverage in bargaining with state legislatures. Even big business will benefit from excessive political fragmentation only in the short run. For the American business community as a whole will suffer in the twenty-first century if the decision of state governments to cut funding for public programs in order to pay for bribes to corporations results in an inadequately educated work force, crumbling transportation systems, and unlivable cities.

Despite the dubious results of federalism, dispersing federal functions to the states has become one of the key elements of conservative "reform." If the devolution of authority were combined with the cutoff of federal funding, this would represent a genuine, if misguided, commitment to a small-government philosophy. But most conservative "decentralists" have something else in mind: maintaining centralized federal funding, but allowing state and local governments (or, alternately, institutions of "civil society" like churches) to decide how the federal funds are to be used.

The idea of allowing local political bodies, or local private-sector groups, to decide how to use allocated federal funds is neither new nor conservative. Although it is now offered as an alternative to the much-maligned Great Society, the combination of federal funding with local discretion was the key element of Lyndon Johnson's creative federalism, which Richard Nixon repackaged as the new federalism. In the late 1960s and early 1970s, the idea of showering states, localities, and community groups with federal dollars which they could then use as they saw fit appealed to both Democrats and Republicans in Congress who wanted to spread largesse to their supporters while avoiding bitter fights over particular programs. "With general revenue sharing," political scientists Matthew A. Crenson and Francis E. Rourke observe, "the substantive objectives of the federal government had finally disappeared almost entirely. The legislation lacked even the perfunctory statement of purpose that customarily served as a preamble for almost all bills introduced in Congress. . . . Nevertheless, [there was] a broad coalition to support the principle that quarterly checks should be sent to the nation's 39,000 subnational governments."[4]

One of the few good things that the Reagan administration did in domestic policy was to abolish revenue sharing. Ironically, advocates of a new version of revenue sharing like Republican presidential contender Lamar Alexander are attempting to repeal one of the major accomplishments of the Reagan administration—and to re-create one of the legacies of Lyndon Johnson.

In doing so, they are simply masking big-government liberalism as small-government conservatism. If these "decentralizers" were sincere, they would insist on abolishing federal programs and entitlements altogether, not merely shifting the locus of decision making to states, localities, and private groups while maintaining a flow of dollars from Washington. Genuine states' rights radicals would insist that money spent in a state be raised entirely within that state. The more Republican schemes for decentralizing federal programs are examined, the less they look like a revolution and the more they look like a conservative version of Great Society liberalism—a kind of interest-group conservatism. "To the victor belong the spoils," was the old Jacksonian motto. Having gained control of the federal apparatus, conservatives may use it to tax their enemies and reward their constituents. Federal funds for antipoverty programs, which paid for local left-liberal "community action" offices under interest-group liberalism, may pay for church-based "civil society" programs under interest-group conservatism. The basic principle—using the taxing power of the federal government in the interests of patronage—is the same in either case. Like Johnson's creative federalism and Nixon's new federalism, this sort of centrally funded federalism is not federalism at all.

Conservatives can make a plausible-sounding case that state and local officials, or even the leaders of nongovernmental private community groups, are better judges than legislators and bureaucrats in Washington of how to use federal funds to combat crime, or reduce poverty, or improve education in their areas. But they leave two other questions unanswered: why should federal money raised by taxing Californians be spent in Mississippi at all? And, if Californians are to be taxed to pay for schools, police, and antipoverty programs in Mississippi, why should the representatives of California in the House and the Senate be denied any say in how the California contribution is to be spent in Mississippi? The conservative case for decentralization sounds appealing, when it is framed in terms of getting government bureaucrats in Washington off the backs of policymakers in Sacramento and San Diego. When it is described as a scheme for sending blank checks from taxpayers in California to politicians or churches in Mississippi, by way of Washington, with no strings attached, the idea suddenly loses much of its appeal.

Many on the right recognize that granting the states more say in federal programs is hardly a return to strong federalism. Indeed, the most radical Jeffersonians and Jacksonians are against government, period—state and local government as well as federal government. Theorists of states' rights in the Jefferson-Jackson Anti-Federalist tradition have never satisfactorily answered the question of why state governments are necessarily a lesser threat to individual liberty than the federal government. On this point, the view of the far right is more consistent, if more radical: no government is to be trusted, not even the city council. Liberty can only be safeguarded by individuals—armed individuals, that is.

Central to the ideology of the far-right paramilitary groups whom the Republican right now courts is the idea that the Constitution forbids any significant limits, by the federal government *or* the state governments, on the right of individuals to amass artillery for the purposes of personal recreation and, if necessary, armed insurrection. On the face of it, this seems improbable. If it were true, then the Founding Fathers would have created a government without the means for its own defense. The federal government—and the state governments, as well—would have no recourse as private armies mobilized on U.S. soil and equipped themselves with an arsenal permitting them to overthrow the state. "The Constitution," Justice Robert Jackson once famously observed, "is not a suicide pact." If the conservatives who argue against the constitutionality (as opposed to the wisdom) of gun control are correct, the Constitution is indeed a suicide pact.

No one reading the Second Amendment without preconceptions would be likely to conclude that it authorizes private, extra-governmental, paramilitary militias: "A well-regulated militia being necessary to the security of a free State, the right of the people to keep and bear arms shall not be infringed." According to established rules of constitutional construction, constitutional provisions must be read on the assumption that they are consistent and coherent. The phrase about the "well-regulated militia," therefore, cannot be dismissed as meaningless verbiage; rather, it must be the basis for any plausible reading of the constitutional right to bear arms.

Conservatives usually claim to support "strict construction" of the Constitution according to its "original intent," ascertained with the help of evidence like debates and usage at the time a provision was drafted and ratified. In the case of the Second Amendment, the evidence as to the intent of the Founders is so abundant that there is little room for disagreement about its meaning. Any doubt as to the purpose of the clause is cleared up by examination of the first draft, which read: "The right of the people to keep and bear arms shall not be infringed; a well armed and well regulated militia being the best security of a free country; but no person religiously scrupulous of bearing arms shall be compelled to render military service in person." As Garry Wills points out, "bear arms" in this context clearly refers to military service; the clause cannot mean "that Quakers, who oppose war, will not be allowed to use guns for hunting or sport."[5] The very phrase "bear arms" is a military term (and was in the eighteenth and nineteenth century—Daniel Boone and Davy Crockett would have been laughed at if they had described themselves "bearing arms" on expeditions to hunt bears or squirrels). The right of the people to "keep" arms referred to the right of the people as an organized polity—that is, the state governments—to maintain arsenals for the use of state militias. It was not intended to give every individual, whether he belonged to a state militia or not, the right to amass assault weapons, bazookas, hand grenades, and land mines in his basement or his front hall closet.

The notion that the Second Amendment prevents any government limits on private ownership of weapons is alien to the practice as well as to the theory of American constitutionalism. Before the Civil War, many of the states banned gun ownership on the basis of race. In the late nineteenth century American conservatives were so fearful of the prospect of armed uprisings by organized labor (Secretary of State John Hay wrote a novel on the theme) that they built fortified National Guard armories in strategic locations. The state militias were seen as checks on abuses by a federal standing army, no doubt; but the Second Amendment does not envision armed individuals, alone or in unofficial paramilitary units, as checks on the state militias. What is more, the contrast between the state militias and the standing army is easily exaggerated; the Constitution makes it possible for the federal government to nationalize the National Guard, as has been done effectively since the early twentieth century.

The Second Amendment prevents the federal government from completely abolishing official state militias—nothing more, nothing less. Nothing in the Constitution prevents the federal or state governments, or both, from outlawing the formation of storm trooper squads on U.S. soil and limiting gun ownership to members of the National Guard. Members of right-wing paramilitary militias, of course, might claim a "natural right of revolution," of the sort invoked by the American patriots in 1776 (and by the Confederates in 1860–61). There is no *constitutional* right to revolution, however. There is, of course, a provision for instances where armed bands amass weapons and attempt to overthrow the federal government. The Constitution permits the death penalty for treason.

On February 23, 1983, on a road in North Dakota, federal authorities stopped Gordon Kahl, a member of the far-right Posse Comitatus who had served time in jail for tax evasion and had refused to pay taxes or obey his probation rules. Kahl, his son, and another passenger engaged in a firefight, in which Kahl's son (whose gun had been fired) was wounded. Kahl shot and killed two deputy U.S. marshals, and left two others wounded on the ground. After driving his son to a doctor, he vanished. A few months later, surrounded in a house in the Ozark mountains, Kahl shot a county sheriff and was then shot and killed, his body burned in the blazing house.[6]

Hundreds of far-right extremists attended the funeral of a man they considered a patriot. But the Republican leadership in Washington did not make the death of Gordon Kahl a cause célèbre. The Senate, then under the control of the Republican party, did not hold hearings into the death of Gordon Kahl. Robert Michel, the House minority leader, did not press the Democrats to hold hearings in which federal, state, and local law enforcement officers could be attacked for their handling of the Kahl case. The major conservative magazines did not question the competence or integrity of the law enforcement officers who were killed or wounded by Kahl and his associates, nor did they offer extenuating arguments on behalf of Kahl and the Posse Comitatus.

On April 19, 1995, 167 people lost their lives in the bombing of the Federal Building in Oklahoma, which was timed to coincide with the second anniversary of the conflagration that engulfed David Koresh and his Branch Davidian followers in their Waco, Texas compound. The arrest and indictment of Timothy McVeigh, a right-wing radical with links to the paramilitary militia movement that has burgeoned in recent years, drew attention to the radical right. The newly elected Republican majority in Congress had a golden opportunity to turn the light of publicity on far-right terrorism.

Despite the efforts of New York Democratic Congressman Charles Schumer, House Speaker Newt Gingrich refused to hold hearings on the militia movement (Schumer had to hold his own private hearings on July 11, 1995). Instead, one of the first acts of the Republican Congress was to pander to the radical white-supremacist and survivalist right by holding theatrical hearings on the events at Waco and at Ruby Ridge, Idaho, where FBI agents accidentally killed the wife and child of a far-right outlaw, Randy Weaver. Between 1983 and 1995, the paramilitary right had changed from a fringe group into one of the major constituencies of the Republican party.

This became clear once again in February 1995, when Larry Pratt stepped down as co-chairman of Patrick Buchanan's presidential campaign after revelations that he associated with white supremacists and anti-government hate groups. Pratt was the leader of Gun Owners of America, an anti-gun control group even more extreme than the National Rifle Association, which claims to have 150,000 members. Pratt was present at an October 1992 meeting in Estes Park, Colorado, two months after the Weaver siege in Idaho ended. The meeting was called by Pete Peters, a leader of the Christian Identity movement, a sect with its origins in nineteenth-century Britain which holds that Anglo-

Americans, not Jews, are the true descendants of the Israelites of the Old Testament. Also present at the meeting were Richard Butler, leader of Aryan Nations, and a variety of neo-Nazis, anti-abortion crusaders, and tax protestors. According to one report, Pratt advised the group to play down political efforts to prevent gun control, in favor of promoting a "national struggle for survival" with "armed militia units." The meeting issued a "Special Report" which included a call for "leaderless resistance"—"All individuals and groups operate independently of each other, and never report to a central headquarters or single leader for direction or instruction. . . ."[7]

In the aftermath of the scandal surrounding his role in the Buchanan campaign, Pratt predictably enough claimed he was not a far-right extremist or a white supremacist. Pratt's presence at the Estes Park meeting—which one authority views as "the birthplace of the American militia movement"[8]—was not an isolated incident, however. In 1993, Pratt joined Pete Peters and other Christian Identity leaders at an annual conference sponsored by the Christian Identity journal *Jubilee*. In 1994, Pratt joined Klan members and skinheads in addressing the convention of the Constitutionalists Networking Center, a far-right organization headed by former Arizona Governor Evan Mecham (who had vetoed legislation mandating the birthday of Martin Luther King, Jr. as a state holiday).

That someone like Larry Pratt should be associated with the white-supremacist and paramilitary fringe and the right wing of the Republican party is disturbing, but not surprising. What is surprising is the sympathy that mainstream conservative intellectuals have begun to show for anti-government hate groups. By a grim coincidence, even as rescue workers were sifting through the rubble in Oklahoma City in their search for bodies in the days following April 19, 1995, the May 1995 issue of the conservative magazine *First Things* was appearing on newsstands across the United States. Bold red and black letters screamed from the cover: "WACO: The Massacre, the Aftermath."[9]

That essay by Dean M. Kelley—the author of books like *Why Conservative Churches Are Growing* and *Why Churches Should Not Pay Taxes*—used innuendo and rhetoric to put federal law enforcement officers in the worst possible light. The attack on law officers began with the use of the term "massacre" for the fire that consumed Koresh and his followers. Since the FBI and ATF officers who stormed the compound, at great risk to their own lives, had no idea that Koresh had booby-trapped it with gasoline drums, they can hardly be accused of engaging in a deliberate "massacre." The term "mass suicide," as in Jonestown, is far more accurate. This libel of law officers, however, was typical of the allegations made in the Kelley piece.

This is what the neoconservative editors of *First Things* chose to publish, as their magazine's most sustained and considered response to the Waco disaster:

> The tone of the Treasury report, despite its criticism of tactical errors, was conveyed by its first page, a black-bordered dedicatory panel bearing the words "In Memory of" and listing the names of the four agents killed [by Koresh's followers] in the assault. (There was no black-bordered page bearing the names of the six members of the religious group killed on the same occasion.) The report repeatedly asserted that David Koresh and his followers "ambushed" the federal agents. "On February 28, [they] knew that ATF agents were coming and decided to kill them." A more accurate statement, however, might be that they decided to fend them off.

It is worth pausing for a moment to examine the implications of this passage. It seems peculiar, to say the least, that a mainstream conservative publication would publish a complaint that the federal government does not mourn the cultists who were killed in a firefight with federal agents along with the federal agents whom the cultists murdered. But then, Kelley opposes the use of the word "cult"—Koresh and his followers were members of a "religious group." What is more, Kelley hints that the members of this persecuted "religious group" were within their rights when "fending off" federal agents serving a lawful warrant by gunning them down in cold blood as they tried to carry out their duty.

Throughout the essay, Kelley argues that the Branch Davidians were misinterpreted and persecuted by an oppressive and authoritarian federal government. Even Kelley, however, must concede that this "religious group" had violent tendencies. Note how he states the facts as though he were Koresh's defense attorney:

> George [Roden] challenged Vernon [Howell, a.k.a. David Koresh] to a duel in 1987 to prove which was the True Prophet. The form of the duel was to see who could bring back to life a long-dead Davidian whose casket was exhumed by Roden. Howell declined the challenge and complained to authorities about the exhumation. When they demanded proof, Howell and seven armed followers stole into the Mt. Carmel premises to photograph

the coffin. Roden caught them, and a gunfight broke out. All eight of the Branch Davidians were tried for attempted murder. Seven were acquitted, and Howell's trial ended in a hung jury. He was never retried.

Poor, misunderstood David Koresh. There he was, trying to help out the authorities by providing evidence of a crime. Of course he and his "armed followers" had committed burglary, but that was just evidence of civic zeal, no doubt. And when he and his "armed followers" engaged in a gunfight with the other cultists—why, no doubt they were just fending them off, as they would later "fend off" the federal officers serving warrants.

One might have expected this disingenuous attempt to exonerate David Koresh to appear in a publication of the neo-Nazi right or the Ku Klux Klan. Instead, the neoconservative editors of *First Things* chose to make this attack on American law enforcement a lead story—and to underline the message, they chose to publish it on the anniversary of the Waco fire. They had no way of knowing that Timothy McVeigh and his fellow conspirators had chosen the same anniversary to send a different version of the same message of hostility to the federal government.

That *First Things* would open its pages to a revisionist, far-right account of Waco in such a manner speaks volumes about the drift to the far right of the conservative movement in the 1990s. Only a few years before, the editor of *First Things*, Richard John Neuhaus, a former liberal Lutheran pastor who has become an arch-conservative Catholic priest, had been at the center of a bitter controversy that pitted neoconservatives against "paleoconservatives." The Rockford Institute, the sponsor of Neuhaus's institute on religious studies, had expelled Neuhaus from his offices after he criticized Rockford for subsidizing the conservative journal *Chronicles*. Under the editorship of Thomas Fleming, Neuhaus and other neoconservatives like Midge Decter complained that *Chronicles* was flirting with the far-right themes of the "fever swamp," including demented conspiracy theories about the federal government and thinly veiled anti-Semitism. No one could have suspected that within only a few years "fever swamp" themes like Waco revisionism would become a central concern of *First Things*.

The derailment of an Amtrak train on October 9, 1995 by a group called "Sons of the Gestapo," which killed one passenger and injured dozens, may be a precursor of right-wing terror yet to come. In the aftermath of the Oklahoma bombing, conservatives (many of whom had initially hurried to blame "Arab terrorists") were quick to take offense at suggestions that decades of denunciations of supposed federal tyranny might have encouraged deluded souls to take all the talk seriously. It would be nice to believe that the bellicose rhetoric and imagery employed by liberals and leftists as well as conservatives never promotes actual violence. Still, one wonders. James Coates, a student of the violent right, observes: "It should be noted . . . that in years when the national trend leaned leftward, such as the 1970s, the violence on the political fringes came more from the ultra-left than from the right wing. . . . Today the crimes are the same, but the perpetrators come from the opposite end of the political spectrum."[10] If conservatives—with some justice, I think—claim that the radicals who talked of "Amerika" and compared Johnson and Nixon to Hitler were inadvertently encouraging far-left terrorists like the Weather Underground, it is hard to see how those on the right who talk of abortion as a "holocaust" can avoid blame for creating a climate in which the bombing of abortion clinics and the murder of doctors who perform abortions can be viewed as noble deeds. The major form of terrorism in the United States since the 1970s, it should not be forgotten, has been the right-wing terrorism perpetrated by the violent wing of the anti-abortion movement.

As long as the Republican party was predominantly a coalition of northeasterners and midwesterners, the supposed right of American citizens to barricade themselves in fortified and booby-trapped compounds and amass assault weapons was not high on the list of GOP concerns. The southern drawl of the new Republican right is thickest when conservatives denounce gun control. Though the paramilitary, survivalist right has recently clustered in Idaho and the Mountain West, the South, even more than the West, has long been the capital of American armed violence and vigilantism. A study by historian Richard M. Brown of American vigilante movements found a striking pattern: 211 of 326 vigilante movements took place in the Highland South, while most of the rest were found in the Mountain States and the lower Middle West. Vigilantism was rare in the Tidewater South, and no case could be found of a vigilante movement in New England, New York, or the Midwest settled by Yankee pioneers. The leading historian of American folk cultures, David Hackett Fischer, makes a compelling case that extra-legal personal and communal violence are not so much part of the American tradition as of *one* American tradition—that of the Scots-Irish who immigrated from Britain between 1717 and 1775, and who shaped the "hearth culture" of the region stretching from West Virginia through Tennessee to Texas.[11]

More and more conservatives these days, in response to the domination of the GOP by white southern voters, are heard complaining that "rednecks" are the last minority whom it is permitted to ridicule. I have a certain amount of sympathy for this claim. A quarter of my ancestors are from the Highland South. Its twanging dialect is my *Muttersprache*. Its customs are those I find familiar and reassuring—from a taste for chicken-fried steak and country music to an enjoyment of target practice and hunting. I grew up using guns, and I subscribed to gun magazines until a few years ago, when I grew disgusted by the same radical, subversive, unpatriotic propaganda line that led President Bush to resign from the NRA.[12] I agree with southern conservatives that the folk culture of the Highland South is all too often and all too easily demeaned (not only by Yankees, but by moonlight-and-magnolia Tidewater types). I also agree, however, with those conservatives who denounce the idea that all "cultures" are created equal. When conservatives criticize "inferior" cultures nowadays, they usually have the subculture of poor urban blacks in mind. It seems to me, though, that as valuable as much of the Highland Southern heritage in matters like music may be, the high tolerance for interpersonal violence and the tradition of vigilantism and paramilitary paranoia that have been part of the tradition for centuries are leading candidates for condemnation as "inferior" cultural relics just as damaging as the inner-city black behavioral patterns that white conservatives are so quick to denounce. Maybe I am too optimistic, but I would like to think that in the next century the living tradition of my fellow "rednecks" will be represented in American consciousness by the sounds of musicians in Nashville and Branson, not by images of overweight commandos shimmying in fatigues through the mud of fortified compounds, rehearsing a war against the leaders we have elected.

After states' rights and the alleged right of citizens to amass high-powered weapons and form paramilitary storm trooper units in preparation for armed insurrection, populist proposals for direct democracy are the most important element of the southern and western Anti-Federalist tradition bequeathed by the Dixie Democrats to today's national Republican party. The Republican right, in recent years, has mastered the art of placebo populism—supporting measures that give a comforting illusion of magnifying the political power of ordinary voters, without actually reducing the domination of the political system by powerful special interests.

The biggest of the harmless sugar pills that the GOP has been prescribing for the American body politic is term limits. If members of Congress could be limited to short terms in office, this would cripple the power of special interests—or so the conservatives claim. In reality, the power of special interests like corporations and trade associations comes from their importance in financing political campaigns—in particular, radio and television advertising. Even if term limits were adopted, challengers taking on incumbents, as well as virtuous, as-yet-uncorrupted freshman legislators, would have to raise vast amounts of advertising money, from the same special interests that flourished before term limits. As befits a true placebo policy, term limits is not a bad idea; it is simply irrelevant.

For an example of genuine populist reform, one must turn to limitations on campaign finance. Despite the popularity of proposals for campaign finance reform with the American public, there was no mention of campaign finance in the Contract with America. Indeed, after the Republicans gained control of both houses of Congress, Republican leaders did their best to squelch any discussion of the topic. "Campaign finance will not be on the agenda," Senator Mitch McConnell (R-Kentucky), the Republican point man on the subject, snapped after the election. "There's no groundswell for it. We won't waste any time on it."[13] Senator Phil Gramm smirked, "I am eager to reform our campaign process just as the Democrats were when they were in the majority." Newt Gingrich proposed postponing a vote on campaign finance reform by turning the subject over to a bipartisan commission for a leisurely study.

Once Republican elected officials have retired from Washington and are no longer dependent on special interests, they can literally afford to be more candid about the need for campaign finance reform. Former Representative Guy Vander Jagt (R-Michigan) suggests that Congress "require that 51 percent of the money raised would have to come from within the congressman's district. With that provision, you'll ipso facto put a ceiling on what PAC's can give. You immediately switch the congressman's attention from PACs here in Washington back to the congressional district and the people he's representing. . . ."[14] Representative Vin Weber (R-Minnesota), who was a leading conservative during his years in Congress, argues that public financing of campaigns "remedies a couple of problems. I think it certainly minimizes the amount of time people have to spend raising money." Weber adds, "I'd have no problem in abolishing PACs."[15] Another retired Republican congressman, Hamilton Fish (R-New York) favors "free access to television and radio."[16] Former House Minority Leader Robert Michel (R-Illinois) believes that as much as 75 percent of campaign contributions should come from the district: "So you don't have the people in Chicago influencing the vote for the man down in Peoria." As for leadership PACs, which permit congressional leaders to contribute money to their fellow representatives or senators, Michel says: "I'm all for eliminating these leader PACs and that type of thing."[17]

While former Republican members of Congress, including conservatives as well as moderates, speak out against the abuses of our corrupt campaign finance system, and while a few Republicans, including Patrick Buchanan, have responded to populist pressure with proposals for reform, the conservative press maintains a united front in opposition to the very idea of limits on the role of money in American politics. When Ross Perot called for campaign finance reform, the editors of the *Wall Street Journal* became apoplectic. According to the *Journal*, campaign finance reform is the cause of special-interest power and not the cure: "In a world without that [$1000 individual] limit, a billionaire like Ross Perot wouldn't have to run himself but could find some other candidate to bankroll. . . ." Now there's a populist reform: make it easier for billionaires to hire politicians, so they do not need to go into politics themselves! The same editorial describes the popularity of campaign finance reform as "one example of the darker side of the Perot phenomenon, which is its susceptibility to the politics of resentment and pessimism." It seems that Americans who are angry at the idea of billionaires buying politicians to represent their interest in the capital are unduly "pessimistic."[18]

An equally strained argument against campaign finance reform has been contributed by George Will. Will, who has written a book endorsing the pseudopopulist reform of term limits, proves himself to be a true conservative by attacking a political reform which (unlike term limits) would not be an ineffectual placebo policy. Will mocks the idea that there should be equality among citizens "even to the point of stopping the voluntary contribution of private resources to support political discourse" (by which Will appears to mean the bankrolling of politicians by special interests and rich supporters). Will argues that all limits on the ability of special interest groups and tycoons to finance campaigns "constitute government rationing of political expression." Not only do campaign finance regulations violate the First Amendment guarantee of free speech, according to Will, but they "illustrate the timeless tension between the pursuit of equality and the preservation of liberty." Any attempt to reduce the role of money in politics, in the United States or anywhere else, will "inevitably . . . shrink the individual's sphere of sovereignty."[19]

If Will is right, and the absence of legislation preventing billionaires from writing themselves or their political hired hands checks to finance political campaigns is one of the key indicators of a free society, then freedom in the world is much more imperiled than anyone hitherto suspected. After all, most democracies today do not have loopholes in their campaign finance laws that permit the sort of political activity by billionaires that Will sees as vital to freedom. Perhaps freedom-loving Americans should try to organize a resistance movement in democratic Europe, to help overthrow governments that limit campaign spending and to restore the right of German millionaires and French billionaires to spend as much as they want on campaigns for themselves or their agents. Will, of course, is in a minority. Very few people in the United States, or in any of the democracies, would think of including the right of Malcolm Forbes, Jr. or Pete DuPont to exhaust his inherited family fortune in running for high office as one of the sacred rights of citizenship for which generations of freedom-loving people have fought and died. None of the drafters of new democratic constitutions in postcommunist Eastern Europe and Russia thought to include a provision guaranteeing the right to unlimited campaign donations by the rich. Only in the United States—and here, only because of a horribly mistaken Supreme Court case, *Buckley v. Valeo* (1976)—is the free flow of money into campaign coffers equated with free debate.

As the contrast between the views of George Will and Pat Buchanan on the subject of campaign finance suggests, this debate illustrates the class conflict within the conservative coalition. Populist conservatives, rather than liberals or leftists, might be the most important beneficiaries of campaign finance reform. The populist right has shown a talent for grass-roots organization, for example, in Patrick Buchanan's upset victory in the New Hampshire primary over the well-funded campaigns of Dole, Alexander, and Forbes. Reducing the role of money in politics would probably strengthen the religious right and the populist right—while weakening the influence in Washington of the Beltway and Wall Street right. No wonder George Will and the editors of the *Wall Street Journal* are so alarmed by talk of reducing the role of money in campaigns.

In the final analysis, the Anti-Federalist theory of government, recycled by the southernized right, is hopelessly muddled. Conservative anti-statism is unconvincing because it confuses the alleged dangers of big government and central government with the genuine dangers of arbitrary government. For half a century, conservatives have been claiming that welfare-state and civil rights legislation would lead to tyranny. Newt Gingrich claimed that the provision of universal health care to American citizens would require a "police state."[20] Barry Goldwater claimed that the Civil Rights Act of 1964 would create a "federal police force of mammoth proportions" and produce an " 'informer' psychology" in which neighbors spied upon neighbors. "These, the Federal police force and an 'informer' psychology, are the hallmarks of the police state and landmarks in the destruction of a free society."[21] In reality, of course, neither the United States nor any other democratic welfare state with a strong central government and liberal civil rights legislation has become a police state. Sweden did not move from welfare-state egalitarianism toward authoritarian rule. The adoption of universal health care by Britain after 1945 did not lead to a reign of terror in the British isles. The Civil Rights Act of 1964 did not lead to an American equivalent of the Gestapo. This is not to say that tyranny is not something to be guarded against in modern states. But where tyrannical regimes have replaced democratic regimes, invariably the chief agents have not been the new welfare-state agencies, but the "old," premodern, security organs—the military and the police. The Weimar Republic was overthrown, not by social-security bureaucrats, but by the German military and police, in collaboration with the Nazi party. If Soviet tyranny had rested solely on socialist economic institutions like collective farms, instead of military and police forces, the Soviet government would have been overthrown long before it was. If ever there were a proposition in social science that has been disproven, it is the conservative claim that the welfare state and civil rights enforcement lead to totalitarian tyranny all the time—or for that matter at any time.

Conservative rhetoric about protecting the individual from the arbitrary and repressive state is much more impressive than the conservative record. During the 1950s and early 1960s, many states in the South created, in effect, miniature police states that spied upon and harassed civil rights leaders, as well as homosexuals and law-abiding citizens with liberal and leftist views. The files of Florida's state-within-a-state, recently revealed, remind one of the secret police of the former Soviet bloc countries. Somehow William F. Buckley, Jr. and the other conservative defenders of individual freedom in the 1950s managed to completely overlook these genuine, homegrown secret police states, while warning about the imaginary dangers of tyranny that would result from the abolition of Jim Crow and the adoption of Medicare and student loans. For that matter, where were all the conservatives who complained that Social Security was "socialist tyranny" when Japanese-Americans were being rounded up and put in concentration camps? Why didn't conservative "individualists" who claimed to prefer state-level to federal reforms march on state capitals in the 1950s and 1960s to demand the abolition of segregation by state law, as an alternative to federal fiat? The depressing truth is that most contemporary American conservatives have no objection to arbitrary government power, at any level, as long as it is exercised in the name of "national security" or "law and order" or the suppression of "vice."

The only liberty that the conservative movement has consistently and ardently defended, in the past half century, is "economic liberty" (defined narrowly as the privileges of property owners and employers and landlords, rather than broadly as the rights of neighbors and workers and renters). The consistency with which conservative intellectuals have supported regimes like Chile under Pinochet and Singapore which have combined police-state repression in the area of politics and civil rights with market economics is further evidence for the contention that conservatives are libertarians when it comes to the marketplace—and authoritarian statists with respect to practically everything else.

The real problem with American government, it can be argued, is not that it is too strong—that is, too independent of society—but rather that it is too weak—that is, too subordinate to the groups and industries it is supposed to regulate. American government at all levels is too easily captured and colonized by the agents of special interests, both conservative and liberal. Government in America is not an ironclad, blasting away at the fragile citizenry, but rather a derelict, captured now by this gang and now by that gang of buccaneers. The solution is not to weaken government, much less to multiply it by division (with roughly 80,000 distinct political units in the United States, it can be argued that we have, not too much government, but too *many* governments, with all the costs that duplication of effort entails). What we need to do is to strengthen the ties between ordinary voters and the democratic state—while insulating accountable government officials from informal pressure by special interests, which disproportionately represent corporations and the rich (the refrain that "every American belongs to a special interest" is self-serving propaganda of the managerial-professional overclass). We have weak, unrepresentative government. We need strong, representative government.

The denigration of government by the right corresponds to the right's idealization of the market. If only the government would get out of the way, conservatives claim, the free market would enrich everyone. According to conservatives, critics of free-market radicalism, when they are not "socialists" or "collectivists" or "statists," are dangerous demagogues attempting to stir up a "class war." In truth, it is the Republican right that is demagogic and radical. And—as I show in the next chapter—the only class war going on in the United States today is the one that has been directed and supported by the right since the 1970s, the quarter-century class war of the American overclass against the American majority.

Chapter 10

Soaking the Middle

*The Conservative Class War Against
Wage-Earning Americans*

Since the 1960s, I have argued, the United States has undergone both a realignment and a revolution. The realignment, triggered by the left's destruction of New Deal–vital center national liberalism, has been a bipartisan conservative political realignment that has marginalized the left wing of the Democratic party and empowered both conservatives like Ronald Reagan and Newt Gingrich and neoliberal Democrats like Jimmy Carter and Bill Clinton. The revolution has been a quiet, slow-motion social revolution—the consolidation of a new national overclass, and the growth of its predominance in both the economy and American politics. Although the conservative political realignment was not the direct result of the rise of the overclass, the economic interests of that class have been served very well for the past quarter century by the confinement of economic choices for the United States to a narrow band with Reagan on the right and Carter and Clinton (both of whom have been more economically conservative than Nixon and Eisenhower) on the "left."[1]

Dramatic public disagreements between neoliberals like Clinton and conservatives like Gingrich, of the sort involved in the budget dispute that led to repeated shutdowns of the federal government in 1995–96, disguise the extent to which there is an elite bipartisan consensus on the American economy. Neoliberals and conservatives offer versions of laissez-faire economic liberalism that differ only in details. They agree in supporting free trade, high levels of immigration, and in opposing sector-specific industrial policy. They also agree that the U.S. welfare state (one of the smallest and least generous in the industrial world) is too big and needs to be either abolished (conservatives) or reinvented (neoliberals). Conservatives and neoliberals alike believe the following theory: high interest rates caused by the deficit lead to low investment, and low investment results in low productivity growth, which in turn leads to stagnant or declining wages; ergo, reducing the deficit will lower interest rates, stimulate investment, encourage productivity growth, and raise the wages of the average worker *even in the absence of strong unions or redistributive government policies.* The only significant disagreements between conservatives and neoliberals involve approaches to reducing the deficit. Both sides agree that deficit reduction is not merely a good idea, but the precondition for all sorts of wonderful developments.

A case can be made that the 1990s panacea of productivity-growth-through-deficit-reduction, even though it is the conventional wisdom of the sober bipartisan establishment, is only slightly less implausible than the 1980s delusion of supply-side economics. Whether that is the case or not, we need not wait to judge the results of the economic orthodoxy that has governed American policymakers in the age of bipartisan economic conservatism that began with Jimmy Carter and continues with Bill Clinton. The ascendancy of Carter-Reagan-Bush-Clinton economic conservatism has coincided with the decline of wages and benefits for all but the top fifth of the U.S. population. Much of this decline may be the result of forces beyond the control of any government (though the powerlessness of central governments, particularly those of major capitalist countries like the United States, is all too often exaggerated by those who have interests that are served by government inaction). There can be no doubt, however, that the economic policies of the right have exacerbated the troubles of the average American wage earner.

In Chapter Seven I discussed the failure of supply-side economics. In this chapter I will describe the right's effort to shift the burden of taxation downward from the top to the middle and the bottom of the population; the silence on the part of conservatives attacking entitlements for the middle class and the poor about the generous "hidden welfare state" that chiefly benefits the affluent; and the conservative attempt to deny or mislead the public about the astonishing rise in economic inequality in the past quarter century. The truth about the conservative class war on the wage-earning majority is damaging to the right—so damaging, in fact, that the right's more astute political strategists naturally want to change the subject altogether to the "culture war" that has been detailed in the previous chapters.

On the subject of taxes, the American right since Ronald Reagan has substituted demagogy for sober analysis. In an earlier chapter, I documented how supply-side economics was developed and disseminated by a small group of influential conservatives centered around the *Wall Street Journal* and the *Public Interest*. Candidate Reagan promised to balance the budget by his second year in office and to produce a $100 billion surplus by his third year. Two-thirds of the national debt that he left George Bush was run up during the eight years of the Reagan administration. As I showed earlier, private nonresidential investment was lower, government was bigger, and combined federal, state, and local taxes were higher on most Americans after Reagan left office than before he was elected. Reagan and his allies did, however, succeed in two goals—they dramatically cut taxes for the rich minority, and they shifted the tax burden downward from the affluent to wage-earning Americans.

Like members of a cult who rationalize the failure of the world to end on the predicted date, many of the supply-side enthusiasts of the 1980s still argue that they were not utterly wrong about supply-side economics. One strategy, adopted by Reagan economic advisor Martin Anderson, is to deny that supply-siders ever made the exorbitant claim that each dollar of tax cuts would produce a corresponding dollar or more in revenue growth.[2] Unfortunately for this extenuating argument, candidate Reagan's claims about the $100 billion surplus in the third year are part of the public record. Jack Kemp, writing in early 1996, was even more disingenuous. "In the 1980s, taxes were lowered from a top marginal rate of 70 percent to 28 percent," Kemp writes. He neglects to mention that for most Americans the Reagan tax cuts were offset by a series of tax increases in the 1980s, particularly in the Social Security payroll tax, which hits working Americans the hardest. The payroll tax, which amounted to only 11.5 percent of the federal revenue base in the 1950s, rose to make up 29.2 percent in the 1980s, as Reagan and his allies succeeded in shifting taxes from the rich and corporations onto wage-earning Americans.

Kemp also tries unsuccessfully to explain away the deficit that the

Kemp-Roth tax cut to which his name is attached did so much to create: "True, nominal budget deficits were higher at the end of the Reagan era. But as a percentage of the gross domestic product, the deficit actually diminished during the 1980s." Kemp neglects to mention that the deficit declined in the later 1980s only after it first shot up to an all-time high as a result of the Reagan tax cuts, from 2.6 percent in 1981 to 4.8 percent in 1982 and an extraordinary 6.3 percent in 1983.

Conservative demagogy about taxes does not end with feeble efforts like Kemp's to defend the discredited doctrine of supply-side economics. For example, in the official Republican reply to President Clinton's 1994 State of the Union address, Republican Governor Christine Todd Whitman called the tax increase passed in 1993 by the Democratic Congress "the largest tax increase in American history." Senator Bob Dole had already called it "the largest tax increase in world history."

This was utterly false. As economist Robert Samuelson pointed out, the 1982 Reagan tax legislation, supported by Dole and other Republican leaders, raised more money (once dollars were adjusted for inflation) over five years than Clinton's five-year budget. Both Reagan's tax increase and Clinton's somewhat smaller tax increase were dwarfed by the enormous tax increases with which the United States financed its struggle in World War II. Though the lie about Clinton's tax increase was exposed, Republicans still denounced Clinton during the 1994 congressional midterm campaign for enacting the largest tax increase in the history of—the United States, the earth, the Milky Way galaxy, or whatever.[3]

Yet another conservative lie about taxes in the United States is the often repeated claim that government is taking a bigger bite out of the average paycheck. The Congressional Budget Office has calculated that the effective federal tax rate on the middle class was stable or declining in the 1980s. In reality, the decline has taken place in pretax income. It is a result of falling wages in the private sector, not big government.[4]

The right's story about what has happened to the U.S. economy in the past generation is a melodrama. Lest I be accused of distorting the conservative message, I will defer to Herbert Stein, the distinguished economist at the conservative American Enterprise Institute, and a former member of the Council on Economic Advisors. Here is Stein's mocking summary of the conventional conservative theory of the American economy:

Most people in the United States are good people, otherwise known as "the middle class." All but about the richest 1 percent and the poorest 15 percent are in the middle class. They work hard, stay with their spouses and rear their children to be like them. If let alone by the government they would prosper and achieve "The American Dream." There are, however, a few people who are not good. These include violent criminals, young women enjoying sex and having illegitimate children, some lawful aliens who are not citizens, and government bureaucrats. For forty years Democratic Congresses have coddled these people and have given them handouts, and this coddling has only increased their number. As a result the middle class has been loaded down with taxes and regulations that have stultified the economy. The American Dream now exceeds their grasp. The great national problem now is to relieve the middle class of these unnecessary burdens.[5]

Contrary to what most Republicans argue, the share of the GDP that is eaten up by federal taxes is no higher than it was under Eisenhower; according to Herbert Stein, "Total federal receipts as a percentage of GDP are now no higher than they were in 1954."[6] Nevertheless, middle-class and working-class Americans pay a higher percentage of the federal tax burden because *since the 1970s conservatives have succeeded in shifting taxation from the rich and business to the middle class.* In particular, the increase in the Social Security payroll tax signed by President Reagan had the effect of increasing the percentage of the federal budget paid for by working Americans.

When Phil Gramm announced his candidacy for the Republican presidential nomination, he noted that average Americans pay far more in federal taxes than they did in 1950. Let us assume that Gramm is right, and the U.S. tax system was superior in 1950. How could we change today's tax structure, to bring it back to the 1950 model?

For one thing, we can raise the top federal income tax rate to 91 percent. That's what it was in 1950, the date that Gramm identifies with "the good old days." Needless to say, loopholes prevented the rich from paying nine out of ten dollars to the federal government. Even so, the effective federal income tax rate for the richest 1 percent of the U.S. population in 1950 was over 45 percent of earnings. In 1990, however—thanks to the Reagan-era tax cuts that Phil Gramm energetically supported—the effective tax rate on the top 1 percent had been reduced to a mere 23 percent of earnings (the top marginal rate, as of this writing, is 39.6 percent).

If we were to have a tax system like the one we had in the good old days of 1950, we would do more than raise the effective tax rate on the super-rich. We would also hike up taxes on corporations. Today corporations pay only about 10 percent of federal income taxes. In 1950, though, a third of the federal income tax receipts came from corporations.

Ordinary Americans pay far more in taxes today not because the federal tax burden has grown as a proportion of GDP (it hasn't), but because much of the tax burden has been transferred from the wealthy few and from businesses to middle-class and working Americans. Conservative claims to the contrary are either misinformed—or misleading.

Recently the centerpiece of conservative proposals for tax reform has been some variant of the "flat tax." Most flat-tax proposals share common features—they would tax wage income (but not capital income) at a single, relatively low rate, and they would abolish most or all tax deductions (including the popular home mortgage interest deduction that helps middle-class homeowners). Most conservative flat-tax plans also share the same drawback—they would result in higher taxes on middle-class Americans and a windfall for the rich.

These drawbacks have been evident since 1983, when two libertarian tax reformers, Robert Hall and Alvin Rabushka, published their book *Low Tax, Simple Tax, Flat Tax*. "Now for some bad news," the authors wrote, after describing their plan. "[I]t is an obvious mathematical law that lower taxes on the successful will have to be made up by higher taxes on average people." To be precise, the adoption of the Hall-Rabushka plan would give a family with an annual income of $3.8 million a tax cut of $500,000 a year, while raising taxes on a middle-income family by $2,000 a year, in 1995 dollars.[7]

The flat tax died during the 1980s, only to be revived in the 1990s by House Majority Leader Dick Armey and would-be Republican presidential nominee Malcolm Forbes, Jr. John Mueller, a conservative economist who once served as an advisor to the Republican sponsors of the Kemp-Roth tax cut of 1978, has criticized the "flat tax" proposed by House Majority Leader Dick Armey and Senator Richard Shelby of Alabama (who converted to the GOP after the November 1994 midterm elections). Mueller describes the Armey-Shelby flat tax as "punishment for the middle class."

Mueller illustrates how Armey's flat tax would hurt middle-class Americans by using two imaginary families, the Joneses and the Smiths. Under the Armey flat tax, the Joneses, a two-career family of four making $20,478 a year, would take home 8 percent less of their paycheck than they would under the current 1995 rate. For the more prosperous Smiths, a two-career couple making $50,411, their take-home pay would drop by $1,609 below what it is today.[8]

Mueller is not the only honest critic of the flat tax on the right. In what he calls "a friendly critique of the flat tax" published in the conservative magazine *Policy Review,* economist J. D. Foster points to a different problem—the unfair exemption of the rich from taxation that would result from a flat tax based solely on "labor income" and excluding capital gains. Foster illustrates the point by using a different pair of Joneses and Smiths:

> Consider two families. The Joneses have a combined salary of $50,000 in wages and salary. Under the Armey plan with a 20 percent tax rate, this family of four would owe $3,700 in tax. Now consider the Smiths, who in retirement consume every dollar of their $1 million in dividend income. Under the flat tax, the Smiths owe no tax at all because capital income is excluded from the tax base. . . .
>
> *When capital income, which would not be subject to personal income tax, is considered along with wage income, average tax rates for higher-income groups are lower than for middle-income groups. . . .* (Emphasis added.)

Foster concludes: "At the proposed rates, the flat tax would impose a tax increase on middle-income taxpayers."[9] The only way to prevent the Armey tax from raising taxes on middle-class Americans would be to make the flat tax even lower (Armey suggests 17 percent). But this would require massive cutbacks in federal spending, far beyond those envisioned by the Republican majority. If, as seems likely, conservatives concentrated their cuts on middle-class entitlements, leaving tax expenditures for the rich and corporate welfare programs intact, middle-class families would lose more from cutbacks in programs like Social Security, Medicare, and student loans than they would save in lower income taxes.

The Republican Congress is not likely to enact Armey's flat tax in the immediate future. The tax legislation it has already proposed is quite bad enough, though. According to Congress's Joint Committee on Taxation, the tax plan approved by the Senate Finance Committee in 1995 would reduce taxes on Americans making more than $30,000 a year—and raise them on Americans whose annual income is $30,000 or less.

No sooner had Armey's flat tax been discredited than Malcolm Forbes, Jr. spent his way toward the top of the pack in the Republican presidential primary, touting his own flat tax. Forbes proposed to replace the present graduated income tax of 15–40 percent, and to abolish all deductions, as well as all taxes on interest, dividends, capital gains, and on inheritances (Forbes inherited his fortune from his father, the late millionaire publisher Malcolm Forbes, Sr.). Under Forbes's flat-tax plan, there would be only a 17 percent tax—levied equally on corporate profits and wages and salaries, coupled with a $13,000 exemption for each adult and a $5000 exemption for each child. The result of the Forbes tax plan, according to calculations by the U.S. Treasury, would be to increase the deficit by $200 billion a year. Like the Armey flat tax, the Forbes flat tax could balance the budget only if the rate were raised—in the process, hiking up taxes on the middle class in order to pay for the enormous tax savings to the rich.

When Forbes began rising in the polls early in 1996, the other Republican presidential contenders, including Bob Dole, Patrick Buchanan, and Lamar Alexander, began attacking his flat-tax plan as a boon for the rich that would hurt the middle class. Desperate to win the support of wage-earning voters, one conservative Republican after another threw conservative economic ideology to the winds and adopted the very kinds of arguments that they denounced as "class war" when liberals made them. Much to the horror of conservative intellectuals and journalists, the country was treated to the spectacle of conservative Republicans rallying to the defense of progressive taxation and claiming to defend the middle class against the selfish rich. In the heat of battle, the desperate Republican rivals did what conservative ideologues have feared the most: they treated the conflict of interest between the rich and the middle class as a fact. When demagogy failed, the opponents of Malcolm Forbes, Jr. did what had been unthinkable since the defeat of the Republican fiscal conservatives by the supply-siders in the 1970s: they told the voters the truth.

After taxes, no subject has inspired more conservative demagogy than welfare. Nothing proves the alienation of today's American right from the classical conservative tradition more than its hostility to the welfare state. The modern welfare state is the product not of intellectual conversion but of fear—fear of revolution. The father of the modern welfare state is Bismarck, an authoritarian conservative who adopted welfare-state policies in order to steal the thunder from his socialist opponents. In the United States, the New Deal was adopted during the greatest crisis of industrial capitalism, when growing numbers of Americans were convinced that liberal capitalism should be abandoned for communism or some version of fascism. Far from being "socialist," the welfare state has been the chief means by which capitalist countries have neutralized potential public support for socialism. Just as a vaccine works by introducing a small portion of the disease into the body in order to stimulate the production of antibodies, so the mildly socialist reforms of modern welfare capitalism have immunized bodies politic against more radical forms of socialism. It is no exaggeration to say that the welfare state is an eminently conservative idea; there is much truth in the old saying that Franklin Roosevelt saved American capitalism. Genuine midcentury American conservatives like Peter Viereck and Dwight Eisenhower recognized the stabilizing, conservative effects of the New Deal's mild and incomplete version of social democracy.[10]

Given the contribution of the welfare state to reconciling citizens to the fluctuations of the business cycle and the vast inequalities that accompany industrial capitalism, one can only wonder at the eagerness with which self-styled "conservatives" are setting about dismantling America's welfare state protections—which are already few and feeble, compared to those of most other industrial democracies. The result of privatizing Social Security, Medicare and Medicaid, and other popular welfare-state programs would be twofold: economic insecurity would dramatically increase for millions of Americans, and social inequality—already greater than at any time since 1929—would rapidly grow. The result, in very short order, would be a backlash against free-market conservatism in favor of a revived liberalism or some sort of right-wing statism of the European fascist or East Asian authoritarian variety. The sooner that conservatives abolish the welfare state, the sooner neoliberals or neofascists will abolish conservatism.

This is a practical argument for the welfare state, of course, not a principled argument. Two kinds of principled arguments for the welfare state can be made. One that is popular on the left is the version of the social-contract theory developed by John Rawls, who argues that a person behind a "veil of ignorance" would design a society in which there was adequate provision for the unfortunate (on the chance that he might be one of the unfortunate). This is a clever but rather academic argument, and less likely to persuade intelligent conservatives than a quite different argument based on the imperatives of republicanism. The republican argument for the welfare state goes something like this:

a republican constitution is much more difficult to establish and maintain than an autocracy or an oligarchy. It requires a fairly substantial population of citizens with the leisure and education to play at least a minimal role in public affairs, as voters and jurors and perhaps as soldiers. Education and leisure, of course, require a certain material base, in the form of income and economic security. This requirement can be met in two ways—by restricting the suffrage to a propertied elite, or by spreading property, or its equivalent in the form of government entitlements, to a mass electorate. Modern welfare states give a stake in society in the form of entitlements to all eligible citizens. The Social Security check and the student loan are the equivalent of the small farm of the "yeoman democrat" in older republican theory.

To this, many conservatives would reply that entitlements are the source of crippling dependence, not of yeoman self-reliance. A citizen's "property" in entitlements is not true property at all. Their argument echoes the reasoning of old-fashioned agrarian republicans—with a crucial (if seldom noticed) difference. Old-school agrarian republicans like Thomas Jefferson favored "real" property—literally, "real estate"— as the basis for civic independence, and were opposed to all dematerialized property, whether it took the form of stocks and bonds or government obligations. In the early twentieth century, Southern Agrarian intellectuals like Allen Tate made a valiant defense of this position, arguing that genuine political independence required that every citizen own his own farm and slop his own hogs (I exaggerate only slightly). There is a consistency in radical agrarian republicanism that is missing from the contemporary conservative attack on welfare-state "dependency." If a steady stream of income from a trust fund or shares in a multinational corporation is just as acceptable a basis for republican citizenship as rents from land, then why isn't a steady stream of income from the government to a pensioner or a student? Indeed, if the republic is conceived of as a great corporation, then why shouldn't citizens be regarded as shareholders, with entitlements representing their minimal share of the earnings? Badly structured entitlement programs, of course, can create perverse incentives, discouraging people from working or saving. But that is a problem with design; properly designed entitlements, like Social Security and the earned-income tax credit, supplement and reward personal effort.

Conservatives themselves abandon their theoretical objection to entitlements altogether, when it comes to education. The centerpiece of contemporary conservative educational reform is school vouchers. In Chapter Seven, I discussed the origins and implications of the conservative enthusiasm for vouchers. Here I raise the subject only to make the point that vouchers represent welfare-statism of the most radical kind. Not only would the federal or state governments give every eligible citizen a subsidy, based on citizenship, but the government—that coercive, repressive, tyrannical government—would tell citizens that the money could be spent only for a particular purpose. The very same conservatives who would denounce the idea of vouchers for health care or housing as socialism run amok have no qualms about proposing one of the most massive and expensive government entitlements ever contemplated in the United States—while calling the school voucher system a "free-market approach."

The conservative enthusiasm for school vouchers is not an isolated exception to the free-market theory of the right. Conservative theorists may be in love with minimal government, but conservative politicians, in power, have nothing against welfare entitlements—as long as their chief beneficiaries are affluent white Republican voters. It is possible to associate with conservative intellectuals and politicians at the highest levels, as I did for nearly a decade, and never hear a single one of their number mention what political scientist Christopher Howard calls "the hidden welfare state." The hidden welfare state is the sum total of all "tax expenditures," or indirect subsidies to individuals and corporations in the form of tax exemptions. The Joint Committee on Taxation of Congress has explained, "Special tax provisions are referred to as tax expenditures because they are considered to be analogous to direct outlay programs. . . . Tax expenditures are most similar to those direct spending programs which have no spending limits, and which are available as entitlements."[11] When tax expenditures are taken into account, according to Howard, "it appears that the true size of the American welfare state is considerably larger than the sum of direct spending programs. The hidden welfare state is roughly one-third to one-half the size of the visible welfare state of direct spending." What is more, when the hidden welfare state is taken into account, "The distribution of benefits toward the middle- and upper-middle classes is even more exaggerated."[12]

Suppose that politicians proposed a direct subsidy that worked on the following principle—the more money you make, the more you will be subsidized by the government. Political suicide, right? And yet that is precisely the principle that guides the indirect tax subsidies that make up the Hidden Welfare State. In the federal mortgage-interest deduction, for example, the bias toward the affluent and the rich is pronounced. The original purpose of this deduction was to make home ownership possible for working-class and lower-middle-class Americans. Today, however, only one in five of the American taxpayers making between $20,000 and $40,000 a year takes advantage of this deduction (the rest either rent or do not itemize because they use the short form 1040). Most of this tax subsidy therefore goes to the well-off who need it least—44 percent to households making more than $100,000 a year, and 17 percent to households with an annual income of more than $200,000. The average mortgage interest deduction for households making $10,000–19,999 is $412; that of households earning more than $200,000 a year, $8,348.

Another pillar of the hidden welfare state is the tax exemption for employer-paid health insurance plans. (Somehow this artificial tax expenditure for health care does not count as "socialized medicine" in conservative eyes). Together, the mortgage interest deduction ($51 billion) and the health-plan exemption ($92 billion) cost the U.S. Treasury $143 billion in lost income in 1994.[13] While the growth of discretionary spending has been frozen by law for the rest of this decade, tax expenditures will continue not only to grow but to grow more than 4 percent faster than the expected growth of the gross domestic product (GDP). By the turn of the century, tax expenditures may equal or surpass all federal spending on discretionary programs.

The conservative war on the welfare state is a war on the visible welfare state (whose programs mostly benefit poor and wage-earning Americans) rather than on the hidden welfare state (whose programs mostly benefit the upper middle class and the rich). The most equitable way to reduce the budget deficit without harming the middle class and the poor would be to impose means-testing on most if not all entitlements—particularly the invisible subsidies that make up the hidden welfare state. The Concord Coalition has issued a plan that would save $190 billion over five years by reducing entitlements for those making more than $40,000 a year, according to a graduated scale.

Such fair and sensible proposals, as one might expect, hold little interest for the party of the rich. Why abolish luxuries for the wealthy, when the burden of balancing the budget can be shifted to the middle-class and the poor? Let them eat tax expenditures. Newt Gingrich has even suggested a tax-expenditure approach to poverty: "Maybe we need a tax credit for poor Americans to buy a laptop."[14] (The Speaker of the House apparently did not realize that most poor Americans, because they pay no income tax, can derive no benefit from tax credits.)

E conomic inequality is another subject on which the right has been anything but straightforward. For most of the past decade, politicians and journalists on the right pretended either that the rise in equality in the United States was a myth, or that it was only a temporary phenomenon. The magnitude of the problem, however, can no longer be denied. Between 1973 and 1995, the wages of the 80 percent of the American work force whom the government classifies as "production and nonsupervisory workers" fell by 18 percent, in dollars adjusted for inflation, from $315 per week to $258 per week. While the economic fortunes of eight out of ten American workers have declined, the real annual income of corporate chief executives rose between 1979 and 1989 by 19 percent—and a startling 66 percent after taxes (thanks to Reagan-era tax cuts).[15] Most of the income gains have gone to a small group within the upper 20 percent of the work force. A mere 1 percent of families in the United States received 79 percent of all the income generated in this country between 1977 and 1990, with much of that bonanza going to the top tenth of that 1 percent.[16]

The phenomenon cannot be blamed on "the global economy," because it is not occurring in comparable industrial capitalist societies, like free-market Britain and social-democratic Sweden. In Sweden, the share of net worth held by the top 1 percent of households declined between 1925 and 1990 from 39.3 percent to 18 percent. In Britain, there has been a similar decline, between 1925 (59.1 percent) and 1990 (20.7 percent). In the United States, too, in the era of New Deal liberalism of FDR and Truman and Johnson, inequality in net worth steadily declined from 39.9 percent in 1925 to around 20 percent in 1975. In the United States, though, unlike in Britain and Sweden, inequality began to climb sharply upward again after the mid-1970s, to reach 35.7 percent—just slightly below the 1925 level—in 1990, without leveling out.[17] Perhaps it is only coincidence that the sharp spike upward in inequality in the United States coincides with the bipartisan conservative political realignment in the mid-1970s that began with the election of Jimmy Carter and continued with the election of Ronald Reagan.

The quarter-century escalation of inequality in America under a series of Republican presidents—and now a Republican Congress—as well as the two most conservative Democrats in a century, Carter and Clinton, is a subject that makes conservatives understandably nervous. The aristocratic conservatives of the past had no difficulty justifying enormous extremes of wealth and poverty. Inequality was part of the providential or natural order. The rich were anointed by God, or belonged to a master race, or played an important role in a "mixed constitution" (commons, lords, and king). Today's conservatives cannot argue in that fashion (though Charles Murray, as we have seen, has revived a version of social Darwinist arguments for hereditary inequality). Contemporary conservatives, after all, pretend to be populists. There are no longer any American conservatives who, in the tradition of Edmund Burke, defend a hereditary elite of rich and powerful families, "great oaks" benevolently spreading their shade over us deferent shrubs. The right, we are told again and again, is the party of the people, of the common man, the enemy of the "elites." In reality, of course, most wealthy Americans have made their money the old-fashioned way: mom or dad died. But you would never know this from conservative propaganda, which treats entrepreneurs and inventors, rather than the hereditary rich or corporate executives, as though they were typical of the rich in America. The "conservative opportunity society" rhetoric of Newt Gingrich identifies the American dream, not with being born rich (like George Bush, Malcolm Wallop, Pete DuPont, Malcolm Forbes, Jr., William F. Buckley, Jr.) but with making one's own fortune (like the Republicans' favorite examples of meritocracy, Bill Gates and . . . Bill Gates and Bill Gates).

Deprived of the aristocratic-conservative argument for the social value of the trust-made man by their own idealization of the self-made man, American right-wingers must fall back on the same utilitarian argument for growing concentration of wealth that they invoke to defend income inequality—we will dam up wealth today, in order to open the floodgates and irrigate the fields tomorrow. Unfortunately for this theory, the historical record is clear: in the past five decades, the American economy boomed under big-government liberalism—and slowed under tax-cut conservatism. In light of the failure of supply-side policies to prove that short-run increases in inequality really benefit everyone in the longer term, many conservatives have tried different rhetorical gambits. Some concede that inequality is indeed rising— but ask, so what? Inequality of both income and wealth, they say, *is not really a problem* in the United States, as it might be in other countries, because Americans are the richest and most socially mobile people in the world.

As it happens, this is not true. Americans on average are no longer the most affluent people in the world. To name only one example, according to 1991 statistics, Canadians in the bottom 55 percent had higher after-tax incomes than the bottom 55 percent of Americans (the average income in the United States is higher—a statistical artifact created by greater extremes of wealth). Although the level of taxation in the United States is lower than the average for all advanced nations, the average American pays more in taxes than the average middle-class citizen in other industrial democracies—and gets less in the form of public services, from education to health care to policing. The United States is a great place to live—if you are rich. But most members of the middle and working classes in the United States would get more for their tax dollars if they lived in Canada or Germany. As for turnover among classes, the United States, which is by far the most unequal of all the industrialized democracies, is about in the middle when it comes to Horatio Alger social mobility.

While median family incomes, adjusted for inflation, rose by about a third in the 1950s and 1960s, during the past twenty years families in the middle have seen their incomes stagnate or decline, and the bottom has seen an absolute decline. While the rising number of single-parent families has contributed to poverty, this factor does not explain the fall in wages that has forced more intact families to become two-earner couples (the number rose during the silent depression of the 1980s by 20 percent). Even worse, the proportion of Americans holding two jobs to make ends meet is higher than it has been in half a century. Only the top 20 percent have gained from economic growth (the top 5 percent in the past two decades have enjoyed an income increase of almost a third). The situation is certain to grow worse if productivity gains are not shared with workers.

If there is any cold comfort to be had, it is in the news that at least inequality of income has not grown as radically as inequality of wealth. According to Edward Wolff, an economist at New York University, between 1977 and 1992, the share of wealth owned by the top 1 percent (the super rich) nearly doubled from 22 percent to 44 percent. The top 20 percent got "only" 76.3 percent of the growth in income during the 1980s—the same one in five received an amazing 98.8 percent of the growth in wealth during Reagan's Golden Age. The trend did not end with the Gipper—the concentration of wealth seems to have reached a postwar high in 1992. What is more, Wolff calculates that 54.2 percent of all bonds, and 46.2 percent of all stocks, are held by the top 1 percent of the U.S. population (average wealth: $2.35 million). Most of the rest is owned by the rest of the top ten percent. The proportion of the stock market held by ordinary people is actually diminishing, as companies reduce the coverage of their employees by pension plans.[18] All of this, of course, is very embarrassing for advocates of trickle-down economics. There has hardly been a drip, much less a trickle.

The facts about rapidly growing income and wealth inequality in the United States trouble conservative polemicists so much that they are tempted to fake their data. In his new book *The Freedom Revolution*, House Majority Leader Dick Armey claims that the poorest Americans in the 1980s were statistically more likely to join the top quintile than to remain in the bottom. From figures showing a degree of upward and downward mobility between income quintiles in the 1980s, Armey infers: "All told, a person in the poorest income group in 1979 was more likely to end the decade in the richest quintile than to remain at the bottom." Really? Was someone making $10,000 in 1979 really more likely to be making $120,000 than $12,000 in 1989? Of course not. Armey, a former professor of economics, has bungled his math, and is trying to pass off his howler as evidence that "Ronald Reagan proved, as John Kennedy said, that a rising tide lifts all boats."[19]

The Treasury study that Armey relies on does not support his argument that America is not a "society where people are either born rich or poor and remain that way through their lifetimes." On the contrary, the June 1, 1992 Treasury study he refers to sheds no light whatsoever on the question of income mobility *between generations.* That study tracks individuals who paid taxes in all ten years from 1979 to 1989, without identifying their social origins; because only about half of all households paid taxes in each of those ten years, the sample is skewed toward the affluent. Even more important, the Treasury study is useless as evidence of social mobility because, absurdly, it treats the movement of high school, college, and graduate school students into the work force as movement out of "poverty" (the median age of the lowest quintile in the study is twenty-two). What the Treasury study shows, at most, is the obvious fact that middle-class Americans tend to make substantially more in their thirties than when they first graduate from college or high school, as in Armey's example of a "recently graduated 23-year-old." What, however, does this tell us about the likelihood that the twenty-three-year-old will rise above the class of her parents—poor, middle-class, or rich? Absolutely nothing. Nor does a 1992 Urban Institute study that conservatives like Armey like to cite tell us anything about social mobility between generations.[20]

There are studies which, unlike the Treasury and Urban Institute studies, *do* examine the question of intergenerational social mobility in the United States. According to Gary Solon, a University of Michigan economist, when relatively optimistic assumptions are made, a child whose father is in the bottom 5 percent of income is roughly eight times more likely to remain poor or near poor than to rise into the top quintile; one whose father is at the fifteenth percentile is about four times more likely to sink into the bottom than to rise to the top.[21] Another University of Michigan economist, Joel Slemrod, has found that generational mobility was no greater in the 1980s than in the 1960s.[22] These studies confirm what common sense would suggest—namely, that Americans who are born poor tend to spend all their lives near the bottom of the income ladder, and that most middle-class and rich Americans end their lives in the same broad income class into which they were born. Armey to the contrary, rags-to-rags and riches-to-riches are much more typical than rags-to-riches or riches-to-rags. Dick Armey has tried to pass off the familiar phenomenon of earnings rising with age after the "poverty" of college or high school as proof of an extraordinary degree of social mobility between generations—mobility which, in reality, remains fairly limited.

Michael Novak, one of the most eminent scholars of the foundation-subsidized right, has tried a different argument in his intervention in the inequality debate. Writing in the *Wall Street Journal,* Novak has argued that inequality of wealth in the United States is genuine, but grossly exaggerated by liberals. Novak points to data showing that over half of those in the top 1 percent in 1979 were no longer there in 1988 (only in America, it seems, is it so easy to move from the ninety-ninth to the one-hundredth percentile). If this is not enough, Novak offers an even more outlandish argument, criticizing those who don't take into account "the publicly owned wealth that belongs to all Americans: the huge expanses of federal lands and forests, as well as those set aside by state and local governments; all federal, state, and local buildings and monuments, research institutions and museums, roads, airports, schools, hospitals; military aircraft and naval vessels; armies and police forces."[23] The homeless may not have a roof of their own, but they are the proud co-owners of Yellowstone National Park.

Though Patrick Buchanan has integrated class-war themes with culture-war conservatism, mainstream conservatives continue to insist with Armey and Novak that all conflicts of interest between the well-to-do and American workers are illusory. The feel-good conservative economic theory of Reagan and Kemp and Gingrich purports to describe a harmonious economic universe, where workers get rich as their incomes go down, where slashing wages creates jobs, where free trade enriches developed and developing countries alike with little or no pain—a laissez-faire world as utopian as the communist society envisioned by Karl Marx, where the state has withered away, no longer needed in a society where technology has eliminated drudgery and people work out of civic enthusiasm instead of need or greed. Like the theorists of communism, the theorists of free-market fundamentalism dismiss common sense, in the name of their economic "science" and its paradoxes: the state must grow stronger before it withers away; wages for much of the population must be lowered today so that everyone can get rich; capitalism will inevitably produce its antithesis in the form of socialism; lower taxes will generate higher tax revenues.

The resemblance between Marxism and the classical liberal economic utopianism of the American right is a family resemblance. Marxism and free-market fundamentalism are squabbling twins, the offspring of the Enlightenment's naive belief in inevitable progress and a "science of society" or a "science of man." In the former communist countries, the high priests of economic dogma were the Marxist dialecticians; in the United States and Britain (though not in Japan or continental Europe), neoclassical economists serve as guardians of the orthodoxy, promising "scientific" approaches to economic progress. Conservatives in the British tradition like Burke and Disraeli and Churchill have been as deeply suspicious of the dogmas of neoclassical economics as they have been of socialism. Today's American conservatives, however, have adopted free-market fundamentalism, in its crudest forms, as their political religion.

It is a false religion. "The market," as a realm of purely economic transactions distinct from the social and political spheres and operating according to quasi-natural "laws," is a figment of the imaginations of academic economists. The extrasocial, extrapolitical "marketplace" that is idealized by American conservatives does not exist, never has existed, and cannot exist, except on the chalkboard. All actual markets are embedded in intertwined networks of government and government-shaped institutions.

Far from being inimical to capitalism, government regulation makes modern large-scale capitalism possible. Consider the basic institution of modern capitalism—the limited-liability corporation. Under the laws that govern modern corporations, shareholders are not individually liable for the losses of a company. In the eighteenth and nineteenth centuries, such laws struck many reasonable people as an abomination. Why should a mere charter of incorporation permit people to escape financial responsibility for the losses of a venture which they own? The answer is not moral, but practical: governments in modern times have favored limited-liability laws because without them, people would not be willing to undertake the kinds of investments in large-scale organizations that make modern prosperity possible. In a true "free market" without a government to encourage the corporate form of commercial enterprise, it seems doubtful that individuals would spontaneously agree to the limitation of liability. Without government legislation encouraging limited-liability corporations, large-scale industrial capitalism might have never gotten off the ground. The world might have been stuck forever at the stage of farms and small shops. (The replacement of debtors' prisons by bankruptcy laws reflects a similar triumph of expediency over commonsense notions of justice.)

Some conservatives might accept the role of government in structuring the institutions of corporate capitalism, from the corporation itself to the banking and insurance industries upon which modern business depends. They might even grant the legitimacy of regulation by the state, in the interest of policing the system against criminals and monopolies. Even if the government is not to be a mere "nightwatchman," it ought to be a neutral "umpire." The government should not discriminate in favor of one industry or sector against another; government should be "rule-oriented," not "results-oriented."

The idea of a government that is indifferent to the outcomes produced by the marketplace may seem plausible in economics faculties on university campuses, or in the editorial offices of right-wing newspapers and magazines. In the real world, of course, governments do take an interest in economic outcomes. If they do not respond to negative trends produced by the operation of national or international markets, they may be voted out of power, or forcibly overthrown—or, at worst, defeated by foreign enemies that are not hobbled by academic inhibitions about government intervention in the marketplace.

The possibility of military defeat and invasion are usually left out of discussions of economics in the United States and Britain. The United States, if one discounts Pearl Harbor (located in what was then a territory, not a state) has not suffered a serious invasion since 1812; Britain, though it has been bombed from the air in this century, has been free from foreign invasion even longer. The exception is the American South, which was defeated in its bid for independence in the Civil War and was occupied by federal forces in large part because its industrial base was so much weaker than that of the victorious North. Elsewhere in the world, political elites cannot as easily separate foreign policy and economics. Germany was defeated in two world wars because its industrial base, even when expanded by conquest, could not mobilize the resources available to the Americans, British, and Soviets. In both world wars Germans starved as a result of blockades and war-related disruption—something forgotten by Americans who blithely advise the Germans and other continental Europeans to abandon agricultural protection and render themselves vulnerable by importing food.

The notion of the separation of economics and world politics is even more alien to Japanese elites. Japan's top-down economic modernization, beginning with the Meiji restoration in the nineteenth century, was a response to a geopolitical imperative—avoiding the fate of other Asian countries that became colonies or protectorates of the western colonial powers. There can be little doubt that the single-minded concentration of the Japanese elite since 1945 on attaining technological parity with the West, and if possible technological primacy, has been motivated largely by a desire to restore Japan's independence and standing in the world. For the Japanese elite (if not for all Japanese), the economy is not a separate realm in which the nationality of corporations and individuals is of no consequence. Rather, the world economy is merely another arena for the competition between nation-states—an arena which has been all the more important, since until recently Japanese military competition with the United States and other great powers has not been an option.

The United States, with its allies, has won three global conflicts, the two world wars and the cold war; it has not suffered military defeat and occupation by foreign troops; its people have not been starved by enemy blockades; its cities have not been bombed into rubble from the air. What is more, the United States was the undisputed hegemon of the world economy, and one of two military superpowers, from 1945 to 1973; even now, in a world of several emerging centers, the United States retains the paramount position. It is all too easy for us Americans to fall into the trap of assuming that the country's experience in the twenty-first century will be as rich in victory and prosperity as the twentieth century has been. Indeed, American conservatives who favor a policy of laissez-faire must assume indefinite world peace—because in a world of serious military rivalries among the great powers, the first casualty would be progress toward a global free market.

Suppose the optimists are wrong. Suppose that today's period of peace among the great powers, in which conflicts are limited to civil wars and purely regional struggles, turns out to be merely an interregnum between Cold War I and Cold War II. Suppose that the twenty-first century sees one or more cold wars in which the great capitalist powers find themselves on opposing sides in rival alliances—America and Europe against Japan, for example, or America and Japan versus China and Europe. In such a world, the national security implications of international trade and investment would outweigh the purely economic aspects. If the United States were to engage in a cold war with Japan or China, the U.S. government would be unlikely to favor the transfer of technology to its enemy—no matter how impressive the arguments for global free trade look on paper. If a German-led Europe emerged as a geopolitical rival of the United States, then the U.S. would have an incentive to minimize its vulnerability to European economic influence, and to pour resources into an effort to surpass Europe in both military and civilian technology. If the great-power conflicts of the future take the form of new cold wars, in which whole economies are pitted against one another, through expensive high-tech arms races, for decades or generations, then the distinction between "national security" and "international economics" is likely to vanish entirely.

We may hope that this bleak vision of a future of geopolitical rivalry between Washington, Tokyo, Berlin, and perhaps other capitalist centers never comes about. Even so, an economic strategy for the United States that simply assumes the existence of perpetual peace and harmony among the great industrial capitalist powers is the one espoused by America's shortsighted, market-worshipping conservatives. Global free trade, based necessarily on perpetual peace among the capitalist powers, is Plan A of the mainstream American right; there is no Plan B. Indeed, radical marketeers on the Republican right seek to abolish the few programs the federal government has for promoting industrial pol-icy—even though in the event of a geopolitical rivalry with capitalist Asia or capitalist Europe, such programs would necessarily be central to America's new cold war arsenal.

Conservatives may reply that they favor defense spending; they are merely opposed to civilian industrial policy. Right answer, wrong cen-tury. The pro-defense, anti-industrial policy conservatives are two or three hundred years out of date. Before the industrial revolution, it was possible for the military sector of a country's economy—its shipyards and arms factories—to exist more or less in isolation from the agricul-tural economy in which most people worked. In a modern, high-tech economy, however, it is not as easy as the conservatives imagine to dis-tinguish "military" from "civilian" technology. The contemporary de-scription of some technologies, like computer technology, as "dual-use" technologies represents a recognition of how difficult it is to separate the gun economy from the butter economy.

Free-market fundamentalists of the *Wall Street Journal* school are fond of saying that if Japan wipes out American high-tech industries by using a protected home market to subsidize its exports, the American con-sumer benefits. As for national defense—well, the Japanese are not going to drop VCRs on Pearl Harbor, are they? Conservatives who argue in this manner ignore the possibility that countries which become leaders in civilian high-tech industries will have an advantage if they choose to convert their technological prowess to military applications. A country like Japan might choose to indefinitely be an economic giant and a military midget. But it is only prudent for the United States to factor in the current civilian sectors of the economies of other major countries in assessing potential military threats in the future. If the Japanese succeed in their project of creating a first-rate space program, it would be folly for American military planners to ignore the possibility that some future Japanese government would pursue military space policies inimical to American interests.

Common sense, then, would seem to dictate concern, in the interest of U.S. national security, about the overall American industrial base—civilian as well as military. On this subject, however, the Republican right has a split personality, espousing utopian views of international har-mony in the area of trade, while at the same time claiming that military threats require the United States to maintain high spending on conven-tional armaments. The only consistent views on this subject are those of guns-and-butter liberals in the tradition of Harry Truman and Lyndon Johnson—who favor both a strong national-security state and a substantial domestic welfare state—and the libertarian isolationists of the right and left, who favor free trade and a small and weak military establishment.

Contemporary American conservatism combines free-market radicalism in theory with support for a generous invisible welfare state that disproportionately benefits the well-to-do. The economic theory of American conservatism—free-market utopianism—is unconvincing. The economic practice of conservatism—lower taxes and higher benefits for the rich, higher taxes and lower benefits for the middle class, the working class, and the poor—is appalling. Having largely created the present budget deficit by means of unnecessary tax cuts for the rich in the 1980s, the Republican elite, in the mid-1990s, is now trying to balance the budget at the expense of middle- and lower-income Americans.

The Contract with America is a triumph of Gingrichian "Newspeak": budget legislation is camouflaged as "The Fiscal Responsibility Act," a proposal for tax cuts (chiefly for the rich) becomes "The Job Creation and Wage Enhancement Act," and a program of slashing benefits to poor people is nicely sanitized as "The Personal Responsibility Act." Underneath all the Orwellian rhetoric is a brutal reality that the numbers reveal. Although only 21 percent of the federal budget is devoted to the poor, programs of the poor will be cut by 37 to 47 percent under the Republican budget plan. While the poor bear a disproportionate burden of cuts, almost half of the $43 billion in tax cuts approved by the Republican Senate, according to the Treasury Department, would go to the 12 percent of Americans whose families earn $100,000 or more.[24] An older, traditional, patrician conservatism believed in noblesse oblige. The privileged, it was thought, should set an example of sacrifice for the lower orders. The attitude of the present generation of American conservatives is more like that of John D. Rockefeller, who reportedly once said, "God gave me my money."

Today's conservatives run for office as populists, and then govern on behalf of the plutocracy. The disengagement of the conservative leadership from the needs and concerns of ordinary working Americans was inadvertently captured in Newt Gingrich's book *To Renew America.* In one passage, the Republican Speaker of the House rhapsodizes about the possibility that millionaires and billionaires in the next century might be able to afford their own space shuttles and to take honeymoon trips in space. "Imagine looking out at the Earth from your honeymoon suite. . . . For those who have everything, a long trip in space will be the equivalent of today's sailboat or yacht or private airplane."[25] While the middle-class majority labors away far below, paying higher taxes under the flat tax system than they once did under progressive taxation, the super-rich will make love in their space yachts in orbit. Who knows? Maybe honeymoons in outer space will be deductible.

Epilogue

Up From Conservatism

Return, for a moment, to the four-way presidential election of 1948. In that election, I argued in Chapter One, the four candidates represented four coherent alternatives for the United States: left-liberalism (Henry Wallace), national liberalism (Harry Truman), neoliberalism or conservative centrism (Thomas Dewey), and extreme conservatism (Strom Thurmond). Three of these tendencies—left-liberalism, neoliberalism, and extreme conservatism—are represented in American political life today. National liberalism, the liberalism of FDR, Truman, Johnson, Humphrey, Henry M. "Scoop" Jackson, Bayard Rustin, and Martin Luther King, Jr., is gone.

This is a tragedy for America, not just for the Democratic party. Practically every worthwhile reform of this century that has extended personal liberty or economic security to ordinary Americans was the work of the national liberals—the FDR-Truman-Johnson Democrats. Try to name one reform, by Taft or Coolidge or Reagan, that has done as much to protect or enfranchise Americans as the Social Security Act of Franklin Delano Roosevelt, Harry Truman's G.I. Bill, or the Civil Rights and Voting Rights Acts that Lyndon Johnson pushed through Congress, along with Medicare, Medicaid, student loans, and Head Start. Most Americans today are better off than they would have been without the work of the New Deal–vital center liberals. Indeed, if conservatives had not succeeded in blocking the completion of the New Deal agenda since the 1960s—guaranteed health care for all Americans, workfare, more generous allowances for the working poor, family allowances—the dramatic increases in inequality and child poverty in the United States that have occurred under a quarter-century of Republican presidential domination might never have taken place.

The point can hardly be stressed too much: on all of the great political debates of the twentieth century, the national liberals were right and their opponents, the left-liberals and the conservatives, were wrong. (Neoliberalism became a coherent philosophy too recently for its adherents to have participated in the great debates.) Consider these controversies:

The Cold War. The left, from Wallace to McGovern, favored unilateral appeasement. The right favored an ill-considered policy of rollback. The national liberals devised and implemented the policy of containment, of siege in Europe accompanied by proxy war and political warfare elsewhere in the world. At the cost of almost 100,000 dead in Korea and Vietnam, the United States and its coalition prevailed, following the containment strategy through to the end. Ronald Reagan and George Bush, who abandoned "rollback" for containment, did not win the cold war. The cold war was won by Harry Truman, Dean Acheson, George Marshall, and Paul Nitze, along with their allies among the statesmen of postwar Europe and Asia.

The national liberals were right about American communism, too. They supported the security measures necessary to monitor and check the activities of Soviet agents in the United States (yes, there were some), just as they had supported measures against agents of Hitler during World War II. Revelations following the fall of the Soviet Union have proven that American communists indeed received direction and money from Moscow at a time when many of their left-liberal defenders claimed they were independent. While they were justified in being wary of the Soviet Union's agents and friends in the United States, the national liberals resisted (though often not strongly enough) the conservative attempt to use anticommunism in order to attack domestic minorities and groups that had nothing to do with the Soviet Union: liberals, democratic socialists, blacks, homosexuals, innovative and provocative artists. Arthur Schlesinger, Jr. got it right in the late 1940s when he observed that communism was a threat to America, not a threat in America. The liberal anticommunists of the center were right about American communism. The conservative anticommunists and the left-liberal anti-anti-communists were wrong.

Civil Rights. The left's civil rights program from the 1960s to the present has been based on the extension into all areas of American life of compensatory racial preferences that discriminate against white Americans. American conservatives supported segregation, and, once that battle was lost, began trying to maximize opportunities for informal segregation by means like school choice. The national liberals were integrationists, opposing both segregation and racial quotas in favor of strict federal anti-discrimination laws. They were right, and the left-liberals and conservatives were wrong.

In the 1980s, conservatives were right to oppose the left-liberal ideology of multiculturalism, though the most persuasive critique of multiculturalism came from a vital center liberal, Arthur Schlesinger, Jr. Critiques of Afrocentrism by integrationist liberals like Schlesinger cannot be dismissed as racist—unlike critiques coming from conservatives who take seriously Charles Murray's pseudoscientific theory that blacks on average are genetically inferior to whites.

The Economy. The left has favored socialism, or an exorbitant social-democratic apparatus. The right has favored laissez-faire and minimal government. The national liberals rejected both socialism and laissez-faire for what used to be called "the mixed economy" and what is now called "the social market"—a system of private property and free enterprise characterized by government entitlements protecting citizens from the vicissitudes of the market and a substantial degree of regulation in the public interest. The model of capitalism that prevailed in the economic competition with communist countries is social-market capitalism, not laissez-faire capitalism. Once again, the national liberals have been vindicated by history, and their leftist and conservative adversaries have been discredited.

In short, the American national liberals in the tradition of FDR, Truman, and Johnson (and, if we go back far enough, of Theodore Roosevelt), the liberals who were too right-wing for the left and too left-wing for the conservatives, have been consistently right. They were right about foreign policy; they were right about civil rights; and they were right about modern industrial capitalism. The left and the right in the twentieth-century United States have both been consistently wrong.

Not that this has mattered. Twentieth-century American national liberals have won all of the great debates—and lost the political war.

Suppose someone told you about a political movement whose leaders describe themselves as radicals and revolutionaries. Suppose, moreover, you were told that these radicals and revolutionaries detested most of the established institutions of American society—including the schools and universities, the courts, the museums, the mainline churches—and considered the federal government a tyrannical police state different only in the degree of its oppressiveness from fascist or communist regimes. Suppose you learned that many of the radicals had given moral support and encouragement to small bands of armed militants who had murdered federal law enforcement officers attempting to serve warrants. You might conclude that you were being told about a movement of the radical left. In fact, the above is a description of contemporary American conservatism—and not just the lunatic fringe, but the new mainstream.

What passes for conservatism in the United States today, I have endeavored to show in this book, has nothing whatsoever to do with conservatism of a kind that Edmund Burke or Daniel Webster would have recognized. Nor is it a "situational conservatism" of the sort that Samuel P. Huntington has described. The right today—as its leaders proudly boast—is a radical right, a revolutionary right.

In a prescient 1982 essay, Samuel Francis called for other members of the New Right to recognize that they were not conservatives at all, but populist radicals. "To call the New Right 'conservative,' then, is true only in a rather abstruse sense," Francis wrote. He suggested that "the political style, tactics, and organizational forms of the New Right should find a radical, antiestablishment approach better adapted to the achievement of its goals."[1] At the time that he wrote this, Francis represented an idiosyncratic minority on the right. More typical were the views of George Will, then a spokesman for "Tory" establishmentarianism who sneered at the "*soi disant* conservatism" of radical anti-statists, and the views of Republican neoconservatives who claimed to be fulfilling, not betraying, the New Deal–vital center liberal tradition.

By the 1990s—ironically, after a decade of conservative successes and domination of the government—the idea of the right as radicalism rather than conservatism had traveled from the fringe of the conservative movement to the center. Michael Joyce, who as president of the Bradley Foundation is one of the most powerful figures of the foundation-subsidized right, told attendants at a conference in Washington convened by *National Review*:

> Now, I'm aware that much of what I'm saying must seem unconservative to you, perhaps even radical. It may sound as if I'm suggesting that conservatism should now engage in the sort of counter-cultural activities that previously dismayed us. I am.

(Laughter and applause).

Given the structure of power in America today, it is time we realized that we are indeed the counter-culture. We are the revolutionaries.

(Applause).

Joyce's claim that "the structure of power" in the United States is hostile to conservatism is surreal. The United States, after all, has the least generous welfare state in the industrial world. Organized labor is weaker here than in any other industrial democracy, with the possible exception of Japan. Beginning in the 1980s, the Democratic party became more dependent on campaign contributions from business and professional associates than from labor. Not one major New Deal or Great Society–style program has been proposed or passed by a Democratic president since Lyndon Johnson; even Clinton's health care program would have established the least statist, most market-oriented system of universal health insurance to be found among the industrial democracies. By the time that Joyce addressed the *National Review* conference, liberalism in the New Deal tradition had been dead for almost a quarter of a century, and left-liberalism had retreated to a few departments on a small number of college campuses. The "liberalism" of Bill Clinton in many ways is further to the right than the modern conservatism of Republicans like Eisenhower, Rockefeller, and Lindsay.

Nevertheless, it would be a mistake not to take an influential figure on the right like Michael Joyce seriously when he says he is a countercultural radical. The radicalism of Joyce and his fellow conservatives is real. Their revolution is one that benefits the rich rather than the middle class or the poor, but it is a revolution nonetheless; history is full of examples of revolutions by ruthless and self-aggrandizing aristocracies and oligarchies seeking to acquire more power and wealth for themselves, at the expense of majorities. The revolutionary right seeks to reduce many of the individual rights that American citizens have won since the civil rights revolution, like protections against racial discrimination and the right to a legal abortion, and to curtail or repeal many of the reforms protecting wage-earning Americans that have been enacted in the last century by Progressives and New Deal and vital center liberals.

The chief beneficiaries of the radicalism of the right, as I have tried to show, are the small number of individuals and families that constitute the economic elite of the United States. Not content with having seen most of the economic growth in the Reagan-Bush era end up in their pockets, the predominantly Republican economic elite seeks to absorb even more of the resources produced by our slow-growing economy, at the expense, if necessary, of the wage-earning majority. The costs of further artificial enrichment of the American overclass by the conservative program will be borne by the American middle class. Middle-class Americans will suffer far more than overclass Americans as a result of conservative cuts in entitlements. At the same time, middle-class Americans will end up paying a higher proportion of their income than overclass Americans in the form of taxes, if conservatives succeed in enacting a flat tax or funding government less out of progressive federal income taxes and more out of the regressive federal payroll tax and regressive state sales taxes on property and food.

Because the United States is a democracy, if only an imperfect one, the economic elite cannot achieve its goals directly (as it could, say, in Chile, under the murderous military dictatorship of General Augusto Pinochet, whom so many American conservatives admire). True, the escalating cost of political campaigns in the United States gives rich individuals and special interests (most of them corporate or professional groups) the power to prescreen candidates and eliminate those who are not acceptable. However, even those candidates who persuade the economic elite to bankroll them still have to be nominated by voters in party primaries and supported by pluralities in general elections. The fact that the electorate is composed disproportionately of upper-income voters helps the candidates of the economic elite. Middle- and lower-income Americans, though, must be persuaded to vote against their economic interests and to vote for the candidates of the right.

As I have argued, conservative strategists try to persuade wage-earning Americans to vote against liberal economic policies that would benefit them and their families by means of "the culture war." The Republican culture war, originating in Richard Nixon's "southern strategy" of coopting supporters of George Wallace, and perfected by Republican strategists like Lee Atwater and William Kristol, is nothing more than an updated version of the political demagogy which the oligarchic Bourbon Democrats of the New South in the first half of the twentieth century employed to divide low- and middle-income southern whites from their potential allies—poor blacks and northern liberals and moderates (Democratic as well as Republican). It is no coincidence that the Republican politicians who have risen to the top in the age of culture-war politics are southern politicians, like Newt Gingrich, Dick Armey, and Phil Gramm, who, even if they were not born in the South, have mastered the characteristic style of southern political culture.

The southern strategy has been more successful than Nixon anticipated. It has led to massive conversions of ex-Democratic white southerners to the GOP. As the weight of white southern converts in the Republican party has increased, and as the influence of old-fashioned northeastern and midwestern Republicans has declined, the party has increasingly adopted age-old southern obsessions about religion, race, guns, and taxes as its own. As the end of the twentieth century approaches, the American right in general has become difficult to distinguish from the southern Jefferson-Jackson right, in its industrialized New South rather than agrarian Old South incarnation.

If liberalism in the Progressive—New Deal—vital center tradition had survived, a radicalized Republican party dominated by white southern and western reactionaries in the tradition of William Jennings Bryan and Strom Thurmond might have been easily marginalized. However, as I have shown, the proponents of the mainstream liberal or national liberal tradition in the United States were defeated in the 1960s by the champions of left liberalism, a movement which had its roots both in upper-middle-class reformism and the socialist and communist traditions of immigrants from Central and Eastern Europe in the northeastern United States. The left's destruction of national liberalism, instead of bringing the left to power, inaugurated a bipartisan conservative political realignment in the 1970s that began with the election of Jimmy Carter. As a result of this conservative realignment, the most successful political factions since the 1970s have been conservatives, running *against* the cultural left, and neoliberals, running *from* the cultural left.

To a large extent the political struggles since the 1960s have represented a three-way feud within the American social elite. The major social trend of our time is not the growth of the black underclass (a phenomenon that is greatly exaggerated) but the growth in wealth and power of a new, credentialed, mostly white national overclass that has emerged from the fusion of the old northeastern elite with upwardly mobile white southerners and westerners and white ethnics. Defined chiefly by advanced education, this new bicoastal establishment of business executives, professionals, and professors shows signs of turning from a class with its own distinct lifestyle and subculture into a segregated, self-perpetuating caste.

All three of the major political positions represented in the contemporary United States—left liberalism, neoliberalism, and conservatism (more specifically, libertarian conservatism)—promote the values, or the interests, or both, of members of the overclass, which accounts for less than 10 percent of the U.S. population. The "radical center," the group of wage-earning Americans who are socially moderate or conservative and liberal in economics, have not been represented in national politics since the defeat of the New Deal–vital center national liberals by the New Politics–New Left left-liberals in 1968–72. Deprived not only of a major party, but even of a major faction within a major party, the middle-class voters of the radical center have flailed around aimlessly. Some have split their votes between Republican presidents (who appealed to their values) and Democratic Congresses (which protected their economic interests); others rallied behind Ross Perot; still others voted for an all-Democratic government in 1992 and then, frustrated, voted for a Republican sweep in 1994. As the years pass and both the values and the pocketbook interests of the radical center are ignored, this group of swing voters has become ever more alienated from the political system and distrustful of a political class that responds chiefly to the overclass left, the overclass right, and the overclass center. Patrick Buchanan's attempt to join the radical center to the far right in a sinister version of populism would not have been possible had the political establishment not neglected the radical center for decades.

The absence of a viable national liberal alternative, then, has done more than permit conservative victory by default. It has engendered a degree of alienation on the part of former New Deal–vital center Democrats that is destabilizing the American political order itself. Restoring national liberalism, in a form that addresses contemporary problems while remaining true to the principles of FDR, Harry Truman, Lyndon Johnson, Hubert Humphrey, and Martin Luther King, Jr. may be necessary not only to defeat the radicals of the southernized right, but also to restore the legitimacy of the American political system in the public mind.

In *The Next American Nation,* I provided a sketch of what a renovated American national liberalism might be. It would combine features of the conventional "left" and the conventional "right." A new national liberalism would favor immigration restriction (to boost wages for low-income Americans) and the outlawing of affirmative action and racial labeling (in favor of race-neutral federal antidiscrimination law). At the same time, a new national liberalism would seek to defend and reform, not destroy, the modern "warfare-welfare state" created by the New Deal and vital center liberals. Against pacifists on the left and isolationists on the right, a new generation of national liberals would defend the interests of the United States as a great power in a dangerous world, and support a strong and appropriate (though not a bloated and inappropriate) military-industrial sector. National liberals would unite their defense of the American national-security state, in the form bequeathed by FDR and Truman, with a defense of the American welfare state or social-market state, whose primary beneficiaries are not the idle poor, as conservatives pretend, but wage-earning, hardworking Americans. The American social-market state should be saved—by replacing welfare with workfare, and by means-testing entitlements to cut costs—and not savaged. Indeed, once existing entitlements are put on a solvent basis, national liberals might support the creation of new entitlements—to universal health care, and to free college education for qualified students. In short, a new national liberal movement would favor a Truman-style policy of guns and butter, paid for by reducing the entitlements and raising the taxes of the wealthy minority, as an alternative to the butter-without-guns policy of the left-liberals and the guns-without-butter policy of the conservatives and the neoliberals.

The obstacles in the way of a revival of national liberalism in the United States are enormous. A new generation of national liberals may find it difficult to raise money, either from conservative business elites or from affluent "limousine liberals" whose cultural radicalism is offended by the stance of national liberals on issues like affirmative action and immigration. For a generation, at least, it seems certain, national liberalism will not be a force in American national politics. The gap in the political spectrum where the liberalism of TR, FDR, Truman, and Johnson was once found will remain.

For the indefinite future, national liberals will have to choose between the existing political alternatives: left liberalism, neoliberalism, and conservatism. In the 1970s and 1980s, the original neoconservatives (that is, liberals in the New Deal–vital center) allied themselves on issues like welfare reform, racial preference, and multiculturalism with the neoliberal-conservative right. This was sound strategy at the time, inasmuch as the left-liberals, as competitors and not just enemies, were the greatest threat to the national liberal remnant. This strategy succeeded—so much so that by the dawn of the 1990s the briefly triumphant left liberalism of the 1970s was in a state of collapse and disarray. The most that the left-liberals could do was to defend existing affirmative-action and welfare programs, even as a growing number of their own ranks joined the neo-conservatives in questioning left-liberal ideology.

Today left liberalism is very close to becoming extinct as a significant force on the national political scene (though it may survive in a few states or cities, particularly college towns). The collapse of left liberalism in the 1990s, following the destruction of national liberalism in the 1960s, means that the major political struggle of our time is the battle between neoliberals (in the Republican as well as in the Democratic party) and conservatives (in the Republican party). To someone in the Progressive–New Deal–vital center tradition, the differences between conservatives and neoliberals seem minor, particularly with respect to economic questions. Both Gingrichite conservatives and Clintonite ne-oliberals support free trade and high levels of immigration. Neverthe-less, it is my conviction that despite disagreements over particular policies national liberals should support neoliberals, both Democratic and Republican, against conservatives. The reason is simple. Conserva-tives reject both the goals and the means of New Deal–vital center lib-eralism, whereas neoliberals reject only the means. Neoliberals claim that the goals of old-fashioned liberalism, like full employment, univer-sal health care, an equitable and efficient public educational system, and racial integration can be achieved by conservative means, like privatiza-tion, decentralization, and tax cuts. In most cases, the neoliberals are mistaken—the goals of big-government liberalism can be achieved only by big-government liberal means. Though the programs necessary to realize liberal goals in the twenty-first century may well be different from the programs of FDR, Truman, and Johnson, they will be equally centralized, and perhaps equally expensive. Even though the neoliberals are wrong, they are only half wrong, whereas the conservatives are wholly wrong.

National liberals, then, should lend their energies to helping the neo-liberals defeat the conservatives (even as attempts are made to establish a new national liberal movement). To use the 1948 analogy once again, in the absence of a Truman, it is necessary to support moderate Thomas Dewey–style conservatism (today's neoliberalism) against right-wing radicalism of the Strom Thurmond variety (today's conservatism, even in its "moderate" forms). Once the radicals of the far right have been defeated, the neoliberals can be allowed to try their nonstatist ap-proaches to realizing liberal goals. If they succeed, then the neoliberals should be congratulated, for achieving liberal goals inexpensively. If they fail, the failure of neoliberalism might then prepare the way for a renaissance of old-fashioned, guns-and-butter national liberalism some time in the second or third decade of the twenty-first century.

And what if the effort to defeat the extremists of the right should fail? What if the radical southernized right succeeds in consolidating its control of the Republican party and, through it, of the federal government? If that should happen, the future of the United States might well resemble the history of the New South from 1875 to 1954, or that of many Latin American countries, where the major political contest has been a struggle between an oligarchic, reactionary right and a populist radical right, each employing the techniques of demagogy, when out of power, and authoritarianism, when in power, in its war with the other. A future in which the alternatives are symbolized by Newt Gingrich and Patrick Buchanan is grim to imagine—but, alas, not all that difficult to imagine.

It is too late to rescue American conservatism from the radical right. But it is not too late to rescue America from conservatism.

Notes

Introduction

1. Quoted in Lloyd Grove, "The Castle Storms Back: GOP Establishment Aims Its Cross-bows at Pat Buchanan and His Hordes," *Washington Post,* February 23, 1996.
2. Irving Kristol, "America's Exceptional Conservatism," *Wall Street Journal,* April 18, 1995.
3. Only two years earlier, for the small and sophisticated audience of *National Interest,* Irving Kristol had sneered at what he called "the American common man": "In any case, my tepid loyalty to 'democratic socialism' did not survive my experiences as an infantryman in the Army. I entered military service with a prefabricated set of attitudes: . . . the common soldiers, for all their human imperfections, represented the potential for a better future. Well, it turned out that, as a provincial from New York, I knew nothing about the American common man. . . . The idea of building socialism with the common man who actually existed—as distinct from his idealized version—was sheer fantasy, and therefore the prospects for 'democratic socialism' were nil"—but not, it seems, for "a democratic populism," Irving Kristol, "My Cold War," *National Interest,* Spring 1993, p. 143.
4. Jerry Gray, "Budget Axes Land on Items Big and Small," *New York Times,* February 28, 1995, p. A14.
5. Richard I. Berke, "Poll Finds Dole Shows Strength on Personal and Political Traits," *New York Times,* Sunday, April 7, 1996, p. A1.
6. Donald Warren, *Radio Priest: Charles Coughlin, the Father of Hate Radio* (New York: Free Press, 1996), advance uncorrected proofs.

Chapter 1

1. Walter Dean Burnham, "Realignment Lives: The 1994 Earthquake and Its Implications," in Colin Campbell and Bert A. Rockman, eds., *The Clinton Presidency: First Appraisals* (Chatham, N.J.: Chatham House, 1996), p. 367.

2. John Zvesper, "Party realignment: a past without a future?" in Robert Williams, ed., *Explaining American Politics* (London: Routledge, 1990), pp. 168–170.

3. Samuel Lubell, *The Future of American Politics*, 3rd ed. (New York: Harper & Row, 1965), pp. 191–192.

4. See Stanley Rothman and S. Robert Lichter, *Roots of Radicalism: Jews, Christians, and the New Left* (New York: Oxford University Press, 1982), pp. 80–145.

5. Byron E. Shafer, *Quiet Revolution* (New York: Russell Sage Foundation, 1983), p. 465.

6. Quoted in Harold Meyerson, "Whither the Democrats?" *American Prospect,* March–April 1996, p. 82.

7. Elizabeth Hardwick, "Mr. America," *New York Review of Books,* November 7, 1968, pp. 3–4.

8. Garry Wills, "Can Wallace Be Made Respectable?" *New York,* March 6, 1972, p. 32.

9. John Judis, following sociologist Donald Warren, has pointed out that the "radical center"—the group I am calling national liberals—are distinct from what Colin Powell called "the sensible center" (neoliberals) and far-right populists. See John Judis, "TRB From Washington: Off Center," *New Republic,* October 16, 1995, p. 4.

10. The data are from the Luxembourg Income Studies, quoted in Seymour Martin Lipset, *American Exceptionalism: A Double-Edged Sword* (New York: W. W. Norton, 1996), p. 73 (uncorrected proof).

11. Donald I. Warren, *The Radical Center: Middle Americans and the Politics of Alienation* (Notre Dame: University of Notre Dame Press, 1976), pp. 20–21.

Chapter 2

1. Arthur M. Schlesinger, Jr., *The Vital Center: The Politics of Freedom* (Boston: Houghton Mifflin, 1949), p. vii.

2. Ibid., p. ix.

3. Ibid.

4. Ibid., p. 31.

5. Ibid., p. 29.

6. See *Meta-Politics: From the Romantics to Hitler* (New York: Knopf, 1941); *Conservatism Revisited: The Revolt Against Revolt, Conservatism Revisited and the New Conservatism: What Went Wrong?, Conservatism from John Adams to Churchill: A History and Anthology* (all published New York: Free Press, 1956; reprinted by Greenwood Press, Westport, Conn., 1978); *The Unadjusted Man: Reflections on the Distinction between Conserving and Conforming* (New York: Free Press, 1956; Greenwood Press, 1973); *Shame and Glory of the Intellectuals: Babbitt Jr. Versus the Rediscovery of Values* (New York: G. P. Putnam's Sons, 1965; reprinted by Greenwood Press, 1978, with supplement on "The Radical Right: From McCarthy to Goldwater").

7. Peter Viereck, *Shame and Glory of the Intellectuals: Babbitt, Jr. vs. the Rediscovery of Values* (New York: Capricorn Books, 1965), p. 249.

8. Quoted in Bob Woodward, *The Agenda: Inside the Clinton White House* (New York: Simon & Schuster, 1994), p. 165.

9. Norman Podhoretz, "The Adversary Culture and the New Class," in B. Bruce-Briggs, ed., *The New Class?* (New Brunswick, N.J.: Transaction Books, 1979), pp. 30–31.

10. Irving Kristol, *Reflections of a Neoconservative: Looking Back, Looking Ahead* (New York: Basic Books, 1983), xii.

11. *Public Papers and Addresses of Franklin D. Roosevelt, 1928–1936,* pp. 771–772, quoted in

Donald Warren, *Radio Priest: Charles Coughlin, the Father of Hate Radio* (New York: Free Press, 1996), p. 43 (advance uncorrected proofs).

Chapter 3

1. Alan Crawford, *Thunder on the Right: The "New Right" and the Politics of Resentment* (New York: Pantheon, 1980).
2. One of the targets of Simon and his partners was Anchor Glass, which managed to save itself from the takeover only by desperately slashing the work force. While many long-time Anchor employees found their lives in ruins, Simon, according to the *Los Angeles Times,* "made more than 100 times his money" (Bill Sing, "Average Return Ranges from 30% to 50%; Players in LBO Game Often Hit Giant Jackpots," *Los Angeles Times,* October 30, 1988, part 4, p. 1).
3. See Peter Coleman, *The Liberal Conspiracy* (New York: Free Press, 1989)
4. James Madison, the namesake of the Madison Center, is also the mascot of the Federalist Society, a nationwide organization of conservative lawyers, students, and professors. One of the early members of the Federalist Society told me that Madison owed his recent and peculiar popularity on the right to the fact that he is neither controversial (like Alexander Hamilton, Madison's collaborator on *The Federalist Papers*) nor completely obscure (like the other contributor to *The Federalist Papers,* John Jay).
5. Samuel Francis, *Beautiful Losers: Essays on the Failure of American Conservatism* (Columbia: University of Missouri Press, 1993), p. 227.
6. Frank Rich, "The Pratt Fall," *New York Times,* February 17, 1996, p. 23.
7. Lionel Trilling, *The Liberal Imagination* (Garden City, N.Y.: Doubleday Anchor Books, 1954), pp. 5–6.
8. Indeed, TR, the presidential candidate of the Progressive party, despised the "muckrakers" (he coined the term).

Chapter 4

1. Pat Robertson, *The New World Order* (Dallas: Word Publishing, 1991), p. 37.
2. Ibid., pp. 68–69.
3. Ibid., p.61.
4. Ibid., p. 123.
5. Ibid., p. 265.
6. Ibid., p. 61.
7. Ibid., p. 121.
8. Ibid., p. 122.
9. Ibid., pp. 80–81.
10. Ibid., pp. 75–76.
11. Ibid., p. 31.
12. Ibid., p. 64.
13. Ibid., p. 10.
14. Ibid., p. 13.
15. Jacob Heilbrunn, "On Pat Robertson: His Anti-Semitic Sources," *New York Review of Books.*

16. Nesta H. Webster, *World Revolution: The Plot Against Civilization* (London: Constable, 1922), p. 8.

17. Robertson, *The New World Order.*

18. Nesta H. Webster, *Secret Societies and Subversive Movements* (London: Dutton, 1924), pp. 230–231, 383.

19. Webster, *World Revolution,* pp. 19–20.

20. Robertson, *The New World Order,* p. 181.

21. Ibid.

22. Webster, *Secret Societies,* p. 368.

23. Robertson, *The New World Order,* p. 123.

24. Ibid.

25. Eustace Mullins, *Secrets of the Federal Reserve* (Staunton, Virginia: Bankers Research Institute, 1954), pp. 4–5.

26. William Guy Carr, *Pawns in the Game* (Toronto: National Federation of Christian Laymen, 1955), p. 154.

27. In 1938 Coughlin helped mobilize a popular campaign to urge Congress to kill an innocuous government reorganization bill. In the words of President Roosevelt, "Members of Congress, the House and the Senate, were flooded with telegrams that this bill would give the President a chance to grab all of the church schools of the Nation, the Protestant church schools and the Parochial school, although I don't know what the President of the United States was going to do with them when he did grab them." *New York Times,* April 29, 1938, quoted in Donald Warren, *Radio Priest, Charles Coughlin, the Father of Hate Radio* (New York: Free Press, 1996), pp. 96–97 (advance uncorrected proof).

28. Coughlin radio address, February 26, 1933, quoted in Warren, p. 134.

29. Coughlin radio address, December 23, 1934, quoted in Warren, p. 120.

30. Coughlin radio addresses, February 2, 1930, and February 26, 1933, quoted in Warren, pp. 132–133.

31. David H. Bennett, *The Party of Fear: From Nativist Movements to the New Right in American History* (Chapel Hill: University of North Carolina Press, 1988), p. 317.

32. Robert Welch, *The Politician* (Belmont, Mass.: privately printed for Robert Welch, 1953), pp. 276–279; quoted in Lee Edwards, *Goldwater: The Man Who Made a Revolution* (Washington, D.C.: Regnery, 1995), pp. 90–91.

33. "The Week," *National Review,* February 6, 1995, p. 10.

34. Norman Podhoretz, "In the Matter of Pat Robertson," *Commentary,* August 1995, pp. 27–32.

35. Quoted in *Detroit Jewish Chronicle,* November 2, 1934; cited in Warren, p. 136.

36. *Detroit News,* August 11, 1973, quoted in ibid., p. 134.

37. Pat Robertson, *The New Millennium,* in *The Collected Works of Pat Robertson* (New York: Inspirational Press/Arrowood Press, 1994), pp. 256–257.

38. Coughlin radio address, November 20, 1938; quoted in Warren, pp. 156–157.

39. Warren, pp. 164–165.

40. Quoted in Bennett, *Party of Fear,* pp. 388–389.

41. "The Charlie Rose Show," October 26, 1995.

42. "Many Jews, it must be said," Hofstadter writes, "might have found Harvey's embraces harder to endure than his slurs." Richard Hofstadter, *The Paranoid Style in American Politics* (Chicago: University of Chicago Press, 1979), p. 301.

43. In 1986, Doug Harlan, a Republican columnist in Texas, warned that "religious fundamentalists are to Republicans what LaRouchites are to Democrats, but the threat to Republicans from the religious right is far greater than the threat to Democrats from

LaRouche." Doug Harlan, "Test of Fundamentalists' Power in GOP 5 Weeks Off," *Houston Post,* May 25, 1986, p. B3.

Chapter 5

1. August 10–17, 1963, pp. 10–12.
2. Quoted in George Brown Tindall, *The Disruption of the Solid South* (University of Georgia Press, 1972), p. 60.
3. Quoted in Lee Edwards, *Goldwater: The Man Who Made A Revolution* (Washington, D.C: Regnery, 1995), p. 361.
4. Robert Alan Goldberg, *Barry Goldwater* (New Haven: Yale University Press), p. 115.
5. Nicol Rae, *The Decline and Fall of the Liberal Republicans* (New York: Oxford University Press, 1989), pp. 75–76.
6. Quoted in Kenneth O'Reilly, *Nixon's Piano: Presidents and Racial Politics From Washington to Clinton* (New York: Free Press, 1995), pp. 285–286.
7. Michael Lind, "The Southern Coup," *New Republic,* June 19, 1995, pp. 20–29.
8. Chandler Davidson, *Race and Class in Texas Politics* (Princeton: Princeton University Press, 1990), p. 212.
9. Michael B. Berkman, *The State Roots of National Politics: Congress and the Tax Agenda, 1978–1986* (Pittsburgh: University of Pittsburgh Press, 1993), p. 72.
10. Daniel J. Elazar, *The American Mosaic: The Impact of Space, Time, and Culture on American Politics,* (Boulder, Colo.: Westview Press, 1994), p. 248.
11. Samuel P. Huntington, "Conservatism as an Ideology," *American Political Science Review,* 51, no. 2 (June 1957), pp. 454–473.

Chapter 6

1. Lee Atwater, "The South in 1984," unpublished memo for the Reagan-Bush campaign, quoted in Thomas Byrne Edsall and Mary D. Edsall, *Chain Reaction: The Impact of Race, Rights and Taxes on American Politics* (New York: W. W. Norton, 1990), p. 221.
2. Quotes from O'Reilly, *Nixon's Piano,* pp. 286–287 (Agnew), 308, 310.
3. Michael Novak, "Morality: How It Became a Four-Letter Word," *Rising Tide,* Sept./Oct. 1995, pp. 10–13.
4. Maureen Dowd, "G.O.P.'s Rising Star Pledges to Right Wrongs of the Left," *New York Times,* November 10, 1994, p. A1.
5. William F. Buckley, Jr., *God and Man at Yale* (Washington D.C.: Regnery Gateway, 1986), pp. 169–170.
6. John Judis, "The Porn Broker," *New Republic,* June 5, 1995, pp. 14–16.
7. James Boswell, *Life of Johnson* (London: Oxford University Press, 1934–50), vol. III, p. 192.
8. Dick Armey, *The Freedom Revolution* (Washington, D.C.: Regnery, 1995), pp. 3–18.
9. Jeane Kirkpatrick, *Dictatorships and Double Standards: Rationalism and Reason in Politics* (New York: Simon & Schuster, 1982), pp. 194–195.
10. Peter Steinfels, "Beliefs," *New York Times,* January 28, 1995, p. 9.
11. Lisa Bannon, "Bazaar Gossip: How a Rumor Spread About Subliminal Sex in Disney's 'Aladdin,' " *Wall Street Journal,* October 24, 1995, p. A1.
12. Some liberals have suggested that the center and the left should reclaim the language of Biblical morality for progressive politics. The last thing we need, at this point in Amer-

ican history, is for liberals too to start invoking verses from the Gospel of Matthew and Deuteronomy on behalf of this or that bill in Congress.

13. John Gray, "Conservatism, Individualism, and the Political Thought of the New Right," in J. C. D. Clark, ed., *Ideas and Politics in Modern Britain* (London: Macmillan, 1990), p. 92.

14. Robert Devigne, *Recasting Conservatism: Oakeshott, Strauss, and the Response to Postmodernism* (New Haven: Yale University Press, 1994), p. 118.

15. Irving Kristol, quoted in Devigne, *Recasting Conservatism*, p. 114.

16. Quoted in Kenneth L. Woodward, "Losing Our Moral Umbrella," *Newsweek,* December 7, 1992, p. 60.

17. Jacob Neusner, "Letter from Inner Israel," *Chronicles,* April 1996, p. 34.

18. Connie Bruck, "The Politics of Perception," *New Yorker,* October 9, 1995, p. 62.

19. Frank Rich, "Gingrich Family Values," *New York Times*, May 14, 1995, Section 4, p. 15; "Victim's Family to Gingrich: Butt Out," combined dispatches, *Washington Times,* November 23, 1995, p. A3.

20. Quoted in Elizabeth Kolbert, "Politics: A Radio Ruckus," *New York Times,* February 24, 1996, p.8.

Chapter 7

1. David E. Rosenbaum, "It's Reaganomics, Alive and Irresistible," *New York Times* Week in Review, February 11, 1996, pp. 1, 5.

2. Peter G. Peterson, *Facing Up: How to Rescue the Economy from Crushing Debt and Restore the American Dream* (New York: Simon & Schuster, 1993), p. 89.

3. Ibid., p. 88.

4. Citizens for Tax Justice, *The Hidden Entitlements* (Washington, D.C.: Citizens for Tax Justice, April 1995), pp. 17–18.

5. David C. Berliner and Bruce J. Biddle, *The Manufactured Crisis: Myths, Fraud, and the Attack on America's Public Schools* (New York: Addison-Wesley, 1995), p. 3.

6. Ibid., pp. 56–57.

7. Ibid., pp. 20–22.

8. Peter Applebome, "Have Schools Failed? Revisionists Use Army of Statistics to Argue No," *New York Times,* December 13, 1995, p. B16.

9. Berliner and Biddle, *The Manufactured Crisis,* p. 44.

10. Richard Rothstein and Karen Hawley Miles, "Where's the Money Gone?" Economic Policy Institute.

11. Berliner and Biddle, pp. 77–83.

12. Barry O'Neill, "The History of a Hoax," *New York Times Magazine,* March 6, 1994, pp. 45–49.

13. Applebome, "Have Schools Failed?" p. B16.

14. Cynthia L. Patrick and Robert C. Calfee, "A Textbook Case of Hype," *Washington Post,* April 7, 1996, p. C4.

15. Quoted in Amy E. Schwartz, ". . . And Progress at a Summit," *Washington Post,* Sunday, April 7, 1996, p. C7.

16. Gerald D. Jaynes and Robin M. Williams, Jr., eds., *A Common Destiny: Blacks in American Society* (Washington, D.C.: National Academy Press, 1989), p. 275.

17. Charles Murray, "The Coming White Underclass," *Wall Street Journal,* October 29, 1993.

18. Barbara Defoe Whitehead, "Dan Quayle Was Right," *Atlantic Monthly,* April 1993.

19. Claudette Bennett, *The Black Population in the United States,* U.S. Bureau of the Census,

Current Population Reports, pp. 20–480 (Washington, D.C.: Government Printing Office, 1995).

20. Christopher Jencks, "Is the American Underclass Growing?" in Christopher Jencks and Paul E. Peterson, eds., *The Urban Underclass* (Washington, D.C.: Brookings Institution, 1991).

21. Marvin Harris, *Why Nothing Works: The Anthropology of Daily Life* (New York: Simon & Schuster, 1987), p. 82.

22. Ibid.

23. Quoted in Tamar Lewin, "Family Decay Global, Study Says," *New York Times,* May 30, 1995, p. A5.

24. Ferdinand Mount, *The Subversive Family: An Alternative History of Love and Marriage* (New York: Free Press, 1992), pp. 15–28.

25. *Public Interest,* Winter 1991.

26. Ibid., p. 4.

27. Ibid., p. 5.

28. See William J. Broad, *Teller's War: The Top-Secret Story Behind the Star Wars Deception* (New York: Simon & Schuster, 1992).

29. Tim Weiner, "Inquiry Finds 'Star Wars' Tried Plan to Exaggerate Test Results," *New York Times,* July 23, 1994, p. 1.

30. William Kristol, "Defeating President Clinton's Health Care Proposal," Memo of December 2, 1993, quoted in Stanley B. Greenberg, *Middle-Class Dreams: The Politics and Power of the New American Majority* (New York: Times Books, 1995), pp. 282–283.

31. Elizabeth McCaughey, "No Exit," *New Republic,* February 7, 1994, pp. 21–25; "Health Insurance for All," *Wall Street Journal,* April 28, 1994, p. A12.

32. Mickey Kaus, "No Exegesis," *New Republic,* May 8, 1995, p. 6.

33. John Schwartz, "Americans Receive New Medicines as Quickly as Others, FDA Reports," *Washington Post,* December 13, 1995, p. A3.

34. The exceptions prove the rule. Herb Stein of the American Enterprise Institute consistently inveighed against supply-side economics. Diane Ravitch, assistant secretary of education under Reagan and Bush, pointed out that the data did not show that private schools are significantly better than public schools. Neither had any influence in modifying the conservative orthodoxy.

35. Irving Kristol, "American Conservatism 1945–1995," *Public Interest,* Fall 1995, pp. 80–91.

36. Berliner and Biddle, *The Manufactured Crisis,* pp. 59–61.

37. Ibid., pp. 166–167.

38. Patrick and Calfee, "A Textbook Case of Hype."

39. R. M. Helskamp, "Perspectives on Education in America," *Phi Delta Kappan* 74, no. 9 (1993), pp. 718–721.

40. Michael B. Katz, *The Undeserving Poor: From the War on Poverty to the War on Welfare* (New York: Pantheon, 1989), p. 153.

41. Robert Greenstein, "Losing Faith in Losing Ground," *New Republic,* March 25, 1985, p. 14.

42. Christopher Jencks, "How Poor Are the Poor?" *New York Review of Books,* May 5, 1985, p. 41.

43. See Charles Lane, "The Manhattan Project," *New Republic,* March 25, 1985, pp. 14–15.

44. Charles Murray, in particular, is identified with a panacea: abolishing welfare. He has offered not one, but two consistent and quite different rationales for abolishing welfare—discouraging illegitimacy and nonwork (in *Losing Ground*) and preventing the de-

terioration of the American gene pool by discouraging the reproduction of the genetically inferior (*The Bell Curve*). If all you have is a hammer, everything looks like a nail.

45. Former Secretary of Education Lamar Alexander, seeking the Republican presidential nomination, came up with his own ingenious solution to the problem of inequitable funding of school districts: "Sometimes there'll just be better places to live than a place with low wealth and high needs. If you're living in an area with a bad school, you move to a place where there's a better school." Alexander did not explain how inner-city parents might afford houses in the affluent suburbs with the best schools. Kevin Sack, "Alexander Builds His Hopes on Some Radical Departures," *New York Times,* February 18, 1996, pp. A1, A18.

46. Left-liberal ideas like these are more plausibly criticized by neoconservative Democrats like Nathan Glazer and centrist liberals like Arthur Schlesinger, Jr. than by conservatives whose favored alternative to Afrocentrism is "creation science."

Chapter 8

1. Mary Melcher, "Blacks and Whites Together: Interracial Leadership in the Phoenix Civil Rights Movement," *Journal of Arizona History* 32 (Summer 1991), p. 209.

2. Quoted in O'Reilly, *Nixon's Piano,* p. 311.

3. H. R. Haldeman, *The Haldeman Diaries: Inside the Nixon White House* (New York: G. P. Putnam's Sons, 1994), p. 53.

4. O'Reilly, *Nixon's Piano,* p. 292.

5. John Ehrlichman, *Witness to Power* (New York: Simon & Schuster, 1982), pp. 222–223.

6. Ibid., pp. 228–229.

7. O'Reilly, *Nixon's Piano,* p. 285.

8. While he was governor of California, Reagan, a millionaire, neglected to pay taxes one year. He blamed his accountant for the oversight.

9. O'Reilly, *Nixon's Piano,* p. 60.

10. Jason DeParle, "How Jack Kemp Lost the War on Poverty," *New York Times,* February 28, 1993.

11. Richard Herrnstein and Charles Murray, *The Bell Curve* (New York: Free Press, 1994); Dinesh D'Souza, *The End of Racism* (New York: Free Press, 1995); Peter Brimelow, *Alien Nation* (New York: Random House, 1995).

12. Charles Lane, "The Tainted Sources of 'The Bell Curve,' " *New York Review of Books,* December 1, 1994, p. 14.

13. Mark Snyderman, "How to Think About Race," *National Review,* September 12, 1994, pp. 78–80.

14. Bob Herbert, "Affront to Black People," *New York Times,* February 12, 1996, p. A15.

15. Quoted in James Ridgeway, "Divided We Stand," *Village Voice,* October 24, 1995, p. 26.

16. "No More Bleeding Hearts," *New York Times, Week in Review,* July 16, 1995, p. 16.

17. Tony Snow, "Post-March Politics: Can the GOP Win Black Votes Now?" *Washington Post,* Outlook, October 22, 1995, pp. C1, C3.

18. Quoted in Dan T. Carter, *The Politics of Rage: George Wallace, the Origins of the New Conservatism, and the Transformation of American Politics* (New York: Simon & Schuster, 1995), p. 83.

Chapter 9

1. Robert B. Reich, "Big Biz Cuts Class: Firms Talk Loud, Do Little for Schools," *Washington Post,* April 21, 1991, p. B1.

2. Berliner and Biddle, *The Manufactured Crisis,* pp. 84–85.

3. Robert R. Kiley, "New York 2020," *New York Times,* February 17, 1996, p. A23.

4. Matthew A. Crenson and Francis E. Rourke, "By Way of Conclusion: American Bureaucracy Since World War II," in Louis Galambos, ed., *The New American State: Bureaucracies and Policies Since World War II* (Baltimore: Johns Hopkins University Press, 1987), p. 157.

5. Garry Wills, "To Keep and Bear Arms," *New York Review of Books,* September 21, 1995, p. 63.

6. Kenneth S. Stern, *A Force Upon the Plain: The American Militia Movement and the Politics of Hate* (New York: Simon & Schuster, 1996), pp. 52–53.

7. Ibid., pp. 35–36.

8. Ibid., p. 36.

9. Dean M. Kelley, "Waco: A Massacre and Its Aftermath," *First Things,* May 1995, pp. 22–37.

10. James Coates, *Armed and Dangerous: The Rise of the Survivalist Right* (New York: Hill and Wang, 1995), pp. 18–19.

11. David Hackett Fischer, *Albion's Seed: Four British Folkways in America* (New York: Oxford University Press, 1989).

12. President Bush's resignation from the National Rifle Association, in response to the description by one of its leaders of federal law enforcement officers as "jack-booted thugs," was the exception to the rule that today's Republican leaders defer to the sensibilities of fanatical opponents of gun control and the survivalist right.

13. Quoted in *Wall Street Journal,* November 18, 1994.

14. Martin Schram, *Speaking Freely: Former Members of Congress Talk About Money in Politics* (Washington, D.C.: The Center for Responsive Politics, 1995), p. 118.

15. Ibid., p. 116.

16. Ibid., p. 129.

17. Ibid., p. 125.

18. "Parsing Perot," *Wall Street Journal,* August 16, 1995, p. A10.

19. George Will, "Long Leap to a Poll Tax," *Washington Post,* April 2, 1995.

20. Friedrich von Hayek, venerated by libertarian conservatives, thought that Soviet-style economic planning was incompatible with personal liberty. He did not think that welfare-state measures were. Hayek wrote: "There is no reason why in a society which has reached the general level of wealth which ours has attained the first kind of security"— which Hayek has defined as "the certainty of a given minimum of sustenance for all"— "should not be guaranteed to all without endangering general freedom.... [T]here can be no doubt that some minimum of food, shelter, and clothing, sufficient to preserve health and the capacity to work, can be assured to everybody.... [T]here is no incompatibility in principle between the state's providing greater security in this way and the preservation of individual freedom." F. A. Hayek, *The Road to Serfdom* (Chicago: University of Chicago Press, 1994 [1944]), pp. 133–134.

21. Quoted in Dan T. Carter, *The Politics of Rage: George Wallace, The Origins of the New Conservatism, and the Transformation of American Politics* (Simon & Schuster, 1995), p. 218.

Chapter 10

1. One family that has done very well as a result of Reagan-era tax cuts is that of George and Barbara Bush. In 1991, the Bushes reported an adjusted gross income of $1,324,456 and paid $209,964 in federal taxes. In the same year, the median American family made $35,035 and paid the federal government $6,116 in taxes. The tax rate on

George and Barbara Bush (15.9 percent) was lower than that on the median American family (17.6 percent). Donald Barlett and James Steele, *America: Who Really Pays the Taxes?* (New York: Touchstone, 1994), pp. 17–18.

2. Martin Anderson, "The Legend of the Supply-Sider," in Martin Anderson, ed., *Revolution: The Reagan Legacy* (Stanford, Calif.: Hoover Institution Press, 1990), pp. 140–163.

3. Peter Carlson, "The Truth . . . But Not the Whole Truth," *Washington Post Magazine*, June 4, 1995, p. 15.

4. Lawrence Mishel, "Rising Tide, Sinking Wages," *American Prospect*, Fall 1995, p. 62.

5. Herbert Stein, "Bill of Goods," *New Republic*, January 23, 1995, p. 24.

6. Ibid., p. 24.

7. Robert S. McIntyre, "A Few Questions for the Flat Taxers," *Tax Notes*, January 29, 1996, p. 609.

8. Amity Shlaes, "Flat-Tax Flap," *Wall Street Journal*, October 20, 1995, p. A12; Jeff Shear, "In Person: John Mueller; The Skunk of the Flat-Tax Party," *National Journal*, January 6, 1996, p. 31.

9. J. D. Foster, "Even Money: A Friendly Critique of the Flat Tax," *Policy Review*, Summer 1995, p. 28.

10. In the words of Peter Viereck, "What's attractive about the useful mess called capitalism (and why it is preferable to socialism and other utopias) is its unsystematic flexibility; it is not an ism, hence open to exceptions, New Deals, humane reforms, trade unions. Being Marxists endimanches, the neo-cons destroy this saving advantage of an otherwise grubby capitalism by making it a rigid dogma, as inflexible as their former Marxism. In general the Republicans of Gingrich would destroy capitalism (turning it into class war) by systematizing it into straight lines." Peter Viereck, private correspondence, February 12, 1996.

11. Quoted in Citizens for Tax Justice, *The Hidden Entitlements*.

12. Christopher Howard, "The Hidden Side of the American Welfare State," *Political Science Quarterly*, Fall 1993, p. 405.

13. "America's Other Welfare State," *U.S. News & World Report*, April 10, 1995, pp. 34–37.

14. Quoted in *Washington Post*, January 6, 1995.

15. Bureau of Labor Statistics figures, January 29, 1996, cited in Simon Head, "The New, Ruthless Economy," *New York Review of Books*, February 29, 1996, p. 47.

16. "Winter of Discontent," *U.S. News & World Report*, January 22, 1996, p. 54.

17. Ibid., p. 50.

18. Edward N. Wolff, "How the Pie Is Sliced: America's Growing Concentration of Wealth," *American Prospect*, Summer 1995, pp. 58–64.

19. Dick Armey, *The Freedom Revolution* (Washington, D.C.: Regnery, 1995), pp. 37–40.

20. Janet Norwood, ed., *Widening Earnings and Equality* (Washington, D.C.: The Urban Institute, 1992).

21. Gary Solon. "Intergenerational Income Mobility in the United States," *American Economic Review* 82 (June 1992): 393–408.

22. Joel Slemrod, "Taxation and Inequality: A Time-Exposure Perspective," in James Poterba, ed., *Tax Policy and the Economy*, vol. 6 (Cambridge, MA: MIT Press, 1992), pp. 105–128.

23. Michael Novak, "The Inequality Myth: What Wealth Gap?" *Wall Street Journal*, July 11, 1995, p. A16.

24. "Class Conflict in Washington," *New York Times*, October 22, 1995, p. 12.

25. Newt Gingrich, *To Renew America* (New York: HarperCollins, 1995), p. 192.

Epilogue

1. Francis evoked not only Jacobinism but Bonapartism when, in the same essay, he wrote, "The New Right, therefore, should make use of the presidency as its own spearhead against the entrenched elite. . . . The adoption of the Caesarist tactic by the New Right would reflect the historical pattern by which rising classes ally with the executive power to displace the oligarchy that is entrenched in the intermediate bodies." "Message from MARS: The Social Politics of the New Right," in Robert W. Whitaker, ed., *The New Right Papers* (New York: St. Martin's Press, 1982), reprinted in Samuel Francis, *Beautiful Losers: Essays on the Failure of American Conservatism* (Columbia: University of Missouri Press, 1993), pp. 70, 75.

Index